Love Signs

Love Signs

LEOPARD

This edition published in 1995 by Leopard Books
Random House, 20 Vauxhall Bridge Road, London SW1V 2SA

Copyright © Sarah Bartlett 1994

Sarah Bartlett has asserted her right to be identified
as author of this work.

ISBN 0 7529 0051 X

Designed by Nigel Hazle
Typeset from author's disks by Clive Dorman & Co.
Printed and bound in Great Britain by
Mackays of Chatham

Contents

Introduction

**Astrology is about *how* we are,
not *why* we are.**

This book aims to be a guide to what you might expect from people as lovers, partners and friends. It also gives you an insight into who you really are, and how others see you. Keep your eyes on the stars and the stars in your eyes, and you won't go far wrong.

Astrology makes no claims to prophecy. It is only a reflection of human psychology: a mirror of us all and the paths we take.

Sun signs divide and generalise, no more or less than any other approach to our existence. They do show the basic qualities we have in common, the emotions and feelings and intellect that we all share and how we use our personal map of life. The map of life is in all of us, and every individual has his or her unique chart. Some areas of our personality are more prominent than others, like on the map of the world, where oceans and continents can be highlighted, or mountains or rivers. Sometimes we project different continents on to that map, other countries of feeling or mentality that are not highlighted on our own personal chart, but are highlighted in someone else.

There are so many other points involved in your natal chart that make you unique, so that when you read this book, remember that talking about a Virgo or a Scorpio can only be a beginning to knowing someone, the larger continents and oceans on their own psychological globe. These reactions and characteristics are not the only way a person will respond to situations. But Sun signs give guidance to the general way we feel, love and interact.

Unless your lover's Sun sign is severely afflicted, or has another

7

more prominent sign in the natal chart, then he or she should be fairly consistent with the Sun sign image, though you may not recognise it instantly.

The sign rising over the horizon at the moment of birth has an equally powerful bearing on our psychological make-up. However, finding this out requires exact and detailed calculations, including certainty of time of birth. That is why our Sun sign is our primary pin-pointer on the map. You may not at first glance recognise yourself, because often your Sun sign reveals characteristics to which you don't want to admit!

As La Rochefoucauld put it so succinctly, 'Not all those who know their minds, know their hearts as well.'

The 12 Signs as Lovers and Partners

THE ARIES MAN

Aries is traditionally the first sign of the zodiac and that means that an Aries man comes first in everything. The Arien lover is bold, demanding, impulsive, and most certainly self-centred, and yet he will take risks in his relationships and in love. Because he cannot stand any kind of restriction to his freedom, you're more likely to find him hanging around motor races, rallies, outdoor activities rather than cutting cigar ends down the local pub. He's looking for adventure and, for the egotistic Ram, love-affairs are as much a challenge to him as hang-gliding.

One of the things that make him an exciting lover is his need to take chances. Romance to this impetuous man involves dragging you round the Himalayas at breathtaking speed and expecting you to eat vindaloo for lunch and dinner when you get back to the local Indian restaurant. He expects weekends in the camper in freezing winter with only each other to keep you warm! He needs a woman with guts both spirited and physically non-combustible to keep up with his vigorous lifestyle.

The arrogant Ram can fall in love easily, and impulsively, and if he genuinely believes that you are the answer to his dreams, he won't hesitate to become deeply involved. His sexual magnetism is tremendous, and he is so aware of his ability to attract women that he sometimes assumes that no one will reject him. This kind of arrogance can lead him into trouble, but his honest, no-nonsense approach always gets him back on top and he doesn't suffer from self-pity, ever.

What you must remember is that Arien hotheads are jealous Fire signs. It's quite all right for him to chat to other women, or even play a touch of harmless flirting, but for you to attempt even a smile at that charming colleague of his across the pub is fatal. In a crowded room you'll know the Aries man because he's the one with the self-confidence and the smile of a dare-devil lover. He might hastily introduce himself, arrogance and impulse working overtime to meet his challenger head-on. But if you crash, watch out for his honest vent to his feelings. It takes a lot to rile an Aries but, if you don't play fair and true, he won't let you forget it.

If you want a permanent relationship with him and can keep up with his energetic sex life you will be rewarded. But never forget that the Ram's egotism governs his need to satisfy himself first, and you second. But if you both can get over his self-centred approach to love and sex, for really he's always searching for an ideal, there is a lot of warmth and honest love waiting in his heart.

THE ARIES WOMAN

The Aries woman usually will want to be the boss in everything, including her love life. Because she is a Cardinal Fire sign, she knows intuitively what she wants. Some Aries girls will come straight to the point and pick you up, if you don't make the first move! Like her male equivalent, an Aries girl has great sexual magnetism, and if you're strong enough to take her on, you'll realise why her hot-headed vanity works.

Undoubtedly she will want to take over your whole life if you fall in with her hard-headed approach to relationships. She will always be ambitious for you, and for where she comes in your life. She is number one, and you will always be number two. If you can bear her egotistic pride then she will be the most loving and passionate partner, but she needs commitment, and she needs to be the centre of your world, or she'll dump you.

Another important consideration is that exclusivity is her *raison d'être*. And that will mean you. Once she's let you into the secret art of ram-shearing then she can get incredibly jealous if you stray out of the sheep pen. She may be a passionate lover, but that passion doesn't make her liberal about free love.

The Ram girl likes men to be young in outlook and appearance. If you've got the energy to go hang-gliding before lunch then you'll be her friend for life. But if you've got a gut hanging out over your trousers and would rather sit in front of the TV with a can of lager, forget having any relationship with her. She needs an energetic man both as a friend, to make impulsive trips and exciting journeys, but also in bed. There is a fire burning in her soul which doesn't need to be put out, it just needs rekindling from time to time. The adventure in her head and the energy in her blood keep her restlessly searching for the next impulsive trip on love. Love is beautiful if she can be the boss, and she can take control, but give her back as much as she puts into a relationship and you'll stay her adventure for life.

THE TAURUS MAN

The natural inclination of Mr Bull at dawn is to force himself out of the bed he cherishes so much. But that's the only bit of forcing he'll do, particularly in any relationship. If he wants you then *you* have to be the one to chase him, but the move will be welcomed. A Taurean male won't actually make many advances and stubbornly waits for those who are worthy of his incredible sensual attention to come running.

For all this laid-back man-appeal it may appear that sex means little to him. But actually that's the catch. The Taurean male's quite seething sexuality, once unleashed on an unsuspecting female who decides to consider him as her partner, can be quite overtly bestial.

He thinks as highly of his body as he does of the next meal or the next bath. The Bull loves the pleasures and luxuries of life and is essentially an implacable part of the earth, intensely sensual, and dependable. He is an Earth sign whose energy and sexual drive originates from all that natural organic goodness that ironically he rarely eats.

There's actually something quite elusive about Taureans. You can never quite fathom out where they've come from, or really exactly where they are going to, probably because they really have no idea, nor care about it themselves. This is why it can take a long time to form a deep relationship with a Bull. If you do get past the horns, this affair could be for life. The placid Bull needs gentle handling, both emotionally and sexually. The trouble is that Mr Bull is often very blind to his own compatibility ratings. He is lured by, and hopelessly attracted to, Fire and Air signs. The Taurean man often gets tangled up with the Airy intellect or impulsive brainstorming of these very opposite types from him. He just can't keep up with the mind-bending improvisation that these signs so naturally use to charm their way through life.

The Taurus man is warm-hearted and affectionate, and he is intensely passionate. But he is a lover of the pleasures of life, a hedonist in every self-indulgence, and every luxury. Sex is a good, basic pleasure which he enjoys as part of a deep and erotic relationship. If after a heavy night of wining and dining he prefers to sleep off the last glass of brandy rather than spend the night with you, it's not that he's selfish, just that he forgot you for a while. After all, there are other sensual things in his life apart from sex, had you forgotten that?

THE TAURUS WOMAN

It's hard to imagine the placid, reliable, earth mother as a hard-edged Bull, but there is a side to her which might have been overlooked! A Taurean female takes a long time to decide if you are worthy of her passion, yet she has the power and the guts actually to initiate the first move in a relationship and should never be underestimated. A bossy girl needs careful handling, and because she is strong-minded and loyal she needs first-class devotion in return.

The Bull lady bears little resemblance to bovine sexuality except for an occasional grumbling temper and a geyser of bubbling anger when she gets overheated by resentment. Pouts grow on a female Taurean's lips very easily. Jealousy is uncommon, but possessiveness is. Her placid, controlled approach to your relationship is her self-protection, her magic eye. She has to impress and be impressed, which is why she often gets tangled up with men with a big cheque book. She likes the sound of champagne corks flying and the permanence of marriage.

Sensuality is the Taurean girl's be-all and end-all. It could be the summer rain pattering on your back as you kiss beneath an umbrella, or making love in the pine forest or beside the babbling stream. She's a creature of the outdoors, of closeness to nature and filling her senses with tastes, sounds and touch.

Venus in cowhide will be delighted equally whether she's having sex, floating in a silky warm ocean, eating pizzas at three in the morning, or cooking you both a cordon bleu breakfast in a tent. Sex is not to be taken lightly and she can get quite prudish with women who are apparent flirts or downright promiscuous. Convinced that a good emotional and sexual relationship is the answer to fulfilment, she might well confide her Mother Earth instincts to you one warm night.

The awkward and niggling little word 'possession' might create a spot of tension but, if you're willing to be a mate for life, or at least more permanent than the fading perfume on her skin, you will have to take sex and love as seriously as she does. If you can offer her honesty and maybe a sound financial future, a superb champagne dinner or a night listening to the owls in the woods, then she will be impressed enough to let you through her tough, resilient Bull-skin.

This girl needs both erotic and sensual communication, a man who can give her a down-to-earth lifestyle and a really warm heart. But make sure you've got the stamina and nerve to accept her blatant honesty if she decides to reject you!

THE GEMINI MAN

The highly versatile, spontaneous and amusing Gemini man is always ready for any mental and sexual challenge. He lives in the air, rather than flat-footed on the ground. Passion and sensuality are a rarity in his love life, for he is the catalyst of communication. The will o' the wisp is inquisitive, and like a child he will want to play games, will move through your life like a shooting star, and never make promises about tomorrow. He is privileged with a youthful appearance and a youthful approach to life. But emotionally, Gemini men rarely let you into their space, in fact they can often seem very cold, in the air, out of their heads and hardly ever in their hearts.

The second problem with which you have to wrestle is that there are always at least two personalities to cope with in one guise. This can be quite alarming when you wake up in the morning with a total stranger, not the man you thought you spent the night with! The seductive and alluring man of the late evening can turn into the clown at breakfast, and never be prepared to stay for lunch. The cherub-like Botticelli twins are actually not so much twins as a couple of conmen, both trying to outwit the other. Because of the mental struggle of trying to figure out his own identity, a Gemini male needs variety and change in his life. This means that he is often promiscuous, often marries at least twice and always wants two of everything. He has this uncanny ability and agility to be all types of lovers imaginable because role-playing stops him from ever being truly himself. And actually he really doesn't know who he is himself.

The double-lover enjoys the company and friendship of females just as much as any intimate physical relationship. Sexually he is the least chauvinistic of the star signs, and would rather spend the evening discussing the world and sipping champagne with you than be down the pub with the boys. He prefers to move on, to change partners, to try out new experiences, whatever forecast is in the wind, and to leave the fog of commitment and emotion far behind him.

If you can give him fun and variety he might even hang around to breathe your kind of fresh air. The Gemini man is often likened to Peter Pan, but if you ask any girl who's been involved with the Twins, she'll say, 'Sure, he reminded me of Peter Pan; but wasn't he like all those lost boys too?'.

THE GEMINI WOMAN

The female twins sparkle at parties, vibrating among other women who would rather keep cool and mysterious and watch this flirting charmer draw men to her like junkies to a fix. That's why a distortion of the facts has arisen and Miss Gemini has been dubbed two-faced in love, and a hypocrite in bed. So it's about time the true nature of this multi-faceted woman was revealed!

They seek out and need constant change in both their social lives and their love lives, not to mention their careers and their home life. Miss Fickle can jump headlong from the trivial to the profound in a split second because she's more interested in actual cleverness than the truth. She may have two or more faces, but they are all *genuine* in her own eyes, and in her own pretty head. Gemini girls are adept at role-playing, from switching from heaven to earth. Give them a character, a *femme fatale*, an innocent virgin, a career woman, you name it, they can play it. If you can keep up with their flighty, pacey, restless way of life, then you'll have more than one woman to keep you company at bedtime.

Apart from the thousand faces that Gemini women possess they are also known to be incredible flirts. It's not so much that she's particularly infatuated with you, it's more likely that she wants to play the game, drink her way through a bottle of champagne and then go home to sleep off the mental exhaustion of it all. She needs a lot of sleep, but a Gemini woman is more likely than any other sign to prefer to sit up all night discussing the latest philosophy, or the latest painting in your collection, or the books on your shelf.

She makes vague attachments, and loves socialising, but very rarely makes deep friendships, particularly with her own sex. Miss Fickle prefers the company of men to women and would rather be one of the boys at the office.

Gregarious girls meet a lot of blokes, so Gemini woman will be well surrounded by a choice selection. But remember, she's attracted to appearances rather than to depth of emotions. She is capable of persuading herself you're the love of her life. Being in love is easy if you talk yourself into it. Why, then, you can talk yourself out of it again when it takes your fancy, or another man does! (By the way, a Gemini girl's heart is a pretty cold place to penetrate, but if you ever get through the surface with

your ice-pick at least you take pleasure in knowing that you
will be remembered in her heart for being the only man that
ever made it!)

The Jekyll girl often has affairs with younger men because
she feels safer; commitment won't be spread across the bed with
the Sunday papers at eleven in the morning after a night of hot
passion. The marmalade men, the electric shavers and the city
bods who need slippers and pipe won't attract her. She is capable of finding something fascinating and appealing in practically all men, but that doesn't mean it will last more than the
second that it takes for her to change their mind, instantly!
Enjoying sex isn't the answer to her dreams, only another dream
can have that solution. And you can't stay her dream for ever –
or can you?

THE CANCER MAN

The Cancerian man is home-loving, gentle and sincere. He
responds deeply to life and to every change in emotion or feelings
around him. His goodness far excels his weaker, depressive side
which can get unbearable and drown an affair in melancholy. His
moods can be touchy, he can be as snappy as an alligator and he
takes everything too personally, fearing rejection. Yet on the
surface he will play the extrovert, be flirtatious, the lunatic everyone loves at the all-night party.

A Crab man is overtly sentimental. He will take a long time to
pluck up enough courage to phone you, until he is sure in his
Crab-like way he can move in for love. Don't forget, Crabs move
sideways, stay in their shells and guard themselves ferociously with
giant claws.

He might seem mildly indifferent: playing guessing games
about his true motives with you when he first takes you out to
dinner.

He loves food, and if you offer him breakfast in bed he might
just agree to scrambling the eggs himself. This man needs smothering with affection, and sexually can be languid and lazy when
it suits him, especially once he feels secure in a relationship.

Typical of Water signs, he feeds on gentle rhythms, quiet arousal and delicate love-making.

Don't ever mention your past boyfriends because he will see vivid mental movies about where you have been, and who you have been with. Cancerians are very possessive, and if you mention ex-partners, he will wallow in self-pity for days.

Don't ever look at anyone once you're married. You are collected, part of his acquisitions and his very personal private collection.

Cancer men hide out in the dark corners of pubs, or at the edge of the in-crowd. If they use their extrovert shell to cover up their weaker personality they can be awkward to spot. Sometimes they hover in the wings, hiding from possible failure, appearing as confident and glib as any fire sign. But around the full moon you can usually spot them when they become touchy and moody, not at all like any Fire sign!

The Crab is easily flattered, and often gullible in the face of a strong protective, woman. He has a cheeky, little-boy-lost appeal that he takes to parties in his search for the perfect soul-mate, and he needs one desperately for all his apparent self-confidence and arrogant manner. It's misleading. Beneath that gregarious shell is a soft heart. There will only ever be one woman at a time for a Cancerian man – at least you can be assured of that.

THE CANCER WOMAN

When you meet the Cancer woman you will immediately know that you have met the most female of all females. The Yin is intense, explosive, warm and genuine, the genie of the zodiac, the sensitive soul, the Moon disabled by love and emotion. You have nothing to fear, except yourself, and the changeability of her deep and dark side. The dark side of the Moon waits for you. Do not disappoint her for the woman with whom you have just become infatuated is the past-mistress of love and romance.

Cancer ladies are easily flattered and at their worst are unstable. Preparation for a life of swaying moods, indistinct emotions and powerful sensitivity have adapted this dippy bird to seek attention and seek out sympathy from a nice guy, one she hopes will have a larger cheque book than her own.

She is protective, gentle, highly intuitive and reflective of others' moods. Yet like the Moon she sways, changing the light of the night from that pale ghostly shadowland to human and loony laughter. A bit touched, a bit sad, occasionally glad, Moon birds need close friends, domesticity and a strong, tender man to support them.

You can only get so close to a Moon bird. She has this intense fear of being opened up like a clam. The big problem for her is that if she doesn't open up then you might reject her like the bad mussels in the cooking pot that get tossed in the bin. Frankly, the Cancerian girl needs a permanent, stable relationship with someone who won't get twisted and confused every time she sulks or goes loopy in the Full Moon. You've been introduced to an apparently hard, tough, thick-skinned woman in the crowd. It really seems unlikely that someone so extrovert and resilient could be reduced to tears by a slight put-down. But she can! She's an extrovert/introvert, a manic depressive and a bundle of fun when she's on one of her highs. She can be downright rude and criticise everything about you from your haircut to your taste in underwear but she won't survive an in-depth dissection of her own deeper and often weaker character. Cancer women will never make the first move, because they sincerely cannot cope with rejection.

A word of warning. This lady can get her claws into you quicker and more deviously than any other Crab this side of the Moon. The claws of a Crab can grab you and, pincer- like, they'll clutch at your heart and possessively monopolise you, as she possesses her books, her kitchen memorabilia and her dog.

Her imagination sizzles in bed, like throwing water on fire. But she needs emotional and sensual fulfilment, a physical experience that will change as easily as her moods. Cancerian ladies don't take to athletic body-building, or get obsessed about their weight, but they will make or break the sexual traditions if it means pleasing the one man they really want to impress.

THE LEO MAN

The Leo man is known for his magnanimous nature and his warm and generous heart. But he is also a prowler, one of the more sexually active signs of the zodiac. Like Capricorn and Scorpio he is motivated by power. The subtle difference is that Leo assumes success in everything he does, particularly when it involves relationships and love. He can't bear the thought of rejection so he never even thinks about it. That's why he blazes his way through life, and that is how he wins.

For all his flash behaviour the tom-cat is actually in need of a lot of stroking. He falls in love easily, but it will often be subconsciously motivated by the desire to impress his companion. The Cat is a show-cat, wherever and whoever he is with. Leos have dramatic tastes, extrovert and extravagant desires, unnerving energy and yet he is so self-opinionated that he can be intolerably conceited and inflexible.

They need to be in the headlines and to draw attention to themselves, so the Leo lover will look for the sort of woman who can enhance his Mogul image and taste for hedonistic delights.

If you're good-looking, independent, can hold your own and be part of his show, then he'll fall in love with you on sight. The one thing you have to remember is that the golden boy, for all his showiness, is actually not very brave. He doesn't take risks like an Arien or Sagittarian, and he generally takes more care about who he gets involved with to avoid hurting his delicate pride. His emotions are fiery, but his judgment is cautious.

For long-term commitment, a Leo will be willing to take the risk only if he gets as much attention as he believes he deserves.

He will have mastered all the techniques of high performance love-making. That is something that he can really impress you with. But while you're enthralled by his energetic love and sexuality, remember that he likes to play the Tom-and-Jerry game. Mostly he prefers to be Tom, but even Tom needs a lot of affection and warmth, for all his boasting conceit. Cold, unresponsive girls can make him temporarily impotent and turn that organised high-flyer to anger; and that's when he can really leave a trail of charred hearts!

THE LEO WOMAN

The Cat woman is one of those girls who is always surrounded by men at social events. She will insist on being the centre of attention at all parties, which is one of the reasons she always organises them. The Leo girl also assumes she will be the nucleus and hotbed in any relationship and, for her, relationships need to be warm, affectionate and full of physical expressions of love. Bear-hugs, stroking her wild hair as if she is a pussy-cat are all gestures that show how she is adored. And she needs that very badly. This naturally vivacious, clever Cat finds men drawn to her like mosquitoes to blood.

This very sexual Cat can at times be overpowering and over-dramatic, but her magnetic personality always catches the lime-light.

Leo was born to lead, and not to follow. If you are strong enough to challenge her, then she may play the role of a sweet innocent for a while. But if she's not the starring role in your life then the loud, extravagant will of her ego will come hurtling out to confront you. And a Leo in full temper and voice is a pretty frightening Big Cat!

Her vanity irritates other women and attracts many men, and she can be arrogant and incredibly stubborn. She is self-opinion-ated, but she is also generous and compassionate, able to create the kind of atmosphere in the bedroom fit for the most sensual and seductive love-making imaginable!

If you can keep up with her energy and delight in passionate and exciting sex, then she might decide to make you a permanent fixture. The Cat woman will scratch for her independence, and won't sacrifice her career or freedom for many men. Although she will flirt her way through a boardroom of old fogeys to assure success in her career, you will have to trust her integrity.

Flatter her and she'll let you closer. Her vanity and her magnetic personality are, ironically, her weakness. But with respect and belief in a Leo woman you can be assured of a loyal and true partner. Never try to control her or play ego games. She needs a strong man who will pamper her; give her the world and in return she'll give you everything back. Attention-getting, and attention-seeking go together, so be prepared for the occasional mild flirtations when she's out at her business lunches, or career parties. If she weren't the star of the show someone else would be, and she really doesn't want anyone else to take that leading part away from her.

THE VIRGO MAN

If anyone could be more accurate, more perfect at time-keeping than a quartz watch, then it would have to be the Virgo man. He is the precision master, the careful and discriminating quiet one in the corner of the bar, who will drink exactly the same amount of alcohol every visit, and who knows precisely the health advantages of wine and the mortality rate of heavy drinkers. This neat and tidy man often pulls weights down the gym rather than girls, and worries about his digestion and whether he should be celibate.

The Virgo man finds warm, emotional relationships difficult, and yet he seeks out quality and the perfect woman. He analyses sex and relationships with the meticulous interest of a stamp-collector. You see, Virgo men don't really need anyone else in their lives. They often panic about their lack of passion, and then devote an awful lot of time worrying about it. (Virgos are constantly fretting about life.) Mr Precision sometimes falls in love with the logic of a relationship, with the actual methodology of it all, but very rarely is deep and genuine emotion involved.

Virgo men have this thing about purity. Not that they are chaste and virginal, but they will search for the purist form of experience and will often sublimate passion for neutrality. This is why if you're not near perfect in his eyes you'll be rejected before he even attempts to test you out. Sex can be a pure and impeccable experience for a Virgo with a girl in mint condition and the right motivation. But is there any life in his soul, any passion or warmth in that apparent cold and solitary physique?

He is very attractive to women because he appears to be a challenge. If you get past that cold shoulder there might just be a sensual, sensational warm heart. He has a heart, but it's as invulnerable as his emotions. On the surface he is the perfect lover and can perform like Don Juan. He is the sexual technocrat of the zodiac. If you can put up with his dissection of your personality, if you like a distant lover and a punctual friend, a lover who is dextrous but unemotional, he might make one of the better permanent relationships. But he compartmentalises life: the past stays the past, the future the future. He carries little sentimental or emotional baggage with him. It's tidier, isn't it?

If you finally get through the cold earth that buries this man you'll find a faithful lover. He's not exactly a bundle of laughs, but the strong silent type who once he's found his perfect partner will never, ever look at another woman again.

THE VIRGO WOMAN

The Virgo girl is quiet, self-aware and keeps her eyes firmly pinned on anything that might remotely interfere with her calculated plans for life. This includes her personal relationships which are as critically analysed and subjected to meticulous scrutiny as if she were conducting a witch hunt or a scientific experiment.

Miss Virgo is not only critical of herself, she is acutely critical of others. She nit-picks rather than knits, and can really infuriate you with her constant reminder that you have a speck of dandruff, or your tie is wonky. She believes that she knows best, and this confident mental sharpness affects all her personal and sexual relationships.

She expects tidiness and perfection around her which includes an organised pristine relationship with her ideal man. The Virgo girl can lack real human warmth at her worst and, because she is such a worrier, even sex can become a chore, and your performance tainted with imaginary faults.

But a Virgo girl loves romance: the first innocent kiss or the love-letters scribbled from a stranger. She can become infatuated with someone over the phone, or by the pure physical beauty in a man. She loves sentiment and delicate love-making. An Interflora sign will make her weep and she's nuts about soppy films, as long as no one is with her when she watches them. If you are too dominant a partner she can become frigid just to suit herself. Coldness is natural to her.

Perfection is wasted on talentless men and she will often be fatally attracted to opposite dreamy types, escapist musicians and artists who, although they fulfil her romantic fantasy, lead her to find fault with every work of art or creation they perform. The Virgo girl is dedicated to pursuing happiness, and her strength is to be able to be both obsessively practical and ridiculously romantic, because love is the purist form of analysis.

Sex will be a delight to her if you keep it light and emotionless, but don't ever be late for a date, or her time-keeping will start clocking you in and out of her bed. She'll never be unfaithful, it's not in her nature. But if you can't enflame that spark of sexuality out of her ice-box she will quite coldly and mercilessly look for it elsewhere. The modest, clever and cautious Virgo girl will be the most affectionate and prudent partner if you can accept her perfectionism. She might decide you're her ideal and throw a party; but she'll stay in the kitchen and worry about the spilled punch. Someone has to haven't they?

THE LIBRA MAN

Libra is the go-between of the zodiac – the man who can be active or passive, will be laid-back, indecisive and fluctuate between love and sex in his head, easy-going, well mannered and everybody's friend. Doesn't that sound like the sort of man you would love to have around? Someone with wit and humour, who curves through life rather than angles through it? He is essentially a relaxed man who is fair and lovely about the world and naturally charming with every female he meets.

He needs harmony, beauty and idealistic truth in his life. For him, life has to fulfil dreams of romance, particularly when love and sex are involved. But this is where he gets confused. Not because he's a soppy sentimentalist, far from it, but because he thinks sex is love and love is sex. You just can't have one without the other, it wouldn't be fair.

This sociable man needs and demands a lot of friends of both sexes. If you get involved with a Libra be prepared to tolerate all the other female friends he spoils. Some of them may even be ex-lovers that he hasn't quite decided whether to see again or not.

But there are times when a Libran won't be forced into making a decision at all and, when it comes to any conflict, emotional or physical, he would rather walk out than fight. The eternal problem for Librans is *not* making a decision. What bugs him is why he has to make a choice about commitment in his relationship, because essentially he hates to reject anything, and that mostly includes his freedom.

He wants the best of both worlds, if he can get it, and flirting his way through life enables him to meet many women, and maybe, just maybe, he'll find the girl of his dreams. He often gets led astray by strong, glamorous females. He can fall instantly in love, but he falls in love with the essence of the affair, rather than the girl. The face value of the romance is all that matters to him initially.

Like Gemini the Ping Pong man is attracted to the appearance of life, not any underlying spiritual meaning.

He's a romantic and a balloon-seller of ideals, releasing them on a windy day to see if they fly alone. He loves the romance of sex, the caresses, the body language, the first meetings. Sexually his head rules his body. His approach is one of airy, cloudless skies and often a languid, lazy love-making. But his soaring passion is an insubstantial mental process, and he often has trouble 'being there' with you.

This sexual egalitarian is a wonderful lover and romantic, but remember, he can fall out of love as easily as he fell into it!

THE LIBRA WOMAN

What if you meet a Libran woman surrounded by a group of adoring friends and she decided you were the most attractive, exciting man in the room? You invite her to dinner and she falls in love with your eyes and your hair and immediately and uncharacteristically accepts the date. An hour later the chances are she'll change her mind, or sweetly point out that actually she is with Tom, an old flame, and really she can't accept because they are already going down the pub that night. What if Tom got upset? And what if Tom really was the man of her life, the ideal she's searching for? And then what if she rejects your offer and you don't make another? This is the terrible dilemma for a Libran woman.

She is lovely, perfectly lovely. Attractive, gregarious, articulate, spirited and independent. A real woman but with a tough head and a strong heart. She's mentally alert and logical about life like any Air sign, but she really hates to reject anything, or anyone. And making decisions just means not having the best of both worlds, doesn't it?

Libran women have deliberately charming smiles which they can turn on when it suits them, to show how wonderfully feminine they can be. But the logical intensity of her mental gymnastics can be slightly off-putting if your intentions are of a deeper or more physical need.

She needs honesty, beauty and truth around her, no heavy emotion and no remorse. She'll cheer you up when you're down, brighten your life with her sparkling humour and will thoroughly enjoy sexual pleasure and hedonistic delights. Don't be a spoilsport or a worm, and if you can't find your way out of a paper bag then you're not her kind of man.

She'll love you for ever if you are her mental equal and her physical mirror image. But remember, this girl can be led astray by beauty and by the idea of love. Like her male counterpart, she can fall in love with the affair before she knows who you are. She'll listen to your opinions about politics, point out her own, then with equal fairness spout everyone else's point of view. That's why getting close to her heart can take a long time. She talks a lot, and she talks for everyone. Can you really find her beneath all those fair judgments?

THE SCORPIO MAN

Apart from a snake or a hypnotist, a Scorpio man has the best chance of fixing his penetrating eyes upon the one he loves or lusts and capturing her. No matter how hard you resist if he gets it in his head to seduce you, this man will hypnotise you before you've got back from the bar with your glass of white wine.

Like any insect, the Scorpio male has the ability to rattle and repel. You can meet him at the standard office party and find him offensive and unnerving, disagree with him about every subject under the sun, but he'll have you, and there's nothing you can do about it!

In Yoga, Kundalini is the serpent who lives at the base of our spine and is awakened upon sexual arousal. Any true Scorpio male's Kundalini is on permanent red-alert. To him sex and love are the whole meaning of life and the answer to every emotion. His attraction to women is motivated by his obsession for finding the truth, and often he falls prey to his own intentions by a touch too much promiscuity. The trouble is Scorpios actually need long-term and stable relationships. But the man is dangerous if you are on his hit-list. He'll pursue you secretively at first. If you find you are the chosen one he can also take over your whole existence.

Sometimes Scorpio will adore you until he actually destroys love, and you, in his mind and soul. It's the regenerative process of the Pluto passion, so you might as well enjoy the attention and the ecstasy while you can before he kills the love he has created.

His jealousy is intense. He lives and breathes every emotion, and with it love. He'll surprise you with spicy and secret rendezvous. In bed he'll be the connoisseur of all things sexual and emotional. He will want sex to be a symbolic, esoteric experience that sometimes falls close to obsession. Sex is big business to him and he can justifiably prove it with his reputation of a discreet but highly dangerous lover. But he has incredibly high standards and you must be spotless, almost virginal. The Scorpio male wants all or nothing, and the longer your mystery is prolonged the more intense the turn-on he gets.

You have to be emotionally and mentally strong to have a relationship with this man. If you think you can handle him, can bear the shock when his eyes start to penetrate another victim's heart across the room, beware! This man is powerful. A boa constrictor takes a very long time to kill its prey – by gently squeezing the life out of it; until it can breathe no more.

THE SCORPIO WOMAN

The powerful seductress of the zodiac takes life seriously, too seriously at times. When she first sets eyes on you she will want to dominate you both physically and emotionally. Scorpio girls have an intuitive awareness of their sexual magnetism and, like sparks of static electricity, you will feel her presence in the room, whether you've met the haunting gaze of her eyes or not.

Watch out when she's about, for this dark, deeply motivated lady can play any charming role, any teasing subtle game that will make you think you are in control, not her.

If she could, the female snake would have been born a man, but as she has to bear the physical weakness of woman, she is more like the Medusa's head than one serpent, and more like a dozen Plutonian meteorites than a simple solitary moon.

For a Water sign she gives a pretty good impression of a Fiery one. Playing the *femme fatale* is easy for she creates subtle intrigue, the mystery and enigmatic power of a genie or a sorcerer. She can be hot and dominating one minute, then an emotional wreck the next. She'll hate voraciously and she'll love passionately. Whatever emotion she feels, she feels with intensity.

If she falls in love with you it will, for that moment, at least be for ever. Playing games with her is fatal, and if you start thinking the relationship should remain casual and lighthearted you might get a shock when she starts calling you on the phone in the middle of the night with tears, threats and demands.

Strength in a man is the Scorpio girl's weakness. The more independent, the more ambitious you are, the more she will love you. Sex and love are like a parasite and its host; without one you can't have the other. Remember, she takes her relationships very seriously and will sacrifice you for another if it means the total fulfilment of her soul.

Power is crucial to her existence and she won't be thwarted. Her strength of character is admirable, and her sexuality is so intense that it could take a lifetime really to know her. Secrets are big words for Scorpio girls, so make sure you have plenty, but keep her own mystery to yourself.

THE SAGITTARIUS MAN

The Archer is born altruistic, bold and voracious. It seems that he has the spirit and the morals of an Angel but watch out, the legendary bowman is more likely to have the soul of a gambler and the morals of a sexual extortionist. With unnerving blind faith and the optimism of Don Quixote this happy-go-lucky man wins his way through life and relationships like a trail of fiery stars. His honest and blunt admission for loving women make him the sort of guy that other men hate and women adore. It's not the egotistic vanity of an Aries, nor the power-driven motivation of a Leo; this Fire sign is genuinely convinced that this is the way things are. He can't help it if he was born beautiful, can he?

He's honest and open about himself, doesn't pretend to be something that he's not, and certainly lets you know if he's had enough of your company. He flirts easily, is really everybody's friend and is lighthearted and easy about life and women.

No strings and no commitments make this man's sense of freedom and need for a blank cheque in personal relationships sacrosanct.

Often the Archer looks for adventure, sexual or otherwise, as long as he can maintain his buccaneering spirit. That is why Sagittarians often resort to casual relationships to make sure there is nothing to stop their capricious wanderings. Meeting challenges head-on is the way the Archer travels through life and love. He responds to the thrill of the chase, of a woman who is hard to pick up. But he is idealistic and if you live up to his high standards he has the uncanny ability to know exactly how things are going to work out with you. If the Archer actually agrees to make an arrangement to meet you the following week and the stars are in his eyes as well as yours, you might think you had instigated the wonderful moment. But Sagittarians have this knack of making you think big, and sharing their expansive nature.

Like the other Fire signs, Sagittarians need outdoor activities and an extrovert lifestyle. If you can keep up with his active and quite fast-paced life he might consider you to be the pal he's looking for. Sex isn't everything to a Sagittarian, he needs someone to play mental and physical games too. He needs an inventive sex life, and his moods can range from passionate and fiery to warm and playful. Sex is fun, not a deep emotional experience.

So don't ever get soppy about him, he really doesn't like the kind of woman who hangs around like a lost doll, or who hasn't a life of her own. The Archer needs someone who is never possessive and rarely jealous, though on occasions he can be.

Watch out for the hailstones though, the Sagittarian can flash in and out of your life like a magnetic storm to avoid those rain-clouds of commitment. But if he's convinced you're as free and easy, as unemotional and as unpossessive as he is, then maybe he'll forget about his unreliable and irresponsible attitude to life, and settle for permanent free love. That paradox is what he really wants.

THE SAGITTARIUS WOMAN

The outspoken Archer woman will insist on letting you know if you don't match up to her ideal, and she'll also pull your ideas apart with frank and brutal honesty which, to the uninitiated, can be a cultural shock. She lives independently and is always happier if her freedom isn't curtailed. Her honesty is genuine but it can sometimes cut through your heart like a butter knife, particularly as she's one of the most vivacious, amusing and popular females.

She prefers the company of men in any social setting and openly flirts in a rather innocent and childlike way. Like her Geminian opposite sign, she has no need for emotional depth to her rela-tionships and prefers the surface attractions, the moles and wrin-kles of appearances, rather than the viscera of human emotion. Friendship and companionship are more important than close emotional ties, and often platonic relationships with men and keeping friendly with ex-lovers is the easiest way to maintain her freedom and ensure an easy-going existence.

She can be so frank, that discussing her ex-boyfriends' intimate

29

inclinations can sound like boasting to your ear, when she was only just letting you know how absurd she finds the whole sexual game. She doesn't mean to hurt anyone, never means to upset or put down a friend, and will end up confused and embarrassed by her own big mouth.

But an Archer girl's optimism spreads through her life and into her partner's with the ease of ripe brie. To be so confident, to be so sure that a relationship will work as long as she has her freedom, is a bonus to any partnership.

Communicating inner emotions and deeper tensions is not part of her vocabulary and that's why she often confuses love with casual friendship. Sex is also not to be confused with love, and she can have a strong physical relationship with a man and just be good friends. Being a pal is easier, doesn't lead to commitments, to arrangements, and traps like that big word 'love' always seems to do. If she's kept you up all night at a dinner-party, played the life and soul, flirted with your dad, and hardly noticed your jealousy, don't expect her to apologise. Her mind is set, and her morals are high, but she does like to have fun, her own way. If you want her to do anything, always ask nicely, never order her or tell her. She won't be bossed, in public or in private, or in bed.

Don't trap this incurable romantic. Don't question her, and you'll find her free love is all for you!

THE CAPRICORN MAN

The Capricorn male is often likened to that goaty god, Pan. On the surface Pan may be a dour, apparently bloody-minded hardliner, but somewhere underneath it all you might find some true warmth and a consistently easy-going nature.

Capricorns are often conventional and rarely let themselves slip into any gear other than the one they have selected. In relationships with women they need to be in control. Even a power-mad Pan's chaos is controlled. In the wild abandon of infatuation his feelings and emotions are held from the precipice of freedom. He will be in charge of his destiny and yours, if you so much as show any inkling of desire for him.

He admires women who can coax him out of his stuffy Goat ways. But he also likes women who are ambitious for him too. Can this bedrock of society really rock the sexual and emotional bed? If he never deviates from his own tethering circle, will he ever have fun? A few women can release him from his rope of cold love. His inner nature often mellows as he ages, and oddly enough the paradox of this man is that as he gets older and more conventional he will also let go of any sexual inhibitions and allow spontaneous 'feelings' to enter his heart.

Pan often gets involved with women just for financial or career advancement. You'll often meet rich and successful females who have been taken advantage of by a Goat. Some of them have the man tethered on the dry arid plain of a monotonous marriage, but most of these Goats are already up there at the top of the mountain. The funny thing is that a Capricorn can digest all the flack you might throw at him for using you. A Goat's stomach speaks for itself!

The Capricorn man is shatterproof and biodegradable. Once he's decided you're the partner for his tenacious way of life, then he'll want to run you as smoothly as his business.

He can seem cold and passionless, restrained and indelicate in sexual communication. He is awfully possessive and it's very hard to change his opinions. But the taciturn Goat has a dry and witty sense of humour and there's always that twinge of inner warmth to draw out. He's not dull, but his approach to sex can be as disciplined and as ambitious as his approach to work. There is a closet romantic in his heart trying desperately to get out, and he needs a wise woman to open the door for him. As long as your relationship is within the boundaries of his own white lines, and he is in control, you'll find the most loyal and reliable partner behind those wardrobe doors.

THE CAPRICORN WOMAN

Don't ever expect a romantic encounter with this woman to last very long. She'll have all those graceful, feminine wiles,

31

make all those suggestive noises about a full-scale affair, but the kissing and the innuendos and the candlelit dinners will last only as long as she wants them to. And that is often shorter than you'd imagined!

The Goat lady is always ambitious and she knows what she wants. If she wants you, she'll look beyond the romantic aspect of love for something more stable, more gutsy and more to do with a business arrangement than an emotional one.

She is often power-mad, whether it's in the office, or in a relationship. There's no point floundering around in bed making wild romantic promises, and sharing ideals when you can go for the real thing. A commitment, a permanent relationship. She doesn't relax in love easily and has a cool approach to sex and emotions. But if you give this Goat the lead she can be intensely passionate and will gradually lose her shyness once she's known you a long time. She has to control the affair her own way, but don't let her fool you into thinking her calm and bossy approach is the only backbone to her heart and her head. Her feathers are easily ruffled and, although she doesn't live in the twilight zone of feelings, she can get jealous and brood quite easily, and sulk if she feels slighted or betrayed.

She needs to know exactly where she's going in life and with you. Self-imposed discipline makes her sometimes pessimistic and will convince her that love is as shallow as your first kiss in the back of the black cab. Capricorn girls find intimate relationships difficult to handle unless they are really in charge, and that's why they make excellent partners or wives, but not very wonderful lovers.

The Goat lady needs her home and her mountain to climb. If she is sure you are worth pursuing she'll also ensure that she is ambitious for you too. A lot of Capricorn ladies are the true reason behind a man's career success! If you can let her take the lead through the chaos of emotion, not burden her with demanding encounters and weak-willed indecision, then she'll stay at the top of the one mountain she yearns to climb with you, called love.

THE AQUARIUS MAN

You have to remember that the space-age man is an unconventional and eccentric freedom lover, and yet wants to be everyone's friend and stick to his own quite rigid lifestyle. Aquarian men set out to find as many friends as they possibly can, rather than worry about love and sex. Love and sex are valid, and part of life, but they aren't the be-all of existence for this fixed Air sign. As long as the Water-Bearer sees change and progress in others, or in the world around him, then he is blissfully happy. He does not particularly pursue or encourage it in himself.

Our Uranus man is an out-of-space man. He's an oddball, a weirdo, often the man you meet at the office disco who doesn't drink and doesn't dance but smokes a pipe and looks like an anarchist. He might also be that man on the commuter train you see every morning who gazes at you with alien eyes and has an aloof and rather cold appearance. He's actually silently working you out, because Aquarians, like Frankenstein, enjoy scientific investigation of the human psyche!

His feelings about women can be as cranky as his habits, but there is one thing he will always do first before he makes any move to attempt a relationship: convince himself that you are strong enough to cope with his inquisitive and probing mind.

He feels it's his right to know everything about the woman of his choice, and the deeper the mystery you stir, the longer you remain an enigma, the more likely he'll want to nose-dive into your secrets. So make sure your game of 'catch me when you can' involves a worthwhile solution!

The secret of the universe, your sexual appetite, you name it, the Aquarian will unravel the truth to expose the answers. Sex is no less, no more, important than any other facet of his active life, and if you're happy to consider sex and love as part of your life too, then you'll stand a better chance of a long-term relationship with this man and all his friends.

Love is impersonal to an Aquarian. He takes it and hands it round with the same degree of feeling (and that's an awfully hard word for him to say) to everyone. Don't ever think that you are special. You can be part of his life, but never to the exclusion of others. Being friends is more important than being lovers. This is how he will choose a soul-mate: sex comes second to this Air sign who lives in his head and rarely in his heart.

He enjoys sex but as for other Air signs it's fun, a mental experience, not emotional, and definitely not soppy. Aquarius is an abstract lover who will blow cold rather than hot. He'll persist until he strips the outer bark of your personality like an icy wind bares the most beautiful and toughest trees. If you're still in one piece and agree to be his pal, that is what counts. Who needs lovers, when you can have a good and permanent friend?

THE AQUARIUS WOMAN

Possessions and possessiveness are not something an Aquarian woman will even consider in her emotional or sexual relationships, particularly from her partner. Her unpredictable and unconventional approach to life is formulated from a stubborn need to be awkward for the sake of it.

She needs mental rapport, companionship, and above all, friendship with a man: someone she can talk to all night and all day, who will stand by her, be loyal and genuine and caring about humanity as well as about the individual long before she'll even consider him as a possible mate in bed or in the home. Aquarian women often live alone better than with a partner and spend a good deal of their lives independently succeeding in careers rather than in motherhood.

The Uranian girl's emotional detachment keeps her free from forming too intense and personal relationships. It gives her an open lifestyle, the chance to encounter as many friends as she possibly can. If you can be her friend and not attempt to own her or try to change her and accept that you have to share her with the world as she shares you with the world, then you may have found a soul-mate. Her apparent lack of passion can be frustrating, but her loyalty is impeccable and her stability is supportive.

Passion implies commitment and intensity, and to an Aquarian girl both are abhorrent. She enjoys sex and physical contact as a pleasurable and warm activity between friends, but she won't ever let you get soppy or slushy. If you do she'll think you're weak and pathetic, and she needs a tower of strength in her bed, not a fragile sandcastle. She can take sex, or leave it.

The essence of an Aquarian girl's love is based on her need to force herself to be different, to be an eccentric. She will, of course, have delved into your mind, wriggled out your intentions, and scanned you with an emotional barium meal to check out if you're worthy of closer inspection. But if friendship isn't in your heart, then love and sex won't be in hers.

THE PISCES MAN

If you've ever gone fishing out at sea, on the glimmering darkling patches of the ocean where the water is black and the bottom of the sea runs deeper than the height of the tallest mountain, then you'll know exactly what a Pisces man is like to catch. Often you have to climb into that diving bell, and take a powerful torch to locate him. Sometimes he'll emerge only to escape from life into fiction and fantasy. He'll often prefer to drown in anything, as long as it's drowning.

Fish men are charmingly romantic and awfully attractive because they are such dreamers; a very different challenge from the passion of Fire signs, the mental agility and lightness of Air or the solid practicality and sensuality of Earth men.

Impressionable to the point of being blotting pads, they will see only what they want to see and cloud their incredible intuitive and psychic senses with careless indecision. Mr Denizen-of-the-Deep lives in a partial eclipse of life no matter what love-encounters throw at him. He is easily led astray by alcohol and women. The Fish will escape into shadowland and pretty dreams, rather than face the mundane reality of life. If he fails in a relationship it's simple: he retreats. For someone who is actually quite gregarious he drifts through life as the zodiacal mop, absorbing and sensing your changing moods.

The Fish men are drawn to very beautiful and very female women. They are easily besotted by physical beauty. Being in love is a good escape from real life, whether it's with a beautiful day, a beautiful drink, or beautiful women. You can lead a Piscean astray more easily than you can get a dog to eat a bag of crisps, and you can get him into an intimate sexual relationship faster than a black-cab meter spends your money.

Sexually he is uniquely gifted. He doesn't need words or books, passion and emotion flow easily and love grows quickly in his deep cave of feelings. But Piscean men are often too far away in their own fantasy, and if you're not open with him you'll get left behind on the shore while he's diving back down into the deepest part of the ocean for the water spirits.

This half-man, half-fish is only ever half-seen. If you are prepared to embark on a sea voyage with him, make sure you've got the sea-legs to follow him to the deepest part of the ocean when he leaves you for his own lonely ecstasy.

THE PISCES WOMAN

The mermaid is half-fish, half-girl, and the Pisces girl is half-way between reality and a dreamworld, far from any logical or mental plane, in a world of intuition and feelings. She is usually poised, beautiful, and compassionate. Love and caring is genuinely felt, and she is kind and uniquely sensitive to others around her. She is the girl who sells sea-shells on the sea-shore, a poetry of emotional fluidity.

Of course this kind of feminine mystique attracts men easily, so she is usually surrounded by a choice of the best fish in the sea. There are many Piscean women who have been badly hurt by rushing headlong into romantic involvements without a thought because they really do not think. The Mermaid suffers intensely from emotional pain, and bitterness can turn her fishy scales to higher melancholy octaves. She can be led astray by the temptation of romance, or by the masks of drugs or alcohol to hide from her own passionate feelings. The Mermaid is deep to find. Like diving for oyster pearls, she will be hidden, unfathomable, and never in shallow water. Her elusive nature is vague and sometimes dithery, and she will always be moving somewhere and never be sure where it is she should be going.

Love is a touch-down, a grounding from reality and she'll fall into it as easily as Alice fell down the rabbit hole. In love she gets carried away by emotion and the prevailing moods of her lover can channel her through the murkiest waters and the shimmering waves like driftwood. Yet sometimes the physical intensity of her sexuality will produce emotional conflicts within herself and she will begin to see the man she thought she loved as just another shell on her lovely sea-shore. She is like the tide that washes across the empty bay, surfing back the shells to find the one that glistens in the sun, rather than the ones that turn to sand. She needs to belong to the sea of love, and to one man, and that man must be strong and protective, and mostly understanding.

The Mermaid often falls for weak, nebulous and gifted characters, a lover who makes love and feels as deeply as she. But together they will drown each other. The tide that carries her on to a better shore is the man who turns up the oyster bed and finds the real pearls inside.

The 12 Signs as Friends

ARIES

The Aries friend is rather like a meteorite landing in your life. Full of energy and enthusiasm for your friendship one day, the next deserting you for another planet, leaving you feeling deserted. Ariens can make and break friendships faster than any other sign. They hate being dependent on anyone and, on the whole, would rather have many acquaintances than close pals. Ariens of both sexes enjoy the companionship of men, and the rough and tumble of fairly lively and noisy gatherings, but they can be quite happy with their own company. They find it difficult to keep platonic relationships with the other sex and are not known for their reliability as friends. They would rather ensure they are the centre of attention so, if others are prepared to tag along with them, they may just be pally while the going is good!

TAURUS

Bulls of both sexes make warm and considerate friends. They need close, intimate friends rather than loose and casual ones and prefer the company of individual pals to social gatherings. They are always generous and would prefer you borrow from them, rather than owe you any favour, yet they are genuinely concerned for your welfare. They need a lot of affection and tactile communication, bear-hugs and cheek-kissing, rather than just a nod, both from friends of their own sex and platonic friends of the other. They like to feel comfortable and will make great efforts to make you always feel at home in their own nests. If you ever need to phone for help, a Taurean is just the sort of person to get you out of trouble, without getting het up, but they may take their time getting there!

GEMINI

Gemini loves a varied and lively social life. Not very reliable when you make arrangements for outings, they are not very fond of very intimate, close friendships. They prefer a wide circle of acquaintances to the serious one-to-one friend. However, they are so adaptable that they will make friends very quickly, chatter about the world and generally enjoy themselves. They can be inconsistent, and also gossips in big circles, so as a close and trusted friend they are not really reliable. Both sexes like platonic friendships, and you often find they have more true friends of the opposite sex than they do of their own. Very gregarious, but not very loyal, they also like to feel they can leave when they want to, rather than have any restrictions to adhere to. They need friends who enjoy intellectual pursuits rather than the great outdoors. But they are adaptable, and will try anything new, for the sake of novelty.

CANCER

Crabs take a long time to make friends and therefore prefer to make firm relationships with people they can trust and have known for a long time. They don't enjoy big gatherings, and rooms full of people they don't know, but will enjoy socialising if it's among small groups of similar-minded people. Can be surprisingly obsessive about maintaining a close friendship and need to feel they can rely on someone to talk through all their own fears and woes. Cancerians are generally cautious about lending money, or any of their possessions, and don't particularly like being asked about their finances. Although they insist on depending on their close friends, they are also easily hurt if let down by others and can take it very much to heart. But they are wonderful at helping in a crisis, and will never let you down.

LEO

The Lion likes to roar and be the centre of attention in any social gathering. They make friends easily with both sexes and will often have a very wide circle of friends to amuse their ego-orientated heads. Leos make good friends and are more reliable than the other Fire signs. They are intensely loyal and will stick up for any one of their acquaintances if they get into trouble, or need supporting. Though not emotionally close to new friends, nor even to the old and trusted, they do need warmth and a fun-loving rapport to stay your pal for long. They are open-hearted and quite generous, but don't ever betray their trust or they can scratch back. Most Leos love socialising and parties, and are often the all-night party goers rather than the dinner party type.

VIRGO

They make difficult friends as they never quite get close enough to anyone, nor accept other people for what they are. They can be cold and judgmental, and also, once they think they know you, can seem quite critical. Yet they are good at socialising on a wider scale, and enjoy casual acquaintances and brief friendships so that they don't get caught up in emotion. On a wider scale they will be lively, fun to be with and enjoy intellectual and stimulating company. They are very cautious about who they invite into their house, and often prefer not to venture into other people's homes: it gets too warm! They like general chit-chat and would prefer to chat to friends in the pub and not make any commitments nor rely on others for anything. They are very single-minded but can be relied upon to organise any event or social gathering. Societies and clubs are their favourite way of keeping acquaintances around them and not getting tied down.

LIBRA

Libra is the most sociable and affable of signs. Librans love parties, social gatherings of all kinds and will always want to make friends with as many people as they possibly can. Librans are also quite a dab hand at keeping in touch with old friends, and they look on casual acquaintances with as much sympathy as they do someone they've known since childhood. Librans need a lot of company and don't enjoy the solitary life. As close friends they can be relied on, but they often have a habit of appearing interested in what you have to say when in fact their mind is somewhere else. They are not particularly deep, nor passionate about forming a close bond unless a friend is prepared to make an effort too. They love gossip and small talk, and don't enjoy lengthy philosophical discussions

SCORPIO

Scorpios are slow to make friends but, when they do, they make them for life. They aren't too fond of large gatherings, but may appear on the surface quite charming and outgoing. Underneath they are probably testing you out to see if you live up to their incredibly high standards! Most Scorpios need very close and intense friendships. Because it takes them so long to decide whether they have found a true and confidential pal, they often find that they lose friends quickly. They don't like to rely on anyone, but they will provide all the emotional support that anyone could need, and have admirable shoulders to cry on. Scorpios can usually and intuitively know if someone is a fair-weather friend but, once a bond is formed, they want it to be unbreakable and don't respond well to casual, light and inconsistent friendships.

SAGITTARIUS

Archers usually have a wide circle of friends, and prefer light and easy pals to any deep and meaningful ones! They move around so much that they are likely to make friends with strangers in the street. They are never suspicious, and never cautious and, if a friend turns out to be an enemy, they can shrug their shoulders and bear no malice, as they just move on to another one. Their open and freedom-loving approach to life makes them fairly unreliable friends to have. Although they can enjoy the company of their own sex and play light amusing games, they aren't good at any form of permanence. They don't like making arrangements and would prefer just to turn up when they feel like it. Both sexes like platonic relationships and feel more comfortable surrounded by many rather than a few.

CAPRICORN

Rather stuck in their ways, Capricorns are not good at making friends and not easy to make friends with! Both sexes prefer the company of men, and would rather form any relationship on a business arrangement than anything looser. They don't need a wide or varied social life and enjoy the company of a few friends who share the same ambitions or mental stimulation. Once they do form any strong friendship, they will try to keep it for life and do not take kindly to being let down. They are not particularly interested in giving or going to parties, and would rather talk in the boardroom or the pub where they feel safer in a neutral environment.

AQUARIUS

Aquarians are naturals at making friends; and keeping them. They love to have a wide variety and circle of friends, and will insist on maintaining endless platonic relationships to ensure that their altruism is genuinely felt. They are in need of mental rapport rather than any sporting or clubby basis for friendship. They are consistent and determined to supply any mental or emotional support they can handle. Although rather cold emotionally, they will always analyse friends' problems and crack the truth, rather than lead you into false promises. Although they prefer people with cranky or eccentric minds like their own, Aquarians enjoy the company of anyone who can stimulate them intellectually. They always say what they mean, and can often be awkward about your judgments. But they will never let you down in a crisis.

PISCES

Pisceans are only slow to make friends as they are a little wary, for all their gregarious nature. They mix well in neutral surroundings and enjoy informal parties and gatherings where they can merge in with the crowd. They enjoy friends of both sexes and prefer to feel relaxed and non-committal rather than have pressures and obligations forced on them. They make wonderful friends when a rapport is established and are genuinely sympathetic, genuinely compassionate and always ready to help with any emotional comfort or support. They prefer a strong mental and intuitive friendship but can be too impressionable and soak up others' problems and bad habits rather than remaining independent of them. They often have a large circle of acquaintances and don't often have many close friends. Pisceans usually have one very old friend to rely on in times of trouble.

Some Famous
Ariens

Ayrton Senna (21 March 1960)
Michael Heseltine (21 March 1933)
Leslie Thomas (22 March 1931)
Marcel Marceau (22 March 1923)
Barbara Daly (24 March 1945)
Elton John (25 March 1947)
Diana Ross (26 March 1944)
Dirk Bogarde (28 March 1921)
John Major (29 March 1943)
Eric Clapton (30 March 1945)
Penelope Keith (2 April 1939)
Marlon Brando (3 April 1924)
Doris Day (3 April 1924)
Bette Davis (5 April 1908)
Gloria Hunniford (10 April 1940)
Alan Ayckbourn (12 April 1939)
Edward Fox (13 April 1937)
Julie Christie (14 April 1940)
Samantha Fox (15 April 1966)
Jayne Mansfield (19 April 1933)

ARIES COUPLES

Business partners, past and present

William Shatner (22 March 1931) and
Leonard Nimoy (Aries – 26 March 1931)
Sir Andrew Lloyd Webber (22 March 1948) and
Tim Rice (Scorpio – 10 November 1944)
Alan Sugar (24 March 1947) and
Terry Venables (Capricorn – 6 January 1944)
Sir Fred Henry Royce (27 March 1863) and the Hon. Charles Rolls
(Virgo – 27 August 1877)
Dudley Moore (19 April 1935) and
Peter Cook (Scorpio – 17 November 1937)
Michel Roux (19 April 1941) and
Albert Roux (Libra – 8 October 1935)
Nicholas Lyndhurst (20 April 1961) and
David Jason (Aquarius – 2 February 1940)

Romantic couples, past and present

Steve McQueen (24 March 1930) and
Ali MacGraw (Aries – 1 April 1938)
Spencer Tracy (5 April 1900) and
Katharine Hepburn (Scorpio – 9 November 1909)
Jane Asher (5 April 1946) and
Gerald Scarfe (Gemini – 1 June 1936)
Emma Thompson (15 April 1959) and
Kenneth Branagh (Sagittarius – 10 December 1960)
Paul Heiney (20 April 1949) and
Libby Purves (Aquarius – 2 February 1950)

Some Famous Taureans

Jack Nicholson (22 April 1937)
Shirley Temple (23 April 1928)
Barbra Streisand (24 April 1942)
Shirley Maclaine (24 Apr i 1 1934)
Al Pacino (25 April 1940)
Ella Fitzgerald (25 April 1918)
Saddam Hussein (29 April 1937)
Joanna Lumley (1 May 1946)
James Brown (3 May 1933)
Audrey Hepburn (4 May 1929)
Eric Sykes (4 May 1923)
Michael Palin (5 May 1943)
Orson Welles (6 May 1915)
Rudolph Valentino (6 May 1895)
Gary Glitter (8 May 1944)
Alan Bannett (9 May 1934)
Maureen Lipman (10 May 1946)
Jeremy Paxman (11 May 1950)
Susan Hampshire (12 May 1942)
Selina Scott (13 May 1951)
Liberace (16 May 1919)
James Fox (19 May 1939)

TAURUS COUPLES

Business partners, past and present

Bing Crosby (2 May 1904) and
Bob Hope (Gemini – 29 May 1903)
Terry Scott (4 May 1927) and
June Whitfield (Scorpio – 11 November 1925)
Fred Astaire (10 May 1899) and
Ginger Rogers (Cancer – 16 July 1911)
Eric Morecambe (14 May 1926) and
Ernie Wise (Sagittarius – 27 November 1925)
Pierre Curie (15 May 1859) and
Marie Curie (Scorpio – 7 November 1867)
Victoria Wood (19 May 1953) and
Julie Walters (Pisces – 22 February 1950)
Pete Townshend (19 May 1945) and
Roger Daltrey (Pisces – 1 March 1944)

Romantic couples, past and present

Adolf Hitler (20 April 1889) and
Eva Braun (Aquarius – 6 February 1912)
HM the Queen (21 April 1926) and HRH Prince Philip, the Duke
of Edinburgh (Gemini – 10 June 1921)
Sir Denis Thatcher (10 May 1915) and
Lady Thatcher (Libra – 13 October 1925)
Emma, Lady Hamilton (12 May 1765) and
Lord Nelson (Libra – 29 September 1758)
Sian Phillips (14 May 1934) and
Peter O'Toole (Leo – 2 August 1932)

Some Famous Geminis

George Best (22 May 1946)
Joan Collins (23 May 1923)
Bob Dylan (24 May 1941)
George Formby (24 May 1904)
Helena Bonham-Carter (26 May 1966)
Jeffrey Bernard (27 May 1932)
President Kennedy (29 May 1917)
Terry Waite (31 May 1939)
Clint Eastwood (31 May 1930)
Edward Woodward (1 June 1930)
Geoffrey Palmer (4 June 1927)
Bjorn Borg (6 June 1956)
Tom Jones (7 June 1940)
Judy Garland (10 June 1922)
Gene Wilder (11 June 1935)
Che Guevara (14 June 1928)
Richard Baker (15 June 1925)
James Bolam (16 June 1938)
Ken Livingstone (17 June 1945)
Delia Smith (18 June 1940)

GEMINI COUPLES

Business partners, past and present

Desmond Wilcox (21 May 1931) and
Esther Rantzen (Cancer – 22 June 1940)
Peter Cushing (26 May 1913) and
Vincent Price (27 May 1911) and
Christopher Lee (Gemini – 27 May 1922)
Bob Hope (29 May 1903) and
Bing Crosby (Taurus – 2 May 1904)
Stan Laurel (16 June 1890) and
Oliver Hardy (Capricorn – 18 January 1892)
Paul McCartney (18 June 1942) and
John Lennon (Libra – 9 October 1940)

Romantic couples, past and present

Laurence Olivier (22 May 1907) and
Joan Plowright (Scorpio – 28 October 1929)
Laurence Olivier (22 May 1907) and
Vivien Leigh (Scorpio – 5 November 1913)
Queen Victoria (24 May 1819) and
Prince Albert (Virgo – 26 August 1819)
Nanette Newman (29 May 1939) and
Bryan Forbes (Cancer – 22 July 1926)
Gerald Scarfe (1 June 1936) and
Jane Asher (Aries – 5 April 1946)
Marilyn Monroe (1 June 1926) and
Arthur Miller (Libra – 17 October 1915)
HRH Prince Philip, the Duke of Edinburgh (10 June 1921) and
HM the Queen (Taurus – 21 April 1926)
Paul McCartney (18 June 1942) and
Linda McCartney (Libra – 24 September 1941)
The Duchess of Windsor (19 June 1896) and the
Duke of Windsor (Cancer – 23 June 1894)

Some Famous Cancerians

Meryl Streep (22 June 1949)
Adam Faith (23 June 1940)
Carly Simon (25 June 1945)
George Orwell (25 June 1903)
John Inman (28 June 1937)
King Henry Vlll (28 June 1491)
Charles Laughton (1 July 1899)
Lord Owen (2 July 1938)
Ken Russell (3 July 1927)
Neil Simon (4 July 1927)
Sylvester Stallone (6 July 1946)
David Hockney (9 July 1937)
Dame Barbara Cartland (9 July 1901)
Virginia Wade (10 July 1945)
Harrison Ford (13 July 1942)
Sue Lawley (14 July 1946)
Linda Ronstadt (15 July 1946)
Donald Sutherland (17 July 1935)
Nick Faldo (18 July 1947)
Diana Rigg (20 July 1938)

CANCER COUPLES

Business partners, past and present

Richard Rodgers (28 June 1902) and
Oscar Hammerstein II (Cancer – 12 July 1895)
Jennifer Saunders (12 July 1958) and
Dawn French (Libra – 11 October 1957)
Ginger Rogers (16 July 1911) and
Fred Astaire (Taurus – 10 May 1899)

Romantic couples, past and present

Esther Rantzen (22 June 1940) and
Desmond Wilcox (Gemini – 21 May 1940)
Prunella Scales (22 June 1932) and
Timothy West (Libra – 20 October 1934)
The Duke of Windsor (23 June 1894) and
the Duchess of Windsor (Gemini – 19 June 1896)
Mel Brooks (28 June 1927) and
Anne Bancroft (Virgo – 17 September 1931)
HRH the Princess of Wales (1 July 1961) and
HRH the Prince of Wales (Scorpio – 14 November 1948)
Tom Stoppard (3 July 1937) and
Felicity Kendal (Libra – 25 September 1946)
Michael Williams (9 July 1935) and
Dame Judi Dench (Sagittarius – 9 December 1934)
Bryan Forbes (22 July 1926) and
Nanette Newman (Gemini – 29 May 1939)

Some Famous Leos

Helen Mirren (26 July 1946
Danny La Rue (26 July 1927)
Jack Higgins (27 July 1929)
Jacqueline Onassis (28 July 1929)
Daley Thompson (30 July 1958)
Frances de la Tour (30 July 1958)
Yves St Laurent (1 August 1936)
Alan Whicker (2 August 1925)
Martin Sheen (3 August 1940)
Joan Hickson (5 August 1906)
Barbara Windsor (6 August 1937)
Robert Mitchum (6 August 1917)
Enid Blyton (11 August 1897)
HRH Princess Anne (15 August 1950)
Madonna (16 August 1958)
Robert de Niro (17 August 1943)
Robert Redford (18 August 1937)
Willie Rushton (18 August 1937)
Coco Chanel (19 August 1883)
Barry Norman (21 August 1933)

LEO COUPLES

Business partners, past and present

Mick Jagger (26 July 1943) and
Keith Richards (Sagittarius – 18 December 1943)
Christopher Dean (27 July 1958) and
Jayne Torvill (Libra – 7 October 1957)

Romantic couples, past and present

Jacqueline Onassis (28 July 1928) and
Aristotle Onassis (Capricorn – 15 January 1906)
Peter O'Toole (2 August 1932) and
Sian Phillips (Taurus – 14 May 1934)
HM Queen Elizabeth the Queen Mother (4 August 1900) and
King George Vl (Sagittarius – 14 December 1895)
HRH Princess Margaret (21 August 1930) and
Lord Snowdon (Pisces – 7 March 1930)

Some Famous Virgos

Martin Amis (25 August 1949)
Sean Connery (25 Augu5t 1930)
Mother Teresa (27 August 1910)
Sir Richard Attenborough (29 August 1923)
Ingrid Bergman (29 August 1915)
Van Morrison (31 August 1945)
Lily Tomlin (1 September 1939)
Raquel Welch (5 September 1940)
Britt Eckland (6 September 1943)
Gwen Watford (10 September 1927)
Barry Sheene (11 September 1950)
Ian Holm (12 September 1931)
John Smith (13 September 1938)
Jacqueline Bissett (13 September 1944)
Freddie Mercury (15 September 1946)
Agatha Christie (15 September 1890)
Greta Garbo (18 September 1905)
Twiggy (19 September 1949)
Michael Elphick (19 September 1946)
Sophia Loren (20 September 1934)

VIRGO COUPLES

Business partners, past and present

The Hon. Charles Rolls (27 August 1877) and
Sir Frederick Henry Royce (Aries – 27 March 1863)
Dick Clement (5 September 1937) and
Ian La Frenais (Capricorn – 7 January 1937)
Peter Sellers (8 September 1925) and
Sir Harry Secombe (Virgo – 8 September 1921)

Romantic couples, past and present

Prince Albert (26 August 1819) and
Queen Victoria (Gemini – 24 May 1819)
Lady Antonia Fraser (27 August 1932) and
Harold Pinter (Libra – 10 October 1930)
Lenny Henry (29 August 1958) and
Dawn French (Libra – 11 October 1957)
Pauline Collins (3 September 1940) and
John Alderton (Sagittarius – 27 November 1940)
Lauren Bacall (16 September 1924) and
Humphrey Bogart (Capricorn – 25 December 1899)
Anne Bancroft (17 September 1931) and
Mel Brooks (Cancer – 28 June 1927)
Jeremy Irons (19 September 1948) and
Sinead Cusack (Aquarius – 18 February 1948)
John Dankworth (20 September 1927) and
Cleo Laine (Scorpio – 28 October 1927)
Sophia Loren (20 September 1934) and
Carlo Ponti (Sagittarius – 11 December 1913)

♎ Some Famous Librans

F Scott Fitzgerald (24 September 1896)
Christopher Reeve (25 September 1952)
Michael Douglas (25 September 1944)
Brigitte Bardot (28 September 1934)
Patricia Hodge (29 September 1946)
Jerry Lee Lewis (29 September 1935)
Richard Harris (1 October 1933)
Groucho Marx (2 Ocxtober 1890)
James Herriot (3 October 1916)
Anneka Rice (4 October 1958)
Jackie Collins (4 October 1937)
Melvyn Bragg (6 October 1939)
Brian Blessed (9 October 1937)
Donald Sinden (9 October 1923)
Charles Dance (10 October 1946)
Edwina Currie (13 October 1946)
Roger Moore (14 October 1927)
PG Wodehouse (15 October 1881)
Angela Lansbury (16 October 1925)
Martina Navratilova (18 October 1956)
Chuck Berry (18 October 1926)
Carrie Fisher (21 October 1956)

LIBRA COUPLES

Business partners, past and present

Ronnie Barker (25 September 1929) and
Ronnie Corbett (Sagittarius – 4 December 1930)
George Gershwin (26 September 1898) and Ira Gershwin
(Sagittarius – 6 December 1896)
Walter Matthau (1 October 1920) and Jack Lemmon
(Aquarius – 8 February 1925)
Budd Abbot (2 October 1895) and
Lou Costello (Pisces – 6 March 1906)
Jayne Torvill (7 October 1957) and
Christopher Dean (Leo – 27 July 1958)
Albert Roux (8 October 1935) and
Michel Roux (Aries – 19 April 1941)
Dawn French (8 October 1957) and
Jennifer Saunders (Cancer 12 July 1958)
John Lennon (9 October 1940) and
Paul McCartney (Gemini – 18 June 1942)
Paul Simon (13 October 1941) and
Art Garfunkel (Scorpio – 5 November 1941)

Romantic couples, past and present

Linda McCartney (24 September 1941) and
Paul McCartney (Gemini – 18 June 1942)
Felicity Kendal (25 September 1946) and
Tom Stoppard (Cancer – 3 July 1937)
Lord Nelson (29 September 1758) and
Emma, Lady Hamilton (Taurus – 12 May 1765)
Rula Lenska (30 September 1947) and
Dennis Waterman (Pisces – 24 February 1948)
Lady Thatcher (13 October 1925) and
Sir Denis Thatcher (Taurus – 10 May 1915)

Some Famous Scorpios

Diana Dors (23 October 1931)
Bill Wyman (24 October 1941)
Sir Robin Day (24 October 1923)
Helen Reddy (25 October 1942)
Jaclyn Smith (26 October 1948)
Bob Hoskins (26 October 1942)
John Cleese (27 October 1939)
Dylan Thomas (27 October 1914)
Hank Marvin (28 October 1941)
Dick Francis (31 October 1920)
Marie Antoinette (2 November 1755)
Lulu (3 November 1948)
Loretta Swit (4 November 1944)
Nigel Havers (6 November 1949)
Joni Mitchell (7 November 1943)
Ken Dodd (8 November 1931)
Neil Young (12 November 1946)
Robert Louis Stevenson (13 November 1850)
Auberon Waugh (17 November 1939)
Jodie Foster (19 November 1963)
Goldie Hawn (21 November 1945)

SCORPIO COUPLES

Business partners, past and present

James Boswell (29 October 1740) and
Dr Samuel Johnson (Virgo – 18 September 1709)
Art Garfunkel (5 November 1941) and
Paul Simon (Libra – 13 October 1941)
Marie Curie (7 November 1867) and
Pierre Curie (Taurus – 15 May 1859)
Tim Rice (10 November 1944) and
Sir Andrew Lloyd Webber (Aries – 22 March 1948)
June Whitfield (11 November 1925) and
Terry Scott (Taurus – 4 May 1927)
Griff Rhys Jones (16 November 1953) and
Mel Smith (Sagittarius – 3 December 1952)
Peter Cook (17 November 1937) and
Dudley Moore (Aries – 19 April 1935)

Romantic couples, past and present

Joan Plowright (28 October 1929) and
Laurence Olivier (Gemini – 22 May 1907)
Cleo Laine (28 October 1927) and
John Dankworth (Virgo – 20 September 1927)
Tatum O'Neal (5 November 1963) and
John McEnroe (Aquarius – 16 February 1959)
Vivien Leigh (5 November 1913) and
Laurence Olivier (Gemini – 22 May 1907)
Katharine Hepburn (9 November 1909) and
Spencer Tracy (Aries – 5 April 1900)
Richard Burton (10 November 1925) and
Elizabeth Taylor (Pisces – 27 February 1932)
HRH the Prince of Wales (14 November 1948) and
HRH the Princess of Wales (Cancer – 1 July 1961)

Some Famous Sagittarians

Boris Becker (22 November 1967)
Billie Jean King (21 November 1943)
Tina Turner (26 November 1938)
William Blake (28 November 1757)
Sir Winston Churchill (30 November 1874)
Bette Midler (1 December 1945)
Paul Nicholas (3 December 1945)
Jeff Bridges (4 December 1949)
Mary Queen of Scots (8 December 1542)
Beau Bridges (9 December 1941)
Kirk Douglas (9 December 1918)
Cliff Michelmore (11 December 1919)
Jasper Conran (12 December 1959)
Dionne Warwick (12 December 1941)
Dick Van Dyke (13 December 1925)
Nostradamus (14 December 1503)
Noel Coward (16 December 1889)
Steven Spielberg (18 December 1947)
Jenny Agutter (20 December 1952)
Jane Fonda (21 December 1937)

SAGITTARIUS COUPLES

Business partners, past and present

Ernie Wise (27 November 1925) and
Eric Morecambe (Taurus – 14 May 1926)
Mel Smith (3 December 1952) and
Griff Rhys Jones (Scorpio – 16 November 1953)
Ronnie Corbett (4 December 1930) and
Ronnie Barker (Libra – 25 September 1929)
Ira Gershwin (6 December 1896) and
George Gershwin (Libra – 26 September 1898)
Keith Richards (18 December 1943) and
Mick Jagger (Leo – 26 July 1943)

Romantic couples, past and present

Billy Connolly (24 November 1942) and
Pamela Stephenson (Sagittarius – 4 December 1950)
John Alderton (27 November 1940) and
Pauline Collins (Virgo – 3 September 1940)
Woody Allen (1 December 1935) and
Diane Keaton (Capricorn – 5 January 1946)
Woody Allen (1 December 1935) and
Mia Farrow (Aquarius – 9 February 1945)
Maria Callas (2 December 1923) and
Aristotle Onassis (Capricorn – 15 January 1906)
Kenneth Branagh (10 December 1960) and Emma Thompson
(Aries – 15 April 1959)
Carlo Ponti (11 December 1913) and
Sophia Loren (Virgo – 20 September 1934)
King George Vl (14 December 1895) and
HM Queen Elizabeth the Queen Mother
(Leo – 4 August 1900)

Some Famous Capricorns

Noel Edmonds (22 December 1948)
Howard Hughes (24 December 1905)
Sissy Spacek (25 December 1949)
Mao Tse-tung (26 December 1893)
Marlene Dietrich (27 December 1901)
Maggie Smith (28 December 1934)
Marianne Faithfull (29 December 1946)
Mary Tyler Moore (29 December 1937)
Rudyard Kipling (30 December 1865)
Anthony Hopkins (31 December 1937)
Bonnie Prince Charlie (31 December 1720)
David Bailey (2 January 1938)
Mel Gibson (6 January 1956)
Gerald Durrell (7 January 1925)
David Bowie (8 January 1947)
Elvis Presley (8 January 1935)
Gracie Fields (9 January 1898)
Rod Stewart (10 January 1945)
Faye Dunaway (14 January 1941)
Richard Briers (14 January 1934)
Princess Michael of Kent (15 January 1945)
Martin Luther King (15 January 1929)
Stefan Edberg (19 January 1966)
Dolly Parton (19 January 1946)

CAPRICORN COUPLES

Business partners, past and present

Terry Vanables (6 January 1944) and
Alan Sugar (Aries – 24 March 1948)
Ian La Frenais (7 January 1937) and
Dick Clement (Virgo – 5 September 1937)
Oliver Hardy (18 January 1892) and
Stan Laurel (Gemini – 16 June 1890)
Phil Everly (19 January 1939) and
Don Everly (Aquarius – 1 February 1937)

Romantic couples, past and present

Humphrey Bogart (25 December 1899) and
Lauren Bacall (Virgo – 16 September 1924)
John Thaw (3 January 1942) and Sheila Hancock
(Pisces – 22 February 1933)
Diane Keaton (5 January 1946) and
Woody Allen (Sagittarius – 1 December 1935)
Aristotle Onassis (15 January 1906) and Maria Callas
(Sagittarius – 2 December 1923)

Some Famous Aquarians

Christian Dior (21 January 1905)
John Hurt (22 January 1940)
HSH Princess Caroline of Monaco (23 January 1957)
Jeanne Moreau (23 January 1928)
Natassya Kinski (24 January 1961)
Virginia Woolf (25 January 1882)
Michael Bentine (26 January 1922)
Lewis Carroll (27 January 1832)
Wolfgang Amadeus Mozart (27 January 1756)
Mikhail Baryshnikov (28 January 1948)
Phil Collins (30 January 1951)
Vanessa Redgrave (30 January 1937)
Tallulah Bankhead (31 January 1903)
Nell Gwynn (2 February 1650)
Charlotte Rampling (5 February 1946)
Patrick MacNee (6 February 1922)
Peter Jay (7 February 1937)
Charles Dickens (7 February 1812)
James Dean (8 February 1931)
Joyce Grenfell (10 February 1910)
Burt Reynolds (11 February 1936)
Abraham Lincoln (12 February 1809)
Oliver Reed (13 February 1938)
Claire Bloom (15 February 1931)
Patricia Routledge (17 February 1929)

AQUARIUS COUPLES

Business partners, past and present

David Jason (2 February 1940) and
Nicholas Lyndhurst (Aries – 20 April 1961)
Jack Lemmon (8 February 1925) and
Walter Matthau (Libra – 1 October 1920)
Don Everly (1 February 1937) and
Phil Everly (Capricorn – 19 January 1939)
Frank Muir (5 February 1920) and
Denis Norden (Aquarius – 6 February 1922)

Romantic couples, past and present

Paul Newman (26 January 1925) and
Joanne Woodward (Pisces – 27 February 1930)
Libby Purves (2 February 1950) and
Paul Heiney (Aries – 20 April 1949)
Mia Farrow (9 February 1945) and
Woody Allen (Sagittarius – 1 December 1935)
John McEnroe (16 February 1959) and
Tatum O'Neal (Scorpio – 5 Novem~er 1963)
Yoko Ono Lennon (18 February 1934) and
John Lennon (Libra 9 October 1940)
Eva Braun (6 February 1912) and
Adolph Hitler (Taurus – 20 April 1889)
Sinead Cusack (18 February 1948) and
Jeremy Irons (Virgo – 19 September 1948)

Some Famous Pisceans

Merle Oberon (19 February 1911)
Jilly Cooper (21 February 1937)
Bruce Forsyth (22 February 1928)
George Washington (22 February 1732)
Samuel Pepys (23 February 1633)
George Harrison (25 February 1943)
Fats Domino (26 February 1928)
Paddy Ashdown (27 February 1941)
Joss Ackland (29 February 1928)
David Niven (1 March 1910)
Mikhail Gorbachev (2 March 1931)
Jean Harlow (3 March 1911)
Patrick Moore (4 March 1923)
Rex Harrison (5 March 1908)
Kiri Te Kanawa (6 March 1944)
Ivan Lendl (7 March 1960)
Yuri Gagarin (9 March 1934)
Prince Andrew (10 March 1964)
Terence Alexander (11 March 1923)
Liza Minnelli (12 March 1946)
Leo McKern (16 March 1920)

PISCES COUPLES

(

Business partners, past and present

Julie Walters (22 February 1950) and
Victoria Wood (Taurus – 19 May 1953)
Roger Daltrey (1 March 1944) and
Pete Townshend (Taurus – 19 May 1945)
Lou Costello (6 March 1906) and
Budd Abbot (Libra – 2 October 1895)

Romantic couples, past and present

HRH the Duke of York (19 February 1960) and
HRH the Duchess of York (Libra – 15 October 1959)
Sheila Hancock (22 February 1933) and
John Thaw (Capricorn – 3 January 1942)
Denis Waterman (24 February 1948) and
Rula Lenska (Libra – 30 September 1947)
Joanne Woodward (27 February 1930) and
Paul Newman (Aquarius – 26 January 1925)
Elizabeth Taylor (27 February 1932) and
Richard Burton (Scorpio – 10 November 1925)
Lord Snowdon (7 March 1930) and
HRH Princess Margaret (Leo – 21 August 1930)

Astro Meditations

FOR YOU AND YOUR PARTNER

ARIES

Being first in everything is being part of everything. Use your energy and impulse creatively, spontaneously. Be you, but learn from gentleness. Fire is cosmic, don't burn others up, set them alight instead.

TAURUS

Hedonistic, jewels of sensuality. Pursue pleasures instead of waiting for them. Resentment builds on regrets. Take notice of energy, ground it if you must. Endurance is an art — respect it.

GEMINI

Seek change, but seek change within. Don't try to look deeper, you can't. The surface is coloured, is covered in shimmering. Let it be superficial, let your sexual love and lightness glide.

CANCER

Be a lunatic but face the truth that you have deeper emotions. Insecurity is instability. Sex and love can unite. Don't hide yourself from your truth — you are an introvert/extrovert. Light a candle to yourself.

LEO

Self-gratification. You love to impress, to make a noise, to have power. Power can be constructive, love and sexuality instructive. Flash warmth. Roar with pride rather than conceit.

VIRGO

Let go of the sex manual. Take a trip on surprise, on unpredictability, that is love. Stop worrying – be dippy. Perfect diffidence, it is as refreshing as your crisp mentality. Jog in bed, dissent.

LIBRA

Romance is born easily. Use charm explosively, no time for hesitation. Fall in love with love, but make it clear to yourself. Clarify romantic attraction and know it for what it is.

SCORPIO

Sentence only your obsessions. Keep others' mysteries as proof of emotions. You feel love as sexuality, as wholeness – the mystery and the answer to life. Fulfil your needs tenderly, administer with light.

SAGITTARIUS

You can expand, let others know. Give yourself freely, without blunt words. Wise to the world, wise eventually in love. Try loyalty, let go of promiscuity. Challenge sexual egotism with altruistic love.

CAPRICORN

Treat sex as an infant, nurture it. Grow with it, not against it. Try reaching out, try giving with the heart. There is no power in restriction, in restraint. Tie sex to love instead of to the bed.

AQUARIUS

Rebellion hurts others. Convention can work. Friendship is your heaven – let others come closer, let others conform if they must. Sex can be part of love, not a trap, it can be free.

PISCES

Ideals, half-seen, half-being. The stray are led astray more easily than the homed. The clouds can open with rainbows on the ocean. Take a deep-sea dive, communicate love instead of drowning.

Love Trends

The inner sections emphasise the important moods and trends through each month of the year with regard to love, friendship, partnership, sex.

Aries

YOUR AT-A-GLANCE CHART

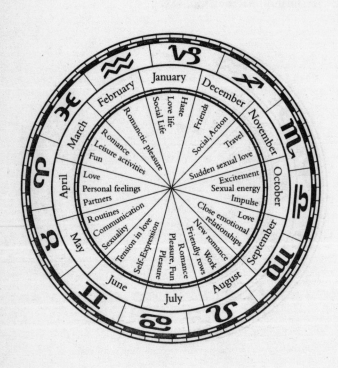

Taurus

YOUR AT-A-GLANCE CHART

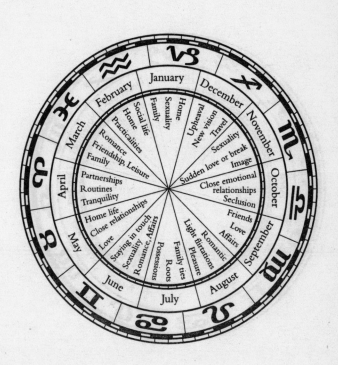

Gemini

YOUR AT-A-GLANCE CHART

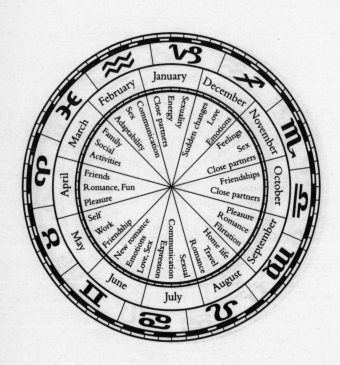

Cancer

YOUR AT-A-GLANCE CHART

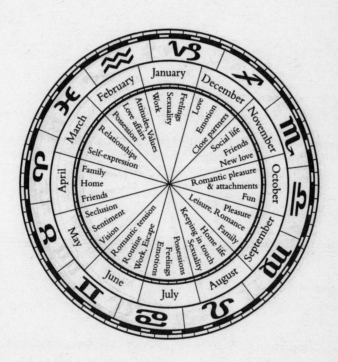

Leo

YOUR AT-A-GLANCE CHART

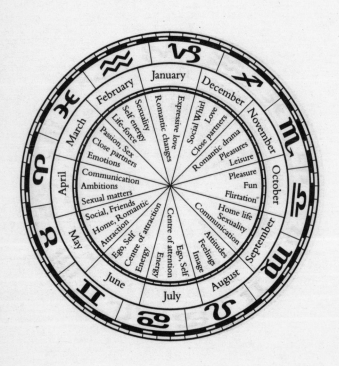

Virgo

YOUR AT-A-GLANCE CHART

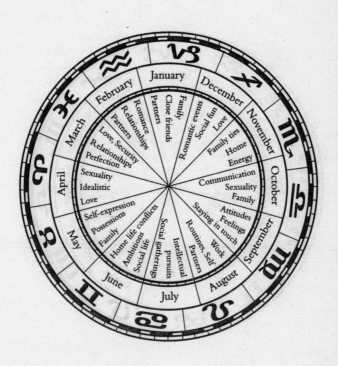

Libra

YOUR AT-A-GLANCE CHART

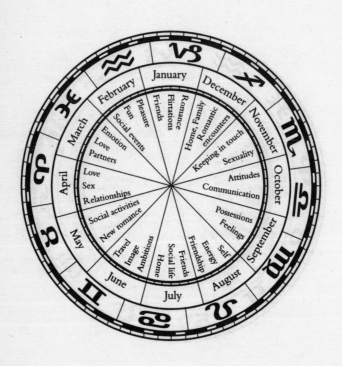

Scorpio

YOUR AT-A-GLANCE CHART

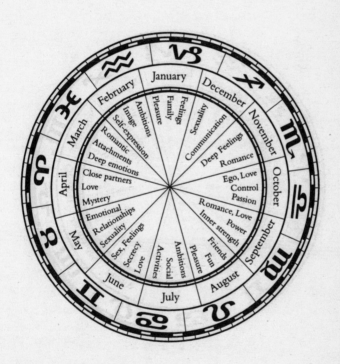

Sagittarius

YOUR AT-A-GLANCE CHART

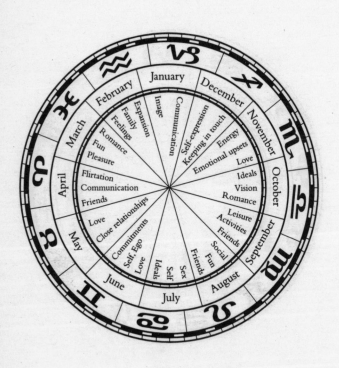

Capricorn

YOUR AT-A-GLANCE CHART

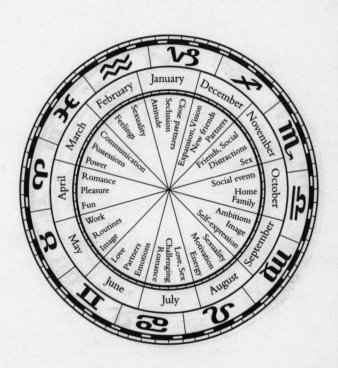

Aquarius

YOUR AT-A-GLANCE CHART

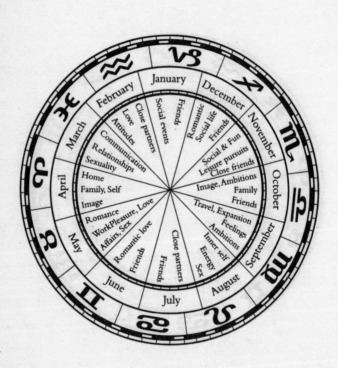

Pisces

YOUR AT-A-GLANCE CHART

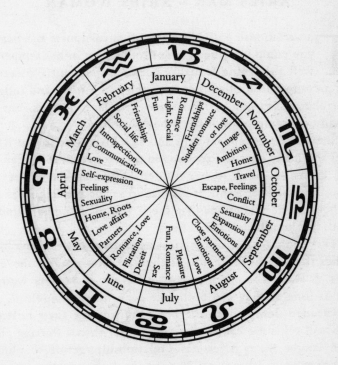

Aries

COMPATIBILITIES

ARIES MAN – ARIES WOMAN

This relationship usually starts off as passionate and fiery as you could imagine. There may be a lot of hot tempers as well as burning sexuality between their initial meetings and a competition of egos to see who can initiate and inflame the relationship quicker. Both get extremely jealous, but are equally contemptuous of the other's jealousy.

She will be as independent and as selfish as he is, but if she tries too many egotistic twists, and threatens him too often, he will either succumb to her sudden child-like charm, or will never speak to her again. If his macho image breaks first it will be because he recognises that she is just as vulnerable underneath her hard little shell as he is.

This could be one of the most passionate and exciting love-affairs if they can both forget their opinions aren't the only ones. A Ram is as much a show-off as she is a career woman. But as long as they can both face each other's impulse and hot-headed desire to be the boss, then maybe their relationship will remain a cautionary tale, rather than a fleeting affair with danger. Many Aries–Aries relationships get off to a better start than most other signs. They are both so sexually magnetic, so ready to rush in before they even think of the consequences, that they probably won't even have time to find out whether they both like beer or spirits. Flirting is part of their child-like behaviour, it enhances their vanity and proves that they are in control. Aries men and women are inordinately selfish in their love-making, and during their initial wild and impulsive romance they may not notice this because they will be so wound up trying to impress one another! If they can learn to be less selfish, to compete less with each other they may not end up going their separate ways. But they never bear grudges, however high their tempers flare.

ARIES MAN – TAURUS WOMAN

Most Taurean woman are hard to spot and impossible to provoke. But an Aries man has the best chance of spotting her hard-edged front and seducing her out of her stubborn attitude that abhors all those things an Aries man is! At a party the Taurus girl will often rather sit alone in the kitchen happily eating the crisps, and an Arien male could find that disturbingly erotic. The Taurus girl's sensuality is foreign to him, which makes her doubly attractive. Her feelings are that sex is good and basic: honest erotic earthiness, a significance of presence, or life. Love is something else, more mysterious and a calling from nature, far deeper than an Aries man can fathom. The high performance level of the ego-driven Ram can be overwhelmingly self-centred and not placid enough for the Bull lady. Aries men aren't particularly good at settling down to play the happy husband, nor the benevolent lover either, both of which a Taurean girl wants in her life. She likes financial security, he likes to take chances, gamble his money, and even his heart, for the pure pleasure of impulsive living. A Taurean girl always wants a simple and comfortable home, a cosy set-up and a sure and steady future, but the Aries man has neither the solidity nor the patience for this kind of relationship. Short-term, it could be sexually fun for him, but neither would get much out of a long-term commitment unless they can adjust to her need for affectionate security and his for spoiled and impetuous living.

ARIES WOMAN – TAURUS MAN

Friction is the name of the game for this odd coupling! Not an easy relationship, especially sexually. Aries women need to release tumultuous energy and deliver themselves into the hands of passionate mind-blowing fantasies. Imagination works alongside physical love with a female Ram and frankly Mr Bull won't find the time to indulge in this kind of exhausting mental and emotional game. The Aries girl likes to express herself openly, the Bull likes to keep everything in the dark. The Bull will dogmatically insist that he is right about everything and, being a positive tenacious hothead, she's more likely to stomp off. The Bull is possessive and very stuck in his ways, which will antagonise the Aries girl more than his eating habits. Her intensely energetic lifestyle won't exactly lock in with his own placid, practical one. He wants life to move along at a slow, easy pace, but she will want to get on the bus before it goes without her.

Another major set-back will be when he wants to handle the cashflow and she would rather just spend it. Most Aries girls are not very clever with their finances, and the Bull's stubborn Monopoly game can create much tension between them. If she can understand that his patience could be her virtue, and he could realise her impetuous nature is fun and honest, and could give him a lot of new challenges in life, then there could be hope for their attraction.

ARIES MAN – GEMINI WOMAN

There is no way that either of these two can resist one another. A Gemini girl is usually out of the house most of the time and is likely to bump into an Aries in any of her many roles in life. Drinking with this man can lead to a relationship quicker than any other social activity! If it's a permanent love-affair they both want, then he can provide the stamina and the passion and she will keep him mentally alert and ready for anything. He will love her changeable, unpredictable nature, and it could be a very sexy relationship, as there will always be adventure between them.

Fire and Air are a potent concoction and they will thrive on each other's body sparks. There will be a lot of passion, and a lively and inventive approach to sex, although the Twin girl may sometimes appear to be on a different planet, which could infuriate the Aries man when he wants her to be sharing his spirited love-making. His ego is in need of polishing most of the time, and usually Gemini girls hate anything to do with housework! Gemini women live in their heads, so he will have to get past her mental puzzles, her teasing provocative crossword games, before he can expect to encounter her true love. Dark and exciting meetings, trips to every possible romantic location, will be shared with equal delight. But don't forget that Aries has that niggling little emotion called jealousy, and that Gemini is one of the more flirtatious women in the zodiac. If she can't resist another game the Aries temper may put out his own fire and, once an Aries man is convinced the relationship has ended, there is no turning back.

ARIES WOMAN – GEMINI MAN

Now an Aries girl with a head full of ideas about where she is going in life often finds herself meeting a charming, irresistible Gemini man and wondering how she can show him she's the most sexually magnetic and vibrant girl of the zodiac. He is likely to be more interested in what goes on inside her head, than in her heart. And certainly he will find her bossy, straightforward approach to life a refresher course in intellectual energy. He likes things to change, to move on, to be constantly a fresh challenge. She will like challenges, but she'll want to improve upon every one she makes. And that often includes improving her Gemini partner. Aries girls are jealous, and Gemini men aren't. In fact they haven't usually a whiff of resentment in their heads. The Aries girl would rather he were jealous; in fact, if he doesn't appear in the slightest bit bothered when she is flirting, the Aries girl can get quite heated and walk out. Their saving grace is that she is just as keen at catching the milkman's eye as he is at falling in love with Doris Day on the TV. His rather detached approach to sex may bother her. When she's in passionate mode, he may be quizzing over the latest contraceptive, or whether the Egyptians made love behind the Pyramids. His is a need for mental and Airy love-making, her need is for fantasy and passion. He may provide the fantasies to enchant her, but he may not produce the passion on demand she so desperately expects.

ARIES MAN – CANCER WOMAN

The Moon girl's initial attraction to this incredibly arrogant man will probably be because of his daring, independent spirit and his incredible good looks. Water and Fire don't mix awfully well, and Fire signs don't like being smothered by anything, particularly a dousing of water; it turns their red-hot passion into a sizzling black ember of bitterness. The Aries man may admit to finding the Cancerian girl's sensuality a temptation of the flesh. He may not at first care about her deep inner self that she cherishes so guardedly, nor her emotional need for a long-term relationship with a protective, dominant male. He is dominant, but not awfully good at protecting, unless he's in the middle of a risk-taking enterprise or adventure, and then he will spring to action like Tarzan. However, the Aries man is basically too reckless with money, and too reckless with most things, for a Cancer girl to stay around long. And equally, his honest, enterprising spirit won't have the patience or strength to play moods with the loony Moon. He may be fascinated for a while by her intensity of feeling and touch, and her deeper secrets may unlock themselves for an Aries man, but a Cancer girl's possessiveness will send him running for the first flight out of commitment. There is always a dangerous battle brewing between sensitivity and arrogance here and he will retreat quickly if he feels those crabby pincers anywhere near him. The last thing he really wants is someone else to worry about his pennies, when he'd like to go out and spend them on anything, as long as it's flash! Sexually, he'll be enlightened by her cool sensuality, but she may not be able to put up with his passion and impulsive, hot-headed love-making.

Cancer women often end up hurt because they pop back into their shells when self-pity takes them out of the frontline. And unless she is a masochist, it is often wiser for the Crab sensibly to retreat from this relationship, before she gets stuck in her shell forever.

ARIES WOMAN – CANCER MAN

Another doomed but potentially explosive relationship! The Aries girl has a direct, no nonsense approach to love. Her feelings are aroused instantly, not latently or later after the flush of passion has subsided. She'll want immediate love, receive immediate attention. The Ram girl may be overwhelmed by the Cancerian man's love of her strength and the pure Fire burning in her soul. They both have, believe it or not, the same goals in a relationship, but neither of them is remotely able to perceive the similarities, only the differences. They both want success, both hunger after a secure relationship and both want to motivate others to love as intensely as they do. Sounds like the perfect formula? Well, it's not.

The Aries girl's love of success is a sunny, bright, optimistic motivation, and the Cancerian man's is fuddled by the Moon, always melancholic, pessimistic, sadly lacking in confidence in any relationship. If the Crab is too cautious, then the Ram is too self-confident. If the Crab plays the extrovert when he first meets the Aries girl (which he usually does quite unconsciously), she will fall desperately in love with the image that he projects so well but refuses to believe he can live up to. He will fall instantly in love with her charm and her impetuous nature. They are both outrageously jealous. The Aries girl won't cope with his smothering possessiveness, and he won't be able to understand her anger if he so much as winks his Crab-like gaze at a distant Moon girl. He will brood, she will lose her Fiery temper. Yet his need for sensationalism in his life may draw her constantly back to his side. Aries women don't forgive easily, nor forget, but the Cancer man is such a mad, sad clown that she might, just for once, return.

ARIES MAN – LEO WOMAN

A thrilling contest of egos battling out for the leading role and the competition to be the centre of the universe! Who comes first? Leo women believe they have to be in charge, and Aries men believe they should be in control in everything, including bed, from day one. The best bet for these two optimists of the zodiac is take it in turns to be on top. The Leo woman is less likely to burn herself out if she lets Aries take the dominating role. Actually if she realises that she is organising his stardom, then to her the battle is already won!

Emotionally they will tumble together like loaded dice. They burn fire with fire and will both love the high they get from this exhausting and frantic relationship full of blazing rows and hurt pride, especially the Big Cat's. The Aries man's troubles may arise from his lack of discretion. He has a rather honest and open way with words, and may open his big mouth when he should be mumbling words of love or adoration to the Leo girl, as she does need a lot of stroking. He might reveal his Leo lady's favourite colour underwear to his mother, when he should have been discreetly suggesting they elope instead. In a blaze of passionate impulse he may turn up on the Ram's doorstep at four in the morning and expect her to share a bath.

Of course this youthful energy will keep them both acting like a couple of kids, but there will be moments when Leo will want more affection, and more emotional strength, from him than he is actually capable of giving. They both love a glamorous and fast lifestyle, would rather live for today than plan too much for tomorrow. Seeking an intense and dramatic involvement will keep them both on their toes, and this could be a loving and permanent relationship if they've both got the energy to survive.

ARIES WOMAN – LEO MAN

The independent Aries woman will get a shock when she first meets a Lion in an extravagant and conceited mood. For the first time in her life she'll be confronted with a man who can give as good as she does, and who won't take no for an answer. Her own bossiness will be burnt away by the Lion's attack (always from behind because he's less likely to get hurt that way), to find herself mysteriously carried away by the way he tells her he knows all the answers, and really how could she ever doubt him if he's decided he has chosen her? His superior and rather condescending approach to women won't unnerve her. Although she may get angry when he tries to explain to her the meaning of life. Leos have this knack of thinking no one, except they, knows the answer to it. Her Martian impulse will rile him frequently, and they are sure to have blazing rows at all times of day and night. Aries and Leo are both Fire signs and they have the same passionate need for a wild and careless sexual relationship. Once they have fallen breathless between the sheets they are more likely than most couples to forget their differences. Unfortunately, it will be the Lion who may on occasion find his pride is hurt more than he can bear and he'll withdraw and become icy. He can inflict pain without thinking and will often quite innocently make frequent comparisons and references to past love-affairs, because he really does believe he is God's gift to women. If she can accept that his arrogance stems from fear of making a fool of himself, and that, like the Lion he is, the bravery is all a front for a warm and loving heart, she might just learn to forgive him in time.

ARIES MAN – VIRGO WOMAN

Now we all know that Virgos have this thing about perfection. Not the heady, sensitive perfection of a Piscean dreamer, but a practical, down-to-earth belief that there is someone out there who can provide Virgos with their heart's desire. Now an Aries out for an entanglement, sexual or otherwise, turning on his favourite virility lesson, can seem the kind of hedonistic turn-on that a Virgo will find both alluring and repellent. The Aries Ram will pick her up for her femininity, think he can save her from a life of dull routine, and is sure she must find him the most beautiful creature. (Fire signs have this rather naïve vanity.) He won't be fond of her cold and rational resentment, although he's got his own jealousy to contend with too. The Aries man will be amused by the Virgo woman's sharp, subtle mentality, and he'll get infatuated with the apparent earthiness of her sexuality. But don't believe that it will keep him coming back for more unless she can inspire him with a bit more heady passion than financial considerations and whether she defrosted the fridge and left the door open. The Virgo girl will want to organise him from day one, and this man really doesn't like anything to be organised, let alone himself!

The coldness of her passion won't be their only obstacle for success. She has this awful ability to appear to disapprove of all the Aries man's most genuine and child-like qualities. He is chaotic, fun-loving, impetuous and risky. She is ordered, a worrier, sensible and concerned with purity, not passion. She is a lover of romance, but once the romance has gone she is happy to work hard for a good solid relationship based on how she sees a perfect marriage to be. Never mind what the Aries man thinks, as far as she is concerned he doesn't think, he merely acts. And the Ram's actions don't usually speak loud enough for her analytical and precise mind.

ARIES WOMAN – VIRGO MAN

The outgoing and tactless Ram girl can seems quite a viable proposition for the Virgo idealist looking for perfection. To be able to control this headstrong woman would seem to him a rather invigorating and mentally challenging business, as long as she doesn't attempt to wash his socks, because he always does it *his* way, and makes sure she cleans up every crumb from the bed before he got into it.

The Virgo man is sometimes unsure of what his ideal is. When he meets an Aries he is, of course, initially infatuated with her very opposite fantasy to his own. But her mystery, however enticing it is to him, can crumble into truth and become an irritant rather like those breadcrumbs between the sheets.

An Aries woman will find his cold, unyielding purity not at first an attraction. But he could be the sort of man she might recklessly have a frantic love-affair with, or just forget him all together. Yet there is something rather strangely magnetic between these two, and often an Aries girl will push back the frontiers of the Antarctic and storm into his heart to try to find if the ice is meltable on her own very high temperature gauge. The Virgo may find her irresistible while the romantic perfectionist is working overtime. His performance in bed will win her over for a while but, once the initial sexual encounter has diminished between them, there is very little left for them to salvage except her independence and his digestive problems.

ARIES MAN – LIBRA WOMAN

Dreamers dream and Aries men put the whole lot into action, if he really believes he can and usually he does! Like any Fire–Air relationship the Libran girl will provide the dreams and fuel for his fire, and because they are opposite signs of the zodiac the attraction will be immediate, sexual and intensely concentrated.

Love grows in this kind of swirl of emotion and physical involvement. The passion will be real and one that neither of these two fun-loving signs will be able to resist in one another.

Libran ladies, however, aren't too keen on making decisions and Aries men are. The impulsive nature of the Aries' rush to reach a quick answer won't always suit the gentle, lovely Libran lady. He believes he is always right, sometimes she won't be too convinced, only because she really won't be sure *after* his leap into the dark, if he were fair in his impetuous and hasty move. On the other hand if the Libran girl doesn't agree with the Aries opinions, which can be downright self-centred and unfair, then she will find it hard to convince him, that as much as she cares what he thinks, other opinions matter too. But like all opposition partnerships this could be a knock-out relationship. Both Aries and Libra will always have a lot to say, a lot to do and places to go. As long as she lets his confidence shine, and his passion pour into her sunshine heart then he will always be there for her.

ARIES WOMAN – LIBRA MAN

The Female Ram is devoted to carnal and passionate pleasures. When she is attracted by a beautiful, charming and apparently expert lover like a Libran man she will think immediately (because she always thinks on impulse) that this man could be the love of her life. She desperately wants someone to understand that beneath her quite frank, bossy and organising nature she is a real, gentle, kind and loving woman.

The Libran man will find her, at first, rather awkward to handle. Used to seducing females with fewer masculine, up-front expectations, he may make a bosh of it and turn her physical attraction for him into an optimism that, maybe tomorrow, she'll meet the man of her life, not just this minute, thank you all the same. Yet because they are opposite signs these two should find that the instantaneous attraction (which stems mostly from the Aries woman) will spark the kind of idealistic romance into the Libran's loins that he had never believed possible. Used to charming his way through life, he will admire her challenging and sometimes naïve self-confidence. She has a way of locking into his Airy ether and reminding him that love is about more than just romance. Sexually they are matched quite beautifully, but she will occasionally feel that he is somewhere else apart from the bed, and he will find her overpowering burning arms can get a little too wrapped around his aesthetic need for dreaming. The Libran needs freedom, and he needs a companion who can understand his social wanderings. She's a burner, he's a dreamer, and their attitudes to life and what it means are very different.

ARIES MAN – SCORPIO WOMAN

The intangible mystery of a Scorpio girl are without doubt one of the most powerful attractions of any sign. The Aries man will respond to those dark sensual messages with true Fiery arousal. Sexual magnetism is a gift to the Arien hothead, his own impulses surge like flames through his heart and soul and to find such a whole, completely sexual woman is his heart's desire! An Aries man who bumps into this woman in one of her more intense and emotional moments may think she is the love of his life. But watch him begin to squirm. Thinking he can understand her every need, because Rams are convinced they are the only men in the universe to have this effect on a girl anyway, he'll get caught out by her sudden emotional and heavy involvement dumped on his own superficial ego. Neither will he carry someone else's load for them, nor will he suffer deep-seated enigmas that can turn into a nest of bitter and twisted vipers. He is a dare-devil, she is fixed in her desires. But she will find him irresistible, and unable to let him go once he has entered her territory. The Scorpio woman is capable of making great sacrifices to hang on to the one she wants, and also making great scenes of misery and despair in her all or nothing desperation. For the fairly straightforward Aries male this can all come as quite a shock if he's not prepared for the vengeance and spite that can turn in this woman's dangerous heart. Essentially this could be a very sexual relationship, but the Aries man may not be able tolerate the secret torments for long.

ARIES WOMAN – SCORPIO MAN

On the surface this is a very sexual relationship. Scorpio men will find the Aries girl's impulsive, carefree, untamed mentality a positive challenge, one that is opposite from his own. Emotionally they could drain each other dry with an intense passion for life. The Scorpio man will want to hit the Aries girl with big truths, deep confessions and expect her to stay in one piece.

Scorpios like dangerous living; they thirst for the darkness and pain of it all. Aries like dangerous living because they don't think about what dangers are actually involved. The risk is what counts: the surface of the danger, not its depth.

The Aries girl may not be emotionally ready for the soul-searching of the Scorpio in the dead of night, but he could prove to be one of the best physical relationships she will ever have. Scorpios must control, and he won't like it when Aries won't be bossed around, can't be overpowered and won't be submissive. It's not in her nature, and she'll probably rebel against his dark and devious, broody moods. He will get het up about her Fiery spirit, and attempt to smother it in his Watery retaliation. Sex is the meaning of life, and the meaning of existence to a Scorpio. It's the whole of life to him, and to an Aries woman it's only part of life. If Scorpio gets into his obsessive gear, then she will have to watch out, even a Ram can get stung by a Scorpion or bitten by a snake!

ARIES MAN – SAGITTARIUS WOMAN

A crazy relationship. Sagittarian women often have energetic and time-consuming careers, so that the chances are she'll probably meet a few of those fast, impetuous Aries men along the same road. The Archer girls have a blunt and headstrong approach to sex and love and an equally passionate lifestyle. That's why the Aries man is often a good bet for understanding her expansive and altruistic nature. The Aries man loves most women, and the Sagittarian woman loves most men. She's a humanitarian, and may well have a host of platonic men-friends which, unfortunately, the Ram will find hard to accept. This relationship can be physically and mentally exhausting for both of these two Fire-eaters. She will want fun, to stay up all night and dance in the summer rain, to experience romance and live in the ideal world of free love as far away from commitment and traps as she can possibly manage. The Aries man may be able to give her most of this, but he really isn't awfully good at being the true romantic. His is the love of passion and the hunger of domination to trim his inflated ego. Hers is to be reminded that fantasy and fairy-tales might come true, even when the party is over. What he can offer her though is honesty and a reckless, free-ranging independence. Sexually they orbit the same planet, and financially and mentally they can ride the same bus and remain friends even when they've both run out of cash and a joke. She'll put up with his egotistic chip on his shoulder; after all, she's not power-driven, just lucky. There will be times when she feels she was unlucky to meet him when their Fiery tempers flare up, they both walk out in a mood and threaten never to speak again. But she'll probably be the first to say she's sorry, and that's what the Ram needs – someone who is true to herself.

ARIES WOMAN – SAGITTARIUS MAN

The Archer looks for adventure, for opportunity round every corner. If he sees a challenge, a woman with strength and an honesty above his own, then he may find the irresistible urge to fall as impulsively in love as she can. He is drawn to lighthearted, independent romantics and would rather flirt than chat to the boys. His encounters with women are often platonic, but there is always an undercurrent of pure sexual masculinity, which he finds hard to cover up, for all his generous friendship and love of sharing his incorrigible charm.

The Aries girl won't be too careful responding to his undoubted charm, after all she is hasty in most things. But she's heard about the Don Juan of the zodiac, and his cheeky, persuasive style. Somehow she can immediately feel vulnerable in this man's presence, perhaps because his values and ideals are matched against such high standards that even an Aries girl feels inferior to his desire. They have much in common, a liking for fun, adventure, an easy-going lightness in a relationship, where 'commitment' and 'for ever' are hardly mentioned. But if they are it will be the Ram girl who first suggests permanence. The Archer rarely allows himself to be put into this position and, for any relationship with a Sagittarian, the Aries girl will have to make sure she never mentions the future, never makes plans, and is herself constantly unavailable and difficult to pin down.

They both have the same ideals in bed. He will be deeply passionate and funny, she will be intensely responsive and warm to his boy-like antics.

Their egos may sometimes clash, but his is based on physical appearance, the way his ego works *through* the world, rather than the Arien ego which needs to feel confident *in* the world.

ARIES MAN – CAPRICORN WOMAN

The logical incompatibility of these two is probably the only thing that will bring them together. A Capricorn girl prefers the stability of home or the solidity of her career and success: a settled existence either way, which means she really has little time for the antics of an Arien ego.

But if she really should take a fancy to a red-hot Ram (he may be a colleague at work, or a long-standing friend who has recently returned to haunt her), she might take a trip out of her ordered existence. As long as she is acting within her own self-imposed restraint she may well allow herself to get involved with the ridiculous impulses of the Aries man.

She will find the impetuous and reckless lifestyle of this man contemptuous, and he won't exactly be nuts about her rather staid and cautious self-reliance. If she lets him into her heart then he might find a suppressed romantic trying to get out. But sexually she is likely to clam up with a man whose ego is bigger than her own. After all, he really is too irresponsible to remember the condoms, so what would it be like relying on him to sign the household cheques, or to make financial decisions?

Her caution will always demoralise his love of spontaneity. Sexually, he could awaken her latent passion, but she needs the purpose of a different order, a neater, perfected regularity in her life, not the fire and brimstone that can burn itself out when it reaches the top of the mountain. Because that is where *she* is going first. An Aries wants to get there too, but he gets high on an awful lot of tangents that lead him to adventures on the way.

ARIES WOMAN – CAPRICORN MAN

Unfortunately for the Goat man the Aries girl will only try so hard to get close to him, and then, like the reactionary Fire sign she is, will give up trying just as she's within inches of his heart. He does have one, for all his apparent stuffy ways and the wheel-clamp of sacrifice to his business or his career. Finding a soul-mate is not particularly part of his life plan. He'd rather get to the top, stay manacled to a reserved existence, or wait till he's older for the fun.

Aries girls like to have fun straight away, as soon as they can, sexually and emotionally. Capricorn men wait prudently and often become train-spotters or computer buffs in their youth to avoid having to face the games and chaos of love and sex.

The Aries woman will turn his head, though. She has this knack of turning his Goaty fortitude into desire and, if she manages to catch the sort of Goat who is able to offer security, friendship and an easy sexual relationship, then he really can be almost, just almost, right for her. The trouble is he's not too hot on communication. That's why Goats are left on the top of their mountains with a trail of broken hearts down the hillside.

His inability to cope with her wild side might mean that they never reach one another. It's sad to see Pan rejected for his impassionate responses, but the Ram won't hang around for staid love. Those two words don't go together in her book, and she hasn't the patience, nor the pride, to hang around for a man who can't keep up with her zest for living.

ARIES MAN – AQUARIUS WOMAN

A brilliant but probably short-lived affair. The Aquarian girl will probably check out everything about this man before even allowing him near her front door, let alone her bed. He will be after a far more physical relationship than she is. But if the Aries man can accept friendship as the most important part of their relationship, they may stand a good chance. Aries men want adventure and excitement in bed, romance and the promise of passionate fulfilment. The Aquarian girl is more likely to be interested in his brain and he may not be quirky enough to amuse her for long. But Aquarian women must defy convention and maybe the sexual antics of this egotistic man will keep her fascinated longer than she imagined. Like most Air signs her boredom level is reached more quickly than anyone else's and, if he can keep her mind active as well as her body, then they will need little emotion in their relationship. Sexual activity is only part of the whole deal to an Aquarian, but to an Aries it represents his ego. She might want an intimate conversation by the Thames at midnight, and an awful lot of respect. He might just want a night making love in a tent on a bare mountain. She is an anarchist, and sometimes Aries can be incredibly old-fashioned. This is where they differ deeply. Intellectually Aries men aren't quite on the same planet; it's almost as if they've been left on Mars when the Aquarian girl took off for the Earth, and a better place. She might encourage him to think laterally, but her individual and quirky habits will leave him cold.

ARIES WOMAN – AQUARIUS MAN

Aries women are number one in their own life, and also number one in every relationship. If she doesn't win the risks and the dice rolls of love that she's set her heart on then she can storm out of a man's life quicker than she stormed into it. With an Aquarian man she is never quite sure if she is winning. He is capable of an almost devious game in which he will never let on who he is, or what he really wants. This can infuriate the Aries girl, but only makes him a more challenging prospect.

His friendship is important, his social life revolves with apparent unselfishness, and yet he is always holding something back. She can never be sure if it's love he feels or humanitarian compassion. The Aries girl wants to be the be-all of his life, but the Aquarian is more generous with his love and would rather share himself and his relationship with the world. This invariably makes an Aries woman jealous, and it can cause a strain whereby she never feels superior, and he really doesn't have the time to begin to care.

Sexually she will enjoy running the show to begin with, but an Aquarian doesn't like being bossed around as much as he doesn't want to be the boss. Eventually their bedtime fun will suffer when his aloof and sometimes cold passion deflates her vulnerable but beautiful ego.

ARIES MAN – PISCES WOMAN

This relationship appears to travel the same route as the doom-laden affair that Romeo and Juliet and many other literary lovers never recovered from. These two are so opposite in temperament and in their motivations and characteristics that it seems unlikely that they should ever meet, let alone stick together. But strangely this can be a pure and perfect sexual relationship at its best. At its worst the Pisces girl is too emotional and can turn the Aries' optimism into a coffin of depression.

The shunting pace and the rushing lifestyle of the Aries man can be at times too demanding for the gentle Pisces girl. If she can be tolerant of his self-seeking and selfish aims, which a Piscean girl often can, then she will have found the strength and honesty that she yearns for in her dreams. He might not be burning the midnight candle for her every night, his self-centred need to explore the world may lead him away further and more often than she might wish. However, he will expect her to be there for him while he's off up the Amazon, or touring Africa in a jeep. It's not necessarily that he doesn't care, it's just that he doesn't *think*.

The doer of the zodiac will be infatuated immediately with the deep stirrings the Piscean woman can make in his heart. In a long-term relationship she could become escapist if he spends too much time out and about, and he could get incredibly bored with her passive and changeable emotions. He could also get jealous of her ability to listen to every soul's problem with the deepest compassion and sympathy, but often won't listen to his own. Joan of Arc martyrdom can cause him to get angry and lose his temper with her, especially if the Fish girl has purposely gone cold on him and herself. He is vivacious and fun and likes male and female company. She is compassionate and gregarious and loves men. An Aries inflamed by fear and jealousy can toss his love on his own funeral fire, and lose a woman who could truly love him.

ARIES WOMAN – PISCES MAN

The Fire and spirit of the Aries girl will find it hard to be inflamed by the sensitive and instinctive behaviour of the gentle Piscean man. She is independent, forceful, bossy and essentially in need of strength and a big-brother type to support her and carry her pain and her vulnerability. The Piscean man is quite able to be all these things to her, but he can irritate her beyond her wildest dreams when he disappears into a dream world. When he takes for ever to get up and out in the morning, when he would rather be playing the piano, or working out why the universe *is*, she would rather be running across the beach or throwing snowballs at the postman. Aries will find his gregarious nature attractive and this is often how they will meet.

Sexually he can stir the kind of emotion and feeling in her that she needs, but her impatience and impulsive nature will want him to be a little more passionate and wild in bed. He finds her upfront and dare-devil approach to life more of a threat to his tranquillity than fun. And a Piscean would always rather retreat than face conflicts head on. Fish can be weak-willed in the face of arguments and an Aries girl is tempting fate if she tries to rile him with words just to stir his drifting emotions. Aries are usually frustrated with the Fish's tendency to escape every time she gets excited about life. He is likely to leave for peace, and a cool lake. The Fish man doesn't take kindly to earthquakes.

Taurus
COMPATIBILITIES

TAURUS MAN – TAURUS WOMAN

These two often resemble a pair of Egyptian sphinxes! They both lie side by side with identical sensual and sexual awareness. Taureans like staying in bed all morning, eating breakfast at noon and counting their money between the sheets. They will be ecstatic about each other's bodies, rather than each other's minds. But they are both rather selfish about their own sensual needs and there will be times when he may want to slob in the bath all night alone with his book and his chocolate orange and she would rather be taken out to the best French restaurant and eat snails. Self-centred distances between them will arise frequently because they are not good communicators, except when it comes to sensual things!

Taureans of both sexes have the same attitude to carefully guarded possession of their finances. When two Taureans form a partnership they will be equally possessive about money, and what to do with it, and there will be times when neither of them will be sure if they should be spending it at all.

Two stubborn Bulls in the same field aren't going to give way very easily, which is why sulking and resentment can be one of the down sides of this quite obstinate relationship. Bulls should learn to open up and tell the other Bull what they really think and feel, or the female Taurean particularly will carry her resentment around like a pair of bruised horns. It will only be in the comfort of their bed that they will eventually be able to forgive and forget. Neither of them bears grudges for long, especially if they can snuggle down beneath the sheets and get on with some Earthy touching. The bovine family are notorious for erotic and basic sex and lots of foreplay, so both will be able to give as good as they get. They'll spend most of their sex life on the horizontal, though. Taureans really don't like wasting too much of their very precious energy.

TAURUS MAN – GEMINI WOMAN

The only thing that a Gemini girl has got in common with a Bull is guts. The Bull has the guts and the nerve to put up with her inconsistent and frequently unpredictable behaviour. And she has the guts to face the Bull head on and get into his brain and find out what is really going on. Having met and perhaps been enticed by the communicator of the zodiac, whether she is fickle or not, the Bull will be faced with the kind of woman who either gets his back up, or forces him silently and patiently to plan a campaign to charge when the moment is right for him. If they become involved she will want a sexual experience based on chit-chat and fun, while the Bull would rather she was firmly devoted to his body and his bed. A woman has to adore this man's body like he was Adonis, not a Bull! But it's not in the Geminian nature to be possessed and, crucially, it is in the Taurean's more Earthy nature *to* possess.

Taurus men often fall madly in love with Air signs, just because they are so ephemeral. It is one of the weaknesses of Earth signs, they are often drawn to the very different types because they are so volatile. Gemini women love to have many men friends in their life. Now the Bull can't tolerate a lot of socialising, and he really doesn't like the idea of his woman (notice I say HIS) sharing her charm. The Taurus man is essentially very proud of his masculinity, and the Geminian flirt is always a seeming challenge to that. These two very different types may find it hard to maintain a permanent relationship. Her intangible attitude, her rather distant and Airy approach to sex doesn't match his tactile and sensual needs. Taurus smells of commitment and, unless the Gemini girl has a more settled area of her natal chart, the chances are that the thought or mention of permanence will have her scarpering. She likes surprises, fun and excitement, a constant change, movement and light. He would rather draw the curtains and smooch to a slow blues.

TAURUS WOMAN – GEMINI MAN

Now Taurean females are known for their need for security, comfort, stability and, most of all, a solid, permanent relationship. When a female Bull meets a Geminian man she knows that this youthful and flirtatious boy is less likely than anyone to be able to provide her with those needs. She can be outrageously attracted to him, just because he is so different from her, and, when a Bull lady falls in love with a casual and easy-going man like a Gemini, she will wait patiently if she has to, until the moment he begins to grow up. But Gemini men never do. He will always be restless, want change, to move on in life, to enjoy new experiences. He is always looking for something, and it doesn't matter what it is. Again the crafted stubbornness of the Taurean female is totally contrary to the Gemini's need for change.

Taurus women love sex like they love love. To a Taurean lady the sensual pleasures of life are a rich and deep experience to be remembered but, to a Gemini man, sex is in his head, not in his heart. He will play the game, have fun, thin experiences with light and air, not thicken it into emotional staticity. For a while they may be able to enjoy each other's differences; she will at least supply him with plenty of humour and emotional determination. To begin with, her strength of character might even interest him. She will attempt to change him if she can, to possess him and mould him into her ideal. Changing a Gemini man is a bad move; the only move and the only change he'll want is away from her.

TAURUS MAN – CANCER WOMAN

The Cancerian woman will love to cook food, and the Taurus man will love to eat it. The only trouble is Mr Bull loves solid, honest, simple food. Meat, chips, eggs and beans will keep most Taureans happy. The Cancer girl, meanwhile, will be into the latest fashion in food, down the delicatessen after quails' eggs and mung beans. Those weren't really the foods the Bull had in mind and insect-sized portions just don't do much for his image. Yet she could keep this affable soul quite happy if she began to understand his very basic needs. Cancerian girls are notoriously jealous, a very different scenario from being possessive. For a while these two will appear to have the same emotions, but gradually the Bull's possessiveness will cause more damage than the Cancerian girl's jealous nature. The Crab girl will imagine more than is true and will often use a man's sexual performance as proof of his love. But to the Earthy Taurus, sex isn't proof of anything, let alone love. Sex is good and natural, body language lives and love is to do with stability and ownership. The Cancer girl can fall in with his line of thought for a while, but her moody, introverted side will fill with imaginary fears. Taurus doesn't really have the energy to listen to emotional wallowing. He cares, but he won't budge from his opinions without a fight. The Cancer girl will love this man for his solidity, and he can keep her balanced when her emotions can't handle the real world.

Taureans usually respect the Cancerian girl's sensitivity, and frankly he will be impressed that she instinctively understands every need of his body. Sexually, Cancer girls usually have a need to be dominated (women's lib or not!). But a Bull is more of an affable, idle and able conqueror with an open-ended gift for inertia. His kind of domination is gentle and caring, more like a sleeping pill than a pick-me-up. Man on top mostly, woman underneath, after all his body is doing the work, isn't that enough?

TAURUS WOMAN – CANCER MAN

The hub of a Crab man's sexuality is his need to be secretly mothered by a woman. Cancerian men take great delight in lying back and letting someone else take the lead, particularly if the woman they are with is beautiful, strong-minded and willing to be the boss. The Taurean woman will quite easily fall into this role. The major problem between them is they both hate making rash and impulsive decisions. In fact any kind of decision is to be avoided and they won't want to rush headlong into any kind of commitment. It can take a Taurean woman years finally to admit she loves a man, and it can make a Crab suffer endless emotional torment to try to admit that the girl he loves is worth taking a sidestep for around his mother's apron strings.

Cancerian men can have hang-ups about their mother which carry on until they marry someone like her. Most get out of this obsession in their teens, but there are a few old ones with a mummy problem. Taurean women have all the mothering characteristics, and if a Crab can just swallow his introverted pride and communicate how he feels then he'll be rewarded. However, sexually they are well matched – she loves sensual, warm sex and he loves emotional, warm sex – there will be trouble when they both retreat over an upset. She goes off and stubbornly sits in her field and waits, he'll pop back into his shell and won't be coming out until the tide turns.

TAURUS MAN – LEO WOMAN

The Lioness will probably chat up the Bull even before he's realised how glamorous and exciting a woman she is. Leo women are drama queens but they are also determined and loyal and if there's something a Bull respects and admires, it is determination and loyalty! Both Bulls and Lions are very conscious of being dominant types, and the chances are that their relationship could turn into a power-struggle and a tug-of-war contest in bed, rather than the simple basic, Earthy relationship that the Bull really wanted all the time. Leo ladies like to be the boss and quite honestly placid Taurus can get a mite fed up with being bossed around, particularly where his sexual satisfaction and sensual pleasures are concerned. He believes he is passionate, not in the roaring, extravaganza way of Leo, but in his sensual and erotic version. She wants action, as well as passion. A Taurean won't actually be very active although, to begin with, he can seem so. He won't want a wrestling match in bed every time she takes the lead. Warning! Wrestling in bed uses up a lot of energy, and this man is an artist of sleep, not of activity.

But, apart from the other Earth signs, a Leo woman is probably the only one who could get away with teasing a Bull, while she humours him by gently stroking his back. Mentally a Leo needs a lot of stimulation which the Bull might find hard to provide. His lack of verbal diarrhoea can also infuriate the more precocious Leo, who loves talking about everything under the sun and knowing the answer to every question. But her bossy, warm air will make him relax and laugh and there will be an easy harmony between them. He can't bear any woman being in control, but somehow the Leo lady might, as usual, get away with it!

TAURUS WOMAN – LEO MAN

Leo men love flattery and to know they are the king. Unfortunately Taurus girls don't take kindly to compliments and very rarely want to get into heated debates or flowery speeches. Yet these two complement each other in ways that may just produce a warm affinity. With the Leo's love of everything big, everything dramatic and glitzy and the Bull's innate desire for a calm passive down-to-earth world, their very different motivations in life can actually benefit one another, if they have the time to communicate. This happens infrequently, because Leo is vainly jousting with every possible event that he can organise and Taurus is generally determined to succeed in a quiet and patient lethargy. Thus their chances for actually sitting down and working out their relationship is about as risky as its original beginning. He may have been attracted by her sensuality, her beauty and cool poise, and she may have been infatuated with his haughty energy and his flamboyant extravagance.

Between the sheets a Leo will find the Taurean girl's sensuality and talent for enhancing his ego more than a delight. He loves sex passionately and sexually their compatibility will outweigh all their differences. She will understand his pride can be hurt by indifference in the day-to-day humdrum of life but, once in bed or wherever they feel comfortable together, they can both make one another feel sexually unique.

TAURUS MAN – VIRGO WOMAN

So you've heard that two Earth signs together makes one big heap of volatile compost? Well, in some respects you're right.

Taurus and Virgo have the same approach to life. Unfortunately the difference is that the Virgo girl has a discriminating approach to sex and love, and Taurus doesn't. The Bull is down-to-earth, but probably too hedonistic for the Virgo girl when it comes to all the earthly pleasures he needs to indulge in. Virgo girls like to analyse sex. Perfection between the sheets is what they want, not the snore of a Bull at dawn and smelly socks on the pillow. The basic raw attitude to life of a Bull is actually not very satisfactory to a Virgo, unless she can control him, and organise him without his even noticing that she is! Taurus isn't a fusspot and doesn't care if the duvet cover wasn't washed since Sunday as long as the bed is comfortable and he gets enough sleep. He can be intolerably untidy and a Virgo is incredibly tidy-minded. She may actually like the Bull's mess, and choose to clear it up or to ignore it, as long as it is ordered chaos, then it's OK. He could actually provide the Virgo girl with her delight for cleaning up and worrying about his dirty collars, and she could be the answer to his sloppy living.

Virgo girls need romance, pretty linen sheets, flowers on their birthday and champagne, which sometimes the Bull forgets and finds hard to provide. If their relationship isn't purely a physical one then it would be better for them both. In fact these two Earth signs make an excellent marriage and then at least the Virgo will have something more to criticise than just the Bull's slobbing in bed till noon.

TAURUS WOMAN – VIRGO MAN

The Virgo man is hypercritical of most women, but there's something very pleasant and comforting about the Taurean girl. It's as if she's as perfect as a woman could possibly be, and that's a standard that he rarely believes he'll find. These two usually meet at work, rather than at play. The Virgo man does little playing and that which he does won't usually involve places where he can be tempted by women.

His hunt for perfection will often lead him to question the Bull's placid nature and strength of purpose and when he realises that he can't pick many holes in her character he will decide, meticulously and analytically, that therefore she must be the most suitable candidate available. He is known to fall in love, but it's a quiet, emotionless experience. Romance is easy for him, because it involves no thread of emotion, only lines from a book. The Taurus girl will think this man a prig at first, conceited, over-obsessive and the plaintive for cold and unresponsive pedantry. Yet when she realises he's got the same motivation and determination, that in fact he is quite resilient and is happy to clarify every situation with analysis, she might even uncover a subtle depth to the sensible way he folds his pyjamas. (A lot of Virgo men do still wear pyjamas, and like them to be ironed.) A domestic-minded Taurus will get on better with him than a career girl, but if she can show enterprise and initiative, not cause emotional scenes, stamp her feet, or leave too many pairs of tights round the bathroom, he might just feel content with her.

Sexually, he can seem cold, and she might take a while to warm him up. But if anyone can, a Taurean's basic sensuality will get him off on a different planet than he's ever known. Could she be the perfection he's been looking for?

TAURUS MAN – LIBRA WOMAN

On reflection, and she'll need a lot of it because a Libran girl likes to spend time deliberating, she could get that Taurean out of his rutting phase quicker than any other sign. She has the charm and all the Airiness that appeals to the strong sense of ownership with which the Bull would like to smother her. Underneath, of course, she is also a woman of the world, and very capable. In fact, if she seduces the Taurean first, she has the guile and the charm to let him believe that he was the one to do the seducing and thus avoid hurting his sexual vanity. He has a lot to offer a Libran and she has a lot to offer a Taurean, both sexually and in love. She might find his habits too self-indulgent, although not far removed from her own, a little too down-to-earth and not much like her more ephemeral and fantasy pleasure-seeking. Libran women are quite adept at getting what they want and, with their natural beauty and their innate restless search for an ideal, they seem dreamlike to the more pragmatic Bull.

Physical connection will probably bring them together. She will appeal to his masculine ego that demands a very feminine attachment and he will appeal to her own rather languid approach to life. They are both hard workers, but once they are out of hours they'll drop everything for sleep, food, or sex. Actually the poor Bull is often fatally drawn to Airy types, because he cannot quite resist their very ephemeral qualities. But the Libra can get bored with the routines that Taurus likes to impose, and also the fact that he will not communicate unless forced out of his field. This can mar their relationship and a Libran will often prove fickle in the eyes of the Bull and he'll retreat stubbornly to his grazing, when if he'd fought a bit harder he might have got her to change her mind.

TAURUS WOMAN – LIBRA MAN

Now a Libra man oozes romance, and so does the Bull lady, in similar quantities, but with dissimilar qualities. Yet they will both agree to differ, which is startling in the first place because the Libran finds it difficult to agree about anything, in case it means rejecting the alternative, and secondly because a Taurean girl usually wants to have the last say and make sure hers is the correct one. The Bull girl's fixed attitude complements his driven one, and their initial relationship will be full of a dimension known only to themselves. They could be locked in a lift together and the Libran will want to make romantic love while they wait for the engineer to turn up. The Bull lady will find it a challenging experience, enlightened by the Libran's sense of love for her wherever he is. The only problems occur when the Libran man decides it is about time he started activating his social life a bit more. As much as he would love to stay at home with the Bull, he would prefer to get out and about, and this can cause much resentment and, at worst, a stampeding Bull.

His charm can delight her; his fatal attraction is his beauty, for, although it is only skin-deep, to the Taurean girl it is as deep as she wants to believe. But the Bull will want decisions about their future, a slow commitment, but a definite one. She will wait patiently for him to choose her as a permanent partner, and yet the Libran man really would rather not make this sort of decision at all. In some ways, he thinks, it wouldn't be fair to rush into any commitment, as much as he wants a partner, because maybe she will regret it. He is, after all, only being fair.

TAURUS MAN – SCORPIO WOMAN

If a Scorpio girl wants passion, and usually she needs an awful lot of it, then the Taurean man will provide more than enough for two. Opposite signs of the zodiac attract with a powerful magnetic force and these two opposites are one of the more potent and potentially disastrous of matches. A Scorpio girl is never easy to live with, particularly emotionally. And a Taurean man isn't easy to live with at times because he doesn't look upon life with the same seriousness and intensity as the Scorpio girl. This relation-ship will always be a love-hate one which can end in love or end in hate.

Scorpios never forgive anyone for a slight, or hurt, neither do Taureans. They are both fixed in their opinions and, like sleeping giants, don't like to be disturbed. The Bull is the giant of indul-gence, the Scorpio is the giantess of danger. They both enjoy deep, sensual sexual experiences, but the Scorpio will want it to be mysterious, sacred, as addictive as danger. This is where they may come unstuck because the Taurean has a quite bawdy sense of humour which he often takes to bed with him. He likes to tease, but Scorpios are really not awfully good at being made fools. The Scorpio girl has to learn to realise that the Bull can get as ecstatic about the next meal in his life as he can about sex, and quite honestly, if you turn heavy on him, he'll turn his backside or you.

Love is living a placid life to a Bull, and love to a Scorpio is always intensively lived.

TAURUS WOMAN – SCORPIO MAN

Taurus girls are known for their possessiveness, Scorpio men for their cruel jealousy. A girl Bull is also known for her sensuality and sexual awareness. It takes her time to fall in love with any man, but if a Scorpio is already out there with his hypnotic eyes fixed on her she had better resolve herself to the ultimate sexual and emotional love-affair. Opposites in astrology usually provide what the other sign needs, or lacks, within itself. For these two signs there will be instant chemical attraction: animal love, no boundaries, love and hate jelly-rolled all into one!

Scorpios have a reputation as lady-killers, but only because they take sex and love so seriously. It's the whole of life's mystery to a Scorpio so the Taurean girl will have to realise that giving herself to this man will involve her whole self and nothing but herself. The Taurus girl will love his passion but will find his emotional penetration of her soul too unnerving at times. Her temper can be roused more easily by a Scorpio, and they will either fight to the bed, or fight until she leaves. Her stubborn pride can win over his fixed purpose and, when a Scorpio has been challenged, he can kill the love within himself faster than a Scorpio can lash its tail. The Taurus girl has patience and the ability to keep her feet on the ground, she may weather any storm clouds the Scorpio builds around him. And when he takes the trouble to look within himself with the same curiosity that he probes his Bull girl, he should find that she holds the real key to opening his heart.

TAURUS MAN – SAGITTARIUS WOMAN

There he goes again, fascinated by the Fire. As the caveman first discovered, so does the Taurean heart yearn to trap Fire's secret and learn why it can burn and tear at hearts. The Bull will be attracted to the Archer girl because she is so wild, so blunt and honest, and full of optimism. If she doesn't mind giving up her freedom, roaming the world and collecting men friends, then she might just manage to remain an indulgence at the Taurean's banquet. But for all his fatal attraction to this Fire sign, he needs someone who will stay put in that messy bed, cook the mushrooms at dawn in the woods, and generally hang around with quiet contentment. The Archer girl hankers after adventure and challenges, and secretly she would like to have the sort of relationship a Taurean can offer her, but her mutability can be dampened by the Bull's possessiveness. Sex can be warm and affectionate and fun, but the Bull might bore her after a while, once she realises that he's not the headless horseman of her dreams. All Sagittarians have a fantasy lover – and Taurus seems at first to fit the role, until she begins to realise that he wants permanence and monogamy. A wild, idealistic love-affair is not in his nature, he would rather settle in bed with those mushrooms and a Fire that he can tame. But that's where he can get hurt, for the Archer girl's fire will never be put out.

TAURUS WOMAN – SAGITTARIUS MAN

A rock-solid relationship is what a Taurus woman wants, not a rocky one. Unfortunately as much as she might fall in love with the Archer's uncanny ability to be optimistic, life's clown and the funniest friend any woman can ever have, she really wants him to be exclusively hers, which to the honest and forthright Archer, is certainly not what life is all about.

Any attempt to curtail an Archer's freedom will make him disappear with alarming speed. He can love, and he wants to love, but freely, and with as many women as he can within human capacity, and he also needs spice and passion. Romance and love to him don't mean a trap, they don't mean commitment and they don't necessarily mean permanence, which of course they do to a straightforward, determined Bull lady. The Archer insists on a strong mental companionship as well as physical lust. He has fun sexually, but he needs a good pal to muck around with, to take on his travels, and would prefer to run in the surf, than knit cuddly toys for the local toddler group. Emotionally he won't submit to possessive women, and certainly doesn't like being shunted into a hole of commitment. To him the Bull lady represents all these things, and he will shudder with fear if she seems to be pointing her horns in his direction. He needs to feel independent, and wants to show the world that his honesty is real. He hates domesticity, and is not very attached to family life, and would rather roam the world with as many friends as he can find. The Bull lady will find it hard to accept this very different man from herself and sexually her quiet sensual approach may not be able to tolerate his open and frank expression of every sexual contact they make.

TAURUS MAN – CAPRICORN WOMAN

The ambitions of a Capricorn girl are usually grounded in her success in finding the perfect partner, to reach the top of her particular emotionless mountain. The mountain may sometimes be a career, or other achievement, but if it involves a man, then he must be part of it too. The Bull man may appear to be the man she's been waiting for so cautiously. And her reservations about his suitability will, even to the normal procrastinating Bull, seem to take for ever to subside.

The Bull himself will be overpowered by her apparent sweetness and charm, her quiet and cautious approach to life and love, and in a way he will want to posses this Goat lady before he even has time to make up his own taciturn mind. Together they both have similar motives in life and in love, but the Bull will always have a more earthy attitude to sex, which the Capricorn girl often finds rather barbaric. It's not that he's over-passionate. Sensuality is fine by her, in small doses, and the Taurean likes very large doses of every sensual experience possible, including sex.

He gives and takes in equal proportions and seems as delighted with an Indian take-away as he does with the way she quietly expresses her enjoyment of sex. They are both practical and self-sufficient, and, if they decide to form a permanent relationship, the Capricorn girl is more likely to end the romantic side of their attachment more quickly, and turn it into a business and friendship arrangement. She can drop being in love, and turn it into a new agenda for partnership. She likes to be in control of any relationship, and a Taurean man is about the only man who doesn't mind too much what she does, because secretly he really likes her manacled devotion. She has no sentimental attachments but, underneath her rather cold detachment, she has a gentle refuge for the stampeding Bull. And silence can turn the Taurean man into the most considerate and no-nonsense lover. That is what she needs.

TAURUS WOMAN – CAPRICORN MAN

The Goat man would rather like to consider himself as a chauvinist at times, and believes that domination is an essential element of success and will provide him with self-approval in his private life. Finding a woman who can live up to his cartel of partnership values, rather than the sloshy sentiment of love and sexuality, is awfully hard. Usually Capricorn men find their best relationships are with other Earth signs; from them there is no threat to topple their male ego and power-driven motivations and they have much in common, practically and sexually.

A Taurus woman has very much the same Earthy drive as the Goat. They are both determined to succeed, both are usually financial wizards and both believe that caution and silence are better ways to success than impulse and passions. The one difference they must face is that the girl Bull is a sentimentalist and a sensualist, and the Goat is not. She might require a lengthier love-affair and a more erotic sexual relationship than he prefers to offer. Basically he will play the robot lover with ease and his feelings, although somewhere lurking in his heart, won't be displayed very often, which most of the time is fine for the Bull woman, who would rather just get on with tactile fulfilment and not worry about emotion.

She will be more affectionate than him, which will suit this no-go area of his heart. But because he has put a curfew on warmth, it might eventually turn her usual tenderness to coldness. He is not lacking in passion, but it's not subtle, Fiery sexuality, it can be cold and empty of love. If neither can communicate on this level then their sexual relationship will suffer, but they will have the strength of friendship and commitment and the security that they both need.

TAURUS MAN – AQUARIUS WOMAN

Aquarians are eccentric and radical, both intellectually and sexually. Taurus is conservative and basic in his own love life. The Airy woman isn't usually turned on by erotic and sensual sex, she also needs mental fantasy, or intellectual excitement, to appreciate the truth of tactile feeling. Aquarians are abstract lovers, and Taureans are direct, forthright and feel the sensual pleasures in life. The Aquarian woman will admire his straightforward motives but, unless she is also in one of her equally direct moods, she can turn him off more quickly than her personal convictions can. This can spill over into their bedtime routine like HP sauce. The Aquarian girl shares with the Taurean the ability to choose stubbornness for its own sake, and why should she clean up their domestic rows, when he makes no effort either? Pig-headed people get on well on the surface but, once they become pig-headed with each other, there's a volatile relationship on the cards.

Taurus will seem incredibly selfish about sex to the rather colder and independent-minded Aquarian who is more interested in the invention of the wheel than the local cookery classes and washing the dishes. She won't be told when to go to bed, any more than she will be told when to get up. The Bull won't be able to cope with her non-conformist sallies down the local pub either. She may be tempted to put him down publicly, her abstraction of his character may seem a simple test to her, but, for a Bull, it will not only outrage his dignity but also his manhood. He has to feel the dominant partner, and it could be very hard with this self-assured woman. Not a very good match as they are both too self-opinionated, and the Bull's pride is easily deflated by the Aquarian girl's lack of warmth or any genuine sexual response.

TAURUS WOMAN – AQUARIUS MAN

The aloof and unresponsive Aquarian man has great trouble dealing with the warm responsive Taurean woman who has just touched his arm and offered to cook him dinner at his place one night. The distance this man puts between himself and a possible romantic involvement is further than Uranus from the Earth, and this is where these two are far apart.

He is Uranus, and she is the Earth: erotic, tactile, needing all the sensual and romantic notions to sharpen her determined and committed motives. A Uranian can only be the awkward, straining, unconventional friend who really would rather study your books and work out your background than fall into bed and into love.

Earthy Taurus will want to put her hand round his as soon as she feels comfortable in his presence. But the trouble with Aquarians is that they really have no need for any physical contact. They live resolutely in their heads and no one's going to change their dippy behaviour, especially not such a warm and trusting woman as a Bull. Some Aquarians have been known to get quickly allergic to a girl's cat, just to avoid getting into a relationship. He needs to live alone with a million friends and a million ideas to test. He wants considerable freedom in a relationship, and a lonely Aquarian is better than a restricted one. Permanency with a possessive woman will cramp his unpredictable and eccentric behaviour. He can find peace with a like-minded being, but the Taurean is too different, too real, and too much of a woman for him. If he falls in love with her it will be short-lived and relies only on the fact that she can tolerate his madness!

TAURUS MAN – PISCES WOMAN

There is an instinctive rapport between these two oddly matching Sun signs. The Piscean girl will immediately feel comfortable and at ease in the basic sensual company of the Bull. She knows that she can wash his socks and he won't get het up about that word commitment. He likes it deeply, and she needs it unfathomably. Mentally they are worlds apart; she lives an ethereal romantic existence, preferring dreams to reality; he is down-to-earth and can be coarse and ungracious. Somehow his strength is what she needs, and her weakness is what he finds attractive and fragile, and in need of protection. His possessiveness can irritate her rather fly-by-night temperament, and she is also a million times more gregarious than he is. But he can accept her desire to escape more easily than with any other girl. Although he doesn't quite understand how she soaks up the world's problems and every feeling in it, intuitively he provides the right tenderness when the Pisces woman reminds him how unthinking and stubborn he can be. She does it with a seductive and child-like vulnerability, and, of course, there he is, to protect and, perhaps clumsily, to prop her up. Both of these signs are very self-indulgent and she can drink him under the table if love is in her eyes. So much ephemeral and misty dreaming about sex and love will probably rouse the Bull from the dinner table more quickly than he is used to. Maybe, after all, love is a more sensual turn-on than food, just this once.

TAURUS WOMAN - PISCES MAN

The Fish man doesn't go looking for trouble and would live in his world of dreams locked away from the rat-race and hurly-burly of real life. When he meets the quiet, dependable Taurean girl he will instinctively and intuitively know that she shares the same love of peace and tranquillity, even though she is tough and determined to succeed. The Taurus woman loves romance, and the Piscean man will fulfil her romantic notions of candlelit dinners, music (she adores music and Pisceans are often very gifted musically) and journeys into faraway lands. She can be a bit too possessive, for the average Piscean needs to escape for a while, even from such a tender woman, and the other quicksand they may fall into is the tendency to be led astray by each other's moods, rather than to lighten the other's darkness with some Airy or Fiery light. There's something almost sombre and shadowy about a Taurus woman and her Piscean. As if down there in the ocean, in the deepest part where the sun never shines, the Bull drowned and never quite recovered her usual charisma.

Sexually they are both sensuous and romantic. They can get lost in his world of fantasy and hers of too much flesh as opposed to feeling. But she will never try to dominate his gentleness, and

119

he's unlikely to want ever to turn into a coldwater Fish with this girl around. He's stronger than she knows, and she is deeper than he believes.

TAURUS WOMAN – ARIES MAN

Most Taurean women are hard to spot and impossible to provoke. But an Aries man has the best chance of spotting her hard-edged front and seducing her out of her stubborn attitude that abhors all those things an Aries man is! At a party the Taurus girl will often rather sit alone in the kitchen happily eating the crisps, and an Arien male could find that disturbingly erotic. The Taurus girl's sensuality is foreign to him, which makes her doubly attractive. Her feelings are that sex is good and basic: honest erotic earthiness, a significance of presence, or life. Love is something else, more mysterious and a calling from nature, far deeper than an Aries man can fathom. The high performance level of the ego-driven Ram can be overwhelmingly self-centred and not placid enough for the Bull lady. Aries men aren't particularly good at settling down to play the happy husband, nor the benevolent lover either, both of which a Taurean girl wants in her life. She likes financial security, he likes to take chances, gamble his money, and even his heart, for the pure pleasure of impulsive living. A Taurean girl always wants a simple and comfortable home, a cosy set-up and a sure and steady future, but the Aries man has neither the solidity nor the patience for this kind of relationship. Short-term, it could be sexually fun for him, but neither would get much out of a long-term commitment unless they can adjust to her need for affectionate security and his for spoiled and impetuous living.

TAURUS MAN – ARIES WOMAN

Friction is the name of the game for this odd coupling! Not an easy relationship, especially sexually. Aries women need to release tumultuous energy and deliver themselves into the hands of passionate mind-blowing fantasies. Imagination works alongside physical love with a female Ram and frankly Mr Bull won't find the time to indulge in this kind of exhausting mental and emotional game. The Aries girl likes to express herself openly, the Bull likes to keep everything in the dark. The Bull will dogmatically insist that he is right about everything and, being a positive, tenacious hothead, she's more likely to stomp off. The Bull is possessive and very stuck in his ways, which will antagonise the Aries girl more than his eating habits. Her intensely energetic lifestyle won't exactly lock in with his own placid, practical one. He wants life to move along at a slow, easy pace, but she will want to get on the bus before it goes without her.

Another major set-back will be when he wants to handle the cashflow and she would rather just spend it. Most Aries girls are not very clever with their finances, and the Bull's stubborn Monopoly game can create much tension between them. If she can understand that his patience could be her virtue, and he could realise her impetuous nature is fun and honest, and could give him a lot of new challenges in life, then there could be hope for their attraction.

Gemini

COMPATIBILITIES

GEMINI MAN – GEMINI WOMAN

A foursome, rather than a twosome, this happy, quick-witted pair will soon play the same mental games and hit it off with wit and humour. They can both adjust to each other's sudden changes and need for stimulating company. Gemini girls will adore flirting with men and Gemini men will adore flirting with women. Neither is particularly jealous by nature, but they can build up niggling resentments if their communication ever breaks down. This is very unlikely to happen. Geminis would rather die than not talk, would suffer if they can't be exchanging ideas and turning their minds to any new adventure. With each other, it always seems a lot more like fun and they really do need a companion in life for all their nomadic existence, especially if it is another nomad. After all, they rarely have to explain themselves in bed and, if one of them wants to sleep (and they do need an awful lot of sleep), the other won't feel hurt by rejection.

If they can both accept that their fickle and sometimes inconsistent behaviour is what they give and what they get, then they will stay friends for life. Unless, of course, love enters the arena. Sometimes both male and female Geminis can get led astray by thinking they are in love again. They are both incredibly attracted to the surface of life, and being in love with love is easy for them. But if they think hard enough and long enough, in between phone calls, they might just realise that love is an illusion in their heads, and really only happens in true hearts.

GEMINI MAN – CANCER WOMAN

When a Gemini man spontaneously suggests dinner with the Cancer woman he's just met at a party she will, of course, be instantly flattered, but will wonder instinctively if he really can winkle out all her secrets. The Crab girl is mysterious and he will like to solve any mental or intriguing puzzle that occurs to him. It's not so much that he has fallen in love with a Cancer girl because of her emotional content, but because she poses the sort of mental challenge that he likes to face. This may sound cold and heartless, but Geminis live in their heads not their hearts. The Gemini man does have one, but he doesn't loan it out until he finds someone who can read its Twin desires and a Cancer girl is probably one of the least likely to do so. They will be drawn sexually to one another quite easily. Geminis are usually youthful in appearance and exciting in bed. Twins like to have fun and to communicate their sexual habits quite openly. The Cancer girl is an extrovert on the surface and so the Gemini might think that he has latched on to a fun-loving Air sign, until he comes across the weaker, emotional wreck that sometimes hides behind this charade of gregarious living.

The Crab girl will take her time to get involved with this up-front, speedy man who may zoom in and out of her life when she least expects it.

She needs stability and seriousness in her life; she wants to feel comfortable with the future and the past. She wants to belong, and the Gemini man doesn't want to belong to anyone. He is the drifter of the zodiac, the nomad of love. If commitment throws its ugly head in hearing distance of his own radar, he'll pack his bags quite happily. Sex isn't important to him, not physically, nor emotionally, only in his head. Unfortunately it can be the very existence for a Moon girl.

GEMINI WOMAN – CANCER MAN

Dreaming of an ideal is something the Twin girl will constantly remember. It stays with her as she restlessly moves through life attempting to find out who she really is. When the dreamy Cancerian, extrovert and so like her (Look, he's even flirting!) suddenly turns into this emotional and highly sensitive Crab who lies in wait for her, one day pretending indifference, the next, passionate love she might change her mind about ideals. The Gemini girl will find this all quite romantic, and possibly enchanting. The Crab might stay up all night with her discussing the latest world news, then offer to play tennis with her at dawn which, of course, is as much fun to her as spending the night in bed with him. His reason for this is to avoid making the first move towards bed, yet she will probably assume he's as detached about sex as she is. She will find his arrogance less apparent than an Aries', less infuriating than a Leo's, and thus more acceptable. She hates arrogance, and she hates egotists. The Cancer man will think he has caught himself a harem. The Gemini girl can be all things to all men, if she wants to, and while she wants to. But this doesn't last long if she gets bored with your routine first.

The truth of the matter comes when the Cancerian finally puts out his grabbing pincers and tries to possess the Twins: she will immediately feel a walkabout coming on. The Cancerian will usually pout, feel desperately sorry for himself and sink into a mood of indescribable self-pity. If she tells him she never really fancied him anyway, perhaps it's because he's asking to be told. It was just a game wasn't it? Geminis are honest, so are Cancerians; but the Gemini is amoral when it comes to emotion, and the Crab can play only by the depressing rules of his introverted habits.

GEMINI MAN – LEO WOMAN

Don't ever tell a Leo woman that her hair is a disaster and her clothes are outdated, unless you are a Gemini man with a little-boy-lost look, an artful creator of the perfect tease. Somehow the Twins will always get away with it. Leo loves trying to tame this rather fickle and glib beast who, she believes, should really have a home and not roam so freely. But Geminis are in need of change and they need their heads to be full of air and ideas, or they become more restless and more liable to promiscuity. A Leo lady can solve this problem if she's got the guts (which she normally has) to show the Gemini cheek: you can have a lovely loyal and true relationship with one person as long as it is her royal highness, the Leo Cat. The reason she manages to convince the Twins is because she believes she is God's gift to men. Men have to want her, have to chase her, have to find her, and the Gemini man who isn't particularly interested in all that preliminary catching will soon find that if he doesn't keep up with her own pussy-cat behaviour, then he'll be suddenly and awkwardly dumped.

Keeping him interested is not as difficult as she might imagine. It comes down to proving that she will always be interesting, never tire of his changeability and never try to pin him down. This last could prove tricky because she does like the idea of permanence. Sexually, the Lion will want more warmth than he can ever give and he won't be as passionate as she would like. But they can keep each other alive and alert, and they both share the need for extravagant living and wild and ridiculous loving. He will live in his head, and she will live in her heart. But the Gemini man can play any role she wants to create for him and, as long as she is centre-stage, then she will create the best parts that give him the most freedom.

GEMINI WOMAN – LEO MAN

The Gemini woman has learnt the art of flattery. Communication is big business to her, and so is flirting, because it really does get her moving through life and gives her the best possible chance of finding the man of her childhood dreams. She loves men very much, like they should be loved, as big brothers, fathers and lovers. But the love is ephemeral, and her cold heart can sometimes turn a big-hearted, forgiving Leo to stone. They both share the same optimism and addictive appetite for living. They will drink their way through the night and postpone love for another day. She will strike a harmonious note on his ego if she wants to and, although he'll constantly remind her that he knows best about everything, it will be to his advantage if he occasionally lets her have her way. He needs a lot of affection, physical as well as mental. Gemini women are pretty hot on mental affection, but they do let the side down with a rather distant, cold approach to anything sensual.

The Gemini girl's mind might well be somewhere else when they are in bed, like writing her next film script, or going through the motions of a dearly loved fantasy. Sex is not all passion and ecstasy for the faint-hearted Leo with a Gemini. He will have to learn that she will never give the whole of herself to him, nor to love, and she will have to learn that he requires more than a cold shoulder on which to rest awhile, otherwise he will quite quickly find another. He is very proud, and very vain, and she is too devious and inconstant for the Fire to stay lit for long.

GEMINI MAN – VIRGO WOMAN

Not a relationship on which dreams are made. The Gemini man certainly won't want to enrich his life with hyper-criticism and meticulous analysis of why he didn't arrive dead on nine o'clock when he was supposed to. The Virgo girl will find herself constantly suspicious, and probably on red alert if he so much as decides to travel anywhere without her. She will also find it hard to understand why he is so casual and so laid-back about life. At first when they meet romantically it might be all birds and bees. They share the same mutability, the same restless desire for knowledge, except the Gemini will actively seek change, and love change, and the Virgo would rather sit down and dwell on it, and then organise it within the compartments she's chosen. Her orderly mind gets the Gemini man reaching for his suitcase pretty quickly. He hates to be told what to do and the Virgo girl *loves* telling people what to do. He also won't want to take the future or their relationship too seriously. Romance is all very well, it has an ending in sight, but a future with a paradigm of virtue sounds to him like the sweetest icing on the biggest wedding cake, and you know how he hates weddings!

Sexually, they have little in common. He is cool, and can fluctuate between sex in his head and no sex. She is in need of romance, of affection, and an Earthy lightness, rather than a mental one. Their Mercury ruler may give them the same ability to analyse and dissect, but the Virgo will turn it to fault-finding and the Gemini will turn it to wondering what he is doing in bed with this serious woman in the first place.

GEMINI WOMAN – VIRGO MAN

The precision-timer of the zodiac will get quickly frustrated when he meets a Gemini woman, mainly because her time-keeping is her own law. If she says she will meet him at eight she will usually bump into an old friend and chat for an hour before she remembers to call him. Her ability to go off at tangents, attempt the impossible and be in two places at once is part of her Mercurial charm.

The Virgo man has little Mercurial charm, he has all life's practicalities Of course, he is a perfectionist, requires a normal amount of affection and a large amount of logic in his love affairs, but really can't waste his precious time with a girl who changes her personality and her job more frequently than a kaleidoscope changes colour.

Virgo men are quite adept at the first inklings of romance. They like to believe they are better at picking up a girl than any other sign. However, because they secretly yearn for a wife, rather than a lover, the Geminian girl will not be awfully good at this kind of partnership. They have little in common, and sexually they will probably flounder fairly soon after any initial infatuation has subsided. The Twins hate to be cornered, and the Virgo man is essentially quite keen on cornering and then dissecting the female of his attention. She may fall for this the first few times, but eventually even the lightness of a Virgo sexual encounter can bore her.

GEMINI MAN – LIBRA WOMAN

An unpredictable and quite wild relationship. Two Air signs can cause a lot of wind, blowing away the dust of boredom, the puddles of emotional indulgence and generally behave like a Force Nine gale through a stick house. When the wolf blew down the piggies' house, he must have been an Air sign, and he could well have been a Gemini actually searching for a Venus girl. Being in love is something that both these signs do equally well, and find they fall into with frequent ease. When it's with one another there's a good chance that the Gemini will understand the beauty and the charm of the Libran woman and accept her need to be right, even when she does find it hard to choose. She will realise that his conman act is only because he's not sure who he is. Instinctively they will share a wonderful rapport for each other's rather Airy and lighthearted sexual needs. Neither of them wishes to be tied by restrictions imposed by a partner, and neither will allow their personal freedom to be jeopardised by love. Because they are both adept at tricks of love, wizardry in the art of charming, it won't take them long to laugh about it, rather than carry on playing magic games.

Sexually they will keep the romance and forget the passion. They both need a light, mental sex life and would rather flit around the country on a bed crawl than stay in some cosy nest for their fornication. Their interest will be in the different places they visit, the change and the newness of the bed, rather than what goes on in it! It will be easier for them both to remember that she takes a long time to make up her mind if she wants a permanent relationship, and to remember that he won't be too fond of the decision either!

GEMINI WOMAN – LIBRA MAN

The flirtatious, spontaneous, witty girl Gemini will be the first to admit that the romantic noises that the Libran man makes are probably the only way she'll be seduced. Usually Gemini women like to do the seducing, which often leads them up paths they wish they'd never chosen. But with a lovely Libra she will often fall hopelessly in love. (For now anyway.) The Libran is a charmer, like her. Both have the ability to realise that the air they breathe is the love they make. But she has a restless soul, and he doesn't. His Airiness is based on finding an aesthetic way through life, to impress and to lead and to attempt to bring fairness and serenity into the world.

This is crucial for the Gemini girl because here at last is someone who really understands her, who can love her without possessing, who can let her go without jealousy and who could well be her mental saviour. (She finds it hard to find intellectual equals.) The Libran male knows too that sexually they will make starlight together, rather than loud shouts of ecstasy and emotional torrents of tears if you leave a kiss behind. He needs romance as much as she does, but they both need to hide behind their masks. Sexually they can take turns on top, and they will both be fascinated by each other as far as they only want to see. She will have fallen for him because of his hair; if he cuts it off she may fall out of love just as quickly as she fell into it. If she tries to make him grow it again, he may begin to find her surface attraction as shallow as his own.

GEMINI MAN – SCORPIO WOMAN

To a Scorpio woman feeling love is being love, is love. It is the whole of her existence, and every emotion and feeling displayed is the serious nature of her relationships. If by chance she should happen to be infatuated with the mental antics and agility of the Gemini man, she will want to consume him with passion first and talk about it later. Unfortunately the Gemini man doesn't like to be consumed with passion, and would rather talk. Neither does he relate very well to the incredible deep-seated emotion and rather serious way this lady looks at love. He might initially find her secretive, rather mysterious power to attract intellectually stimulating. She has hypnotic eyes and she draws you in like a snake ready to strike. He is confident enough to try her out but they both can become hopelessly entangled in a trial of love and hate, rather than the lightness and liberation of the kind of relationship a Gemini would rather have. Physically they will be addicted to one another from the start. First meetings will either be full of his overwhelming attraction for her, or she will fix her mind and her emotions on him until he can't resist. This can be an excessively sexual relationship, which is of course odd for any self-respecting Gemini. His apparent coldness will make her even more responsive, even more determined, to get to the heart and the soul of this butterfly man. But she never will, and that is often where they part company, she feeling betrayed, willing to destroy the love that has grown inside her, and he glancing across the room at another adventure.

GEMINI WOMAN – SCORPIO MAN

This is an extremist relationship. She will hate his guts because he seems so arrogant, full of chauvinist attitudes, and she will be unable to tolerate his secrecy, even though she may secretly admire it. The Scorpio will find her irresistible at first, amused by her charm and her butterfly mind, but don't snakes and Scorpions eat butterflies?

The Gemini woman likes sex as much as any other of her million pastimes, and that is why Scorpio will find her such a delightful challenge. To teach a woman the secret of sex, that it is the total fulfilment, is life itself. It is what inspires the Scorpio to attempt to pull this girl together. But Geminis don't like being taught lessons, and change is in her nature like blood. She doesn't take easily to a concentration of sexual activity. Sure, it's part of the whole, but so is the wind on a summer's day. A lot goes on in a Gemini girl's head that a Scorpio will find hard to comprehend. He likes to unravel mysteries, and the mental gymnastics of the Gemini girl will amuse him for a long time. But he won't want her chatter in bed when he should be moving the earth for them both, and he will want to dominate her restless spirit, believing he can control it in his Serpent's mouth. This could be a successful sexual relationship, as long as she is prepared to drop all her friends, all her role-playing games and actually take him seriously. He's too jealous and she won't want to spend so much time having sex, it can make her short of air.

GEMINI MAN – SAGITTARIUS WOMAN

An opposite attraction between different sexes is powerful, magnetic and this is one of the most exciting and crazy relationships in the zodiac. The Gemini man is a genie of charm. He is astute and clever and witty enough to tempt the brave and honest Archer girl into his arms. They will both feel the magnetic pull of the zodiacal opposition instantly, across crowded rooms, very social gatherings where they are both likely to be. They may have fun to begin with, throw themselves around like a couple of kids and generally misbehave when they should be cautious. They have an irresponsible effect upon each other. But the Gemini man can at times be critical of the Sagittarian girl's big mouth, and she can turn her Fiery nature on him if he flirts more than she does. They both don't suffer from ego problems, so they will happily take turns at being the boss. She may at times wish he'd shut up so she could talk, but they both have trouble closing their minds, and closing their mouths. He has so much to say, and she has so much to do.

They both have a gregarious spirit, and a fear of loneliness. Because they are essentially extroverts they will draw a wide circle of friends around them and, although the Gemini man isn't particularly jealous of the Archer's fondness for male company, she may get a little heated when he brings some female colleagues round for a drink. She needs more emotional support than, frankly, he can give her, for, although she seeks freedom in relationships as much as he does, there is always a wistful part of her which longs to have a base, somewhere to start from, and somewhere to come back to. For the Gemini, beginnings and endings have no place in his life, unless they are temporary.

GEMINI WOMAN – SAGITTARIUS MAN

These two opposites will adapt to each other from the word go. And they may well always be on the go, seeking new adventures together, travelling the world if they could and spending money like it was free. Their child-like and capricious behaviour runs through every facet of their relationship together. If the Gemini female is led astray by anyone it will be with a Sagittarian male. She is known for her wiles and guiles, but, for every trick he plays on her (and Sagittarians love playing tricks and demonstrating their love with surprises and jokes), she will respond with something better. The challenge between them is intense and can provide amusement for onlookers too!

Outwitting each other is another game they will play, quite consistently. Sexually they are capable of finding a rare and perfect harmony, considering she lives in her head and his passion is a mixture of hitting the arrow where he intends and wishing occasionally he could try for a new bull's-eye. In a way that is why the Gemini woman is probably the only one who can keep a Sagittarian man as more or less a permanent fixture, not that either of them like the word commitment. She'll learn pretty quickly that to make any kind of arrangement with a Sagittarian is like trying to arrange a marriage in his eyes. So she will have to wait for his phone calls and his surprises and this can sometimes be an infuriating aside in their truancy games. But they make a good partnership in everything and, if one of them does prefer the freedom of the road and wanders off one day into the sunset, they will always remain friends. Neither carries bitterness nor remorse in their open hearts.

GEMINI MAN – CAPRICORN WOMAN

When a Gemini man meets a Capricorn woman he will realise what it is like when an unstoppable force meets an immovable object. For the constant flit of the Gemini, a woman so quiet and solid, so inflexible and stable seems like a positive millstone. There is calm in her heart, and practical common sense, and there is even power and ambition. The Goat lady will find the flippant ambiguity of the Gemini interesting to begin with but will usually, with good common sense, retreat. She may find his smile and his charm irresistible, but she won't be conned for one minute. There might be a few sexual sparks flying but she is cold and so is he. The man who lives in the clouds may suit the cold romance of the Capricorn caution but, at the same time, her need for an ambitious and reliable turn-on won't be forthcoming. A man who is succeeding, whether it is because of fanaticism or just good honest spunk, is more attractive as a partner than one who can fulfill her minor need for romantic love.

They will share the same need not to get too close physically, or emotionally, and thus at times this can be a harmonious relationship. She may find that he provides her with a chance to laugh and to escape the inflexibility of her chosen lifestyle for a while. But the Gemini is unlikely to want a permanent fixture like a Goat on his own mental mountain, and she is quite incapable of accepting his woman-trotting escapades, and knight-errant insecurities.

GEMINI WOMAN – CAPRICORN MAN

The newness of every experience, how it is and how it works, is also how the adaptable Gemini girl responds to life. If she should meet a Capricorn man, which is usually not by chance but merely by introduction, or works with him, then she will find his immediate response to her may appear to be love at first sight. Serious business, the ladder to success and a self-opinionated ego make this man appear incredibly chauvinist to a very male-minded woman like the Gemini. She will probably detest his strutting bigotry, when really he is only trying to convince her that flexibility is dangerous. The Goat is tethered to his own career stick, and finds love and sex a difficult motive for romping in the rain forests. He would rather end all that romantic trifling and get on with the real business, that is, controlling her life and controlling the relationship his way. Her changeable and unpredictable behaviour is a chaos he would like to order. As much as he appears to be in love, it is only his obsessive power-struggle to quash equivocation. And the Gemini girl represents exactly that.

Sexually they may be able to give each other a rather distant love, which they actually both can find rewarding. The Gemini girl hates emotion in bed, and Capricorn likes to make sure that sensuality is avoided. At a later date, when he's older and wiser, yet younger and spirited, released from his own self-denying chains, she may welcome his less pig-headed self and, as they both are capable of remaining friends, could find one another again young at heart at a ripe old age.

GEMINI MAN – AQUARIUS WOMAN

The nosy Gemini man will find a great deal of genuine, though not emotional sympathy, from the equally inquisitive Aquarian girl. She will immediately want to dissect the bright, witty man she's found at the party, and he will at once be talking non-stop about everything, teasing her with words and playing a game of his own, while at the same time checking out what she is all about. They both have the same easy attitude to life, although at times the Aquarian can be downright stubborn and downright awkward if she chooses. Being awkward is not a Geminian trait. He will always want to express himself, and getting out of tricky situations is as much fun to him as getting into them. Getting into a nosegay of Aquarian eccentricity is better than good; not only will her unpredictability keep him on his toes, but her mentality can champion his own. But the Uranian girl will at times find the mood changes of this youthful rogue just as capricious as her own change in stance. She needs a friend first, and a lover second. And for a Gemini this is the perfect balance for his wide variety of free-range ideas. He has emotions that change with the wind and she has emotions that remain constant but cold. Together they can unlock each other from their shared fear of sexual failure.

GEMINI WOMAN – AQUARIUS MAN

Both Air signs, but she is mutable and restless, he is fixed and stubborn, wanting the world to change rather than himself. Luckily for the Aquarian man the Gemini woman rather likes flitting from job to job, or desire to desire. But unluckily for the Gemini girl the Aquarian man, although mentally in tune with her, can seem dull and too regularly stuck in the mud. At first she will be amused by his strange advances. Not like most men who instantly attempt to guide her towards the bedroom, but more like Frankenstein, who would love to create a monster out of her mind! The Aquarian actually finds her impossibly devious, has a hard time picking her brain, and, of course, the further he has to delve, the more likely he is sure that she will prove an intellectual equal and perhaps even be worth considering for a permanent relationship. Neither of them desires commitment. The Aquarian has a need for a rather oblique loneliness and independence. He has to have friends, or he'll die, but within that circle, however close, he will remain aloof and free-spirited. Tying herself to an Aquarian may be the funniest thing she's ever done. She will adore his sudden and weird behaviour, and he will get turned on by her spontaneous and Airy lightness about life, including him. She will at times take him too lightly, maybe frustrated by his commitment to emancipation, but ironically this can often keep her sparked and interested. For her restless nature feeds on diffidence as long as it is not her own.

Sexually they are fairly similar, emotion and sensuality aren't particularly necessary in bed. In fact they would both prefer to talk all night about the universe, set their deckchairs up on the lawn at midnight, and watch the stars.

GEMINI MAN – PISCES WOMAN

The ups and downs of the Gemini man's changeable and restless nature can cause a few eddies in the quiet and passive pool of the Pisces girl's heart. He never seems to sit still and is always on the go when she would rather slide into a dream or a good book than be organised into another outing, or another party. It's not that she doesn't socialise, far from it, she is as gregarious as the Gemini, which is probably how they met. He will play the little-boy-lost and she will play the wistful, beautiful, dreamy woman that a Gemini man really can't resist. To begin with her rather dreamy existence may fascinate him, because it seems so unlike his own rather factual approach to life. And then there's the dozy way she can seem so compassionate and caring, emotions and feelings well up inside of her and she is quite charming.

But, after a while, the Gemini man may find it all rather frustrating, because she never seems to get anywhere for all her psychic awareness. The Piscean girl could also soon tire of the gossiping and the witty remarks, the surface dusting of life that he wipes across every comment she makes.

Sexually, Water and Air signs can often find much in common. When the Piscean girl first climbs into bed with the teasing, lighthearted Gemini man she may begin to feel like she is alive. The human side of her Mermaid existence won't be floundering for long, and the Gemini Man might conclude that perhaps feelings and intuitive love is not so bad after all. They both believe in personal freedom, and neither will be possessive. But she can be too slow, too laid-back and dreamy, when he would rather be solving another fascinating riddle in life, or rushing off on another trip, just for the sake of change.

GEMINI WOMAN – PISCES MAN

When the Fish first catches a glimpse of the Gemini girl above the murky water, she may be shimmering on the surface like a maggot on a line waiting to catch him. She is fascinated by talent, by beauty and by that elusive quality that, although part of her own make-up, can seem doubly attractive in someone else. To begin with, Fish and Gemini girls communicate well and both are adept at socialising, although the Piscean man actually finds it quite exhausting. The Gemini woman has more energy to invest than the Fish because then life will always be changing, always be moving on. The Fish will be infatuated by her energy, her wit and her little-girl appeal. He is gentle and undemanding, and Gemini women don't like bossy, dominant, or chauvinist men. She is attracted by the surface things remember, by the way he might play the piano, or the way his hair falls across his ears. And the Pisces man has always some surface mystique which will make her instantly infatuated. In bed the Gemini woman isn't as sensual as the Piscean man would like. She can be romantic when it suits her, passionate if she thinks it's time to play the role of a Leo, and downright bored with sex on the next occasion. This can puzzle the gentle, loving Piscean soul and at times her lack of feeling can hurt him. The Pisces will always want to dream, to escape from any truth or reality, he is the undercurrent of the ocean, and she is the surface of the same sea. They will frustrate each other because of this. She can get quite annoyed by the way he takes all morning before he's finished shaving, when she is already out walking the dog within minutes of showering. They have many differences, but they have similar attitudes to life. The Gemini woman needs a man who can understand her search for herself, and the Fish man is probably the only one apart from another Gemini who can.

GEMINI MAN – ARIES WOMAN

Now an Aries girl with a head full of ideas about where she is going in life often finds herself meeting a charming, irresistible Gemini man and wonders how she can show him she's the most sexually magnetic and vibrant girl of the zodiac. He is likely to be more interested in what goes on inside her head than in her heart. And certainly he will find her bossy, straightforward approach to life a refresher course in intellectual energy. He likes things to change, to move on, constantly to be a fresh challenge. She will like challenges, but she'll want to improve upon every one she makes. And that often includes improving her Gemini partner. Aries girls are jealous and Gemini men aren't. In fact, they haven't usually a whiff of resentment in their heads. The Aries girl would rather he was jealous; in fact, if he doesn't appear in the slightest bit bothered when she is flirting, the Aries girl can get quite heated and walk out. Their saving grace is that she is just as keen at catching the milkman's eye as he is at falling in love with Doris Day on the TV. His rather detached approach to sex may bother her. When she's in passionate mode, he may be quizzing over the latest contraceptive, or whether the Egyptians made love behind the Pyramids. His is a need for mental and Airy love-making, her need is for fantasy and passion. He may provide the fantasies to enchant her, but he may not produce the passion on demand she so desperately expects.

GEMINI WOMAN – ARIES MAN

There is no way that either of these two can resist one another. A Gemini girl is usually out of the house most of the time and is likely to bump into an Aries in any of her many roles in life. Drinking with this man can lead to a relationship quicker than any other social activity! If it's a permanent love-affair they both want, then he can provide the stamina and the passion and she will keep him mentally alert and ready for anything. He will love her changeable, unpredictable nature, and it could be a very sexy relationship as there will always be adventure between them. Fire and Air are a potent concoction and they will thrive on each other's body sparks. There will be a lot of passion, and a lively and inventive approach to sex, although the Twin girl may sometimes appear to be on a different planet, which could infuriate the Aries man when he wants her to be sharing his spirited love-making. His ego is in need of polishing most of the time, and usually Gemini girls hate anything to do with housework! Gemini women live in their heads, so he will have to get past her mental puzzles, her teasing provocative crossword games, before he can expect to encounter her true love. Dark and exciting meetings, trips to every possible romantic location, will be shared with equal delight. But don't forget that Aries has that niggling little emotion called jealousy, and that Gemini is one of the more flirtatious women in the zodiac. If she can't resist another game the Aries temper may put out his own fire and, once an Aries man is convinced the relationship has ended, there is no turning back.

GEMINI MAN – TAURUS WOMAN

Now Taurean females are known for their need for security, comfort, stability and, most of all, a solid, permanent relationship. When a female Bull meets a Geminian man she knows that this youthful and flirtatious boy is less likely than anyone to be able to provide her with those needs. She can be outrageously attracted to him, just because he is so different from her and, when a Bull lady falls in love with a casual and easy-going man like a Gemini, she will wait patiently if she has to, until the moment he begins to grow up. But Gemini men never do. He will always be restless, want change, to move on in life, to meet new experiences. He is always looking for something, and it doesn't matter what it is. Again the crafted stubbornness of the Taurean female is totally contrary to the Gemini's need for change.

Taurus women love sex like they love love. To a Taurean lady the sensual pleasures of life are a rich and deep experience to be remembered but to a Gemini man sex is in his head, not in his heart. He will play the game, have fun, thin experiences with light and air, not thicken it into emotional staticity. For a while they may be able to enjoy each other's differences; she will at least supply him with plenty of humour and emotional determination. Her strength of character might even interest him to begin with. She will attempt to change him if she can, to possess him and mould him into her ideal. Changing a Gemini man is a bad move; the only move, and the only change he'll want is away from her.

GEMINI WOMAN – TAURUS MAN

The only thing that a Gemini girl has got in common with a Bull is guts. The Bull has the guts and the nerve to put up with her inconsistent and frequently unpredictable behaviour. And she has the guts to face the Bull head on and get into his brain and find out what is really going on. Having met and perhaps been enticed by the communicator of the zodiac, whether she is fickle or not, the Bull will be faced with the kind of woman who either gets his back up, or forces him silently and patiently to plan a campaign to charge when the moment is right for him. If they become involved she will want a sexual experience based on chit-chat and fun, while the Bull would rather she was firmly devoted to his body and his bed. A woman has to adore this man's body like he was Adonis, not a Bull! But it's not in the Geminian nature to be possessed and, crucially, it is in the Taurean's more Earthy nature *to* possess.

Taurus men often fall madly in love with Air signs, just because they are so ephemeral. It is one of the weaknesses of Earth signs, they are often drawn to the very different types because they are so volatile. Gemini women love to have many men friends in their life. Now the Bull can't tolerate masses of socialising, and he really doesn't like the idea of his woman (notice I say HIS) sharing around her charm. The Taurus man is essentially very proud of his masculinity, and the Geminian flirt is always a seeming challenge to that. These two very different types may find it hard to maintain a permanent relationship. Her intangible attitude, her rather distant and Airy approach to sex doesn't match his tactile and sensual needs. Taurus smells of commitment and, unless the Gemini girl has a more settled area of her natal chart, the chances are that the thought of mention of permanence will have her scarpering. She likes surprises, fun and excitement, a constant change, movement and light. He would rather draw the curtains and smooch to a slow blues!

Cancer

COMPATIBILITIES

CANCER MAN – CANCER WOMAN

When two Crabs meet on the beach their usual instinct is to avoid each other's pincers as quickly as possible. But two Cancerians will meet and instantly recognise the flaws in one another rather than their claws. Because they are both slow in making the first move, and only because they are fearful of rejection, it can take a long time before they actually get involved. But the qualities they both possess: of loyalty, stability and a home-loving passion only strengthen their relationship when they finally do get together. He will be more likely to suggest dinner before she does. A Cancerian girl will certainly accept, and she is quite capable of appearing as glib about it as he is, but underneath those brave faces are panicking crustacea with the chance of the Full Moon round every corner.

The Cancer man can understand this manic-depressive girl better than anyone and yet, once they decide to form a permanent bond, they can actually make each other more melancholic, and more miserable together, than they were apart. He will criticise her as a safety-valve for his own rejection, and she will grouse the same kind of remorse back at him. Crabs are notorious for picking holes in other people once they feel safe with them. Unfortunately for these two they will both suffer pangs of rejection at every cutting remark. If they find depression a way of life in the kitchen, then in the bed they may find the rejection game an even harder play than they bargained for. It might take all night for him to pluck up courage to suggest they make love, and she might crawl off to the spare bedroom to drown her self-pity in the pillow, while he lies and waits and wonders if perhaps he should offer his arms. Once they finally agree that they do both want love, rather than just sex, then they may share the security they both seek. Their problem is that because they hate to be open about themselves – two Crabs are equally evasive, equally secretive – then it might take a long time for them to find out what the other Crab wants.

CANCER MAN – LEO WOMAN

Leo women are renowned for their bossiness and their need to organise everyone else's life. When a Lion lady meets a sensitive Cancerian man she usually thinks that here is a kind, weary soul who needs organising, will be affectionate, loving and just the kind of man to have around to boost her ego. Yet she may find out to her horror that actually a Crab, for all his sulky moods and rather side-saddle enthusiasm, wants to be the leader in their relationship. The shock for both of them is that while Leo can still do the organising, Cancer will instinctively let her get on with it, convinced secretly that he is in charge. The Crab knows that the Lioness must feel that she is in control, even if he is actually running the show. The Crab man will be instantly attracted to this woman's Fiery, proud and intensely loyal good-ness. For all her know-it-all attitude, she actually means well and has a generous heart, with a real warmth that can liberate even a Crab in a deep depressive sulk. She will be the one who can lift him out of depression and coax him into an optimism that is her true spirit. The Sun and the Moon are classic in their differ-ences, the Moon moody and silent, sensitive and emotional, the Sun passionate, vibrant and glitzy.

A Leo woman needs someone who can understand her deep sexual desires, and a Crab man does because he has the intuition and the emotional strength to reflect it right back at her. One of their major set-backs can be that he is liable to smother himself in self-pity if the Leo lady rejects him. The Leo can sulk and proudly turn frigid, like the Sun being eclipsed by the Moon, for very long periods, if she thinks his retreat into his shell is a snub against her. It usually isn't, and there is enough warmth in this relationship to make sure that the Crab and the Lion both feel secure in the truth.

CANCER WOMAN – LEO MAN

The ego of a Leo man in search of a relationship is usually the first thing that confronts a Cancerian girl, alone and vulnerable. She will play a game of elusive interest and probably be fascinated enough by his proud boasting to realise that, actually, he may not be so bad when he calms down. He is arrogant, and he is definitely convinced he knows the answer to every subject under the stars, including the deep secrets of the Crab girl. But she will remember in her deepest fears that he's forgotten to mention himself in this scenario. What she fears most is getting tangled up and then being rejected. She'll play a challenging game to seduce him, though. And because a Moon girl senses the heat that scorches the Lion's ego she knows that he might just be the sort of man she needs. A Cancer girl wants a strong, protective Fire around her, not wishy-washy dreamers who may sink her further into her depths of despair. She wants to admire a man for his abilities, for his energy, for things that are very much part of her own strength, but often sublimated by the moods of the Moon. He will find her feminine, sensitive mystique instantly loveable and his natural protective instinct and his masculine pride will find an easy scapegoat for his boasting vanity, because he knows he will be pampered, in the kitchen, and in the bedroom.

Back in the bedroom the Leo can be over-demanding and too impulsive in his love-making and the Crab lady can be too passive and emotionally wound up. If she's in one of her moods and retreats to the kitchen for solace in a Crab sandwich then the Leo's pride can be deeply hurt. He is vulnerable, actually a lot more vulnerable than he appears. The secret is that his is a stubborn belief that he is right, always right and, like the Lion, his bravery is only as courageous as the prey he is chasing. The Crab has a very tough shell of protection; the Lion doesn't.

CANCER MAN – VIRGO WOMAN

Modesty and refinement walk hand-in-hand usually. One will support the other and they both will work hard to carry and to share the load. With a Crab man and a Virgo girl there is a lot of modesty on both sides, and refinement from the Virgo tastes in life. They may first meet through a third party. Cancer men don't often pick up girls, and Virgo women are very fussy about whom they talk to. A Crab will as usual be extremely cautious about revealing the darker side of his nature. He will flirt his extrovert side around quite casually and the Virgo girl can be genuinely infatuated by the bright, strong leadership quality of this sensitive and genuine man. She likes genuine people, honesty and truth. The Virgo girl will then settle down to analyse the Cancerian man. After much deliberation she reaches a decision that he may actually suffer from emotional trauma, he is affected by the Moon, but she can understand why his behaviour can change with his moods. She will suggest a relationship that can be assured permanence. He will admire her for her mental and highly intellectual reasoning power. It seems she's the sort of girl he needs, a woman who can remind him of the logic behind his deep and complicated search for truth, and someone who can keep him secure and contented. He may find after a while that her analysing turns to criticism, and that her bright and fresh intellect is too crisp and clear-cut for his more emotional, swaying one. Sexually they will complement each other unless her Virgo criticism extends to the bedroom and then the Cancer will turn as frigid and cold as the Moon.

CANCER WOMAN – VIRGO MAN

The Virgo man seeks perfection in a woman. Occasionally he comes across a woman who he thinks may be the answer to this niggling problem, but very rarely. The Crab lady certainly appears the sweetest, most charming, feminine and deeply emotional woman he has ever met, but there is something he can't quite reason about her, and he does love to reason everything. The Crab girl has the same approach to life and money as the Virgo, in many ways. They both like to look after their money, and they both need to maintain a certain privacy in their personal lives. The Virgo man, however, is cold emotionally and, although the Moon girl has her frigid moments, she needs a warmth that might not be returned from this rather old-fashioned and hyper-critical man. He worries too much about his health, and the Moon woman will know every cure in the book, intuitively she will be able to sense his headache coming on, will reach for the aspirins before he's even noticed and be at his side with a port and brandy when he's got a sneeze. They both are very attentive towards each other, but the Virgo's perfection-seeking might begin to niggle her. The Crab won't be able to take his caustic comments for long, and she certainly won't like to be organised like a telephone directory. There will be many breakdowns in their sexual communication. For, although the Crab is perceptive, the Virgo can get mighty restless about being in the same bed as anyone, even the one who he thought was so perfect. He does like his crisp white sheets and the window open in the winter. The Crab will quickly retreat and the Virgo will cool down, and the sexual perfectionist might even turn to celibacy if he feels that the Moon girl has abandoned his icebox.

CANCER MAN – LIBRA WOMAN

The social Libran girl doesn't have much trouble finding men to enchant her, nor a partner among all the choices who would like to have her as their lover. As the life and soul of the party, her charm and her wit draw all sorts of signs to her, and particularly the Cancer man, who does love beauty. Again, he can be as light and flirtatious as she, and, when he first meets her, will throw in those wisecracks and loony humour for which he is better known. The balanced and harmonious girl has the gentleness and strength of the Cardinal Air sign she is. The Crab is a Cardinal Water sign and together they can blend the right amount of companionship and understanding to stay together. Emotionally the Libran is well suited for the ups and downs of the Crab's temperament. She won't judge and she won't ever criticise him when he's down. He will be impressed, and he does need to be impressed, by her level head. He never thought someone so charming and lovely could actually be so tough and so clear-thinking, so full of life and not screwed up!

The Cancer man will never rush into anything, particularly a love-affair, or a commitment, unless he first makes very sure deep inside that he is right. (Some Crab men will ring their mother to check up with her.) The only problem with the Libran is that she really is quite hasty about being in love with love. She won't dare make a commitment unless he makes it first, but then, if she does involve herself in a permanent relationship, what if she's missing out on her freedom? The Crab may get jealous and possessive because the Libran girl does need a lively social life, whether it's with men or women. This in turn will irritate her. He really doesn't have to be suspicious of anyone. Libra will always be honest and open. A Crab often finds it hard to express himself, because he really hasn't quite worked out if revealing his true feelings will lead him into deeper waters than he can handle.

Sexually they may not get on after the initial giddy infatuation. She can be lightheaded, and lighthearted about every night, and he can get too intense and emotional for her touch.

CANCER WOMAN – LIBRA MAN

On the surface a harmonious and gentle relationship that, with time, can turn into peaceful contentment. Learning to compromise is the greatest challenge for this strangely matched pair. The Cancer woman is eternally pessimistic, and the Libran man is always optimistic. However, they can both bring each other to a realistic approach about their day-to-day affairs, because extremists are linked by the Air in the middle of their differences.

The Libran falls in love instantly and really believes (each time) that it will be for ever. The born romantic will swerve through life, in a charming and sometimes arrogant manner, convinced that all women will fall at his feet in a swoon at the twinkle of his eye. They often do. But the Crab lady will be the first to be seduced quickly back into her shell by a Libran. She will retreat instinctively because she can intuitively sense that the Libran man has done this before, can fall head over heels with the surface attraction and then give up when the harmony ends and the bitterness begins. But why should it with a Cancer girl? For a start she is a home-lover, not a daytripper. She doesn't dampen personal freedom and, for her, commitment is security. The Libran needs warmth and stability, but he also needs to venture forth, to play the romantic whenever he can or he becomes stifled and resentful towards his partner. If the Crab can let him go when he wants, doesn't question him or get emotionally possessive, then they have a chance. Essentially they are both kind, and peace-loving. Arguments would only be caused by the Cancerian girl's frigidity or the Libran's rather tactless self-opinions and lack of direction. Sentimentalists can share the past, but, unless the Crab can steer clear of suspicious and possessive emotion, and the Libran man can try to let her share his social wandering so that she has no cause for grouching, they will have little nostalgia to enjoy together.

CANCER MAN – SCORPIO WOMAN

A highly charged magnetic and sexual attraction formed from basic empathy. The Scorpio woman may realise that the deep emotional caves of the Cancer man's inner psychology are the kind she can reach, and only she alone. Both are so emotionally tuned in to each other that it is possible that they can destroy one another too quickly. The Cancer man will find her powerful personality a little overwhelming at times. She will want to control him, and not be the one to follow. However, the Cancer man will want to be in charge and this can cause the Scorpio woman to lash out when she would be better trying to understand her own insecurities. Their differences are great, but their passion will override most of their day-to-day problems. Blackness is something a Cancerian man can sink into, as easily as he can lift the clouds of depression with his laughter and mad, loony humour. These moments of madness the Scorpio needs in her life. She is known for her gravity about everything, and her intensity in everything she feels and does. This makes the Cancerian begrudging and melancholy at times because he really deserves more lightness in his own mopish lamentations.

Sexually, she will melt his side-steps into a dance of ecstasy. Not many women can really get a Cancerian man going, but this one will, and it will be a buzz he will remember all his life. One of the reasons is that they are both secretive to the point of facing the firing-squad rather than admitting the truth. But neither of them will accept secrets being withheld from them, and there could be a lot of interrogations from either side. He is possessive, she is innately jealous, and her tail can strike with alarming ease if she feels his aloof retreats from her could be anything to do with the suspicions she's cast upon him. He is equally suspicious, but her intense passion for him, or her intense rejection, will either sever their relationship completely or create a deeper bond between them. Hers is a passionate and often destructive love, and the Cancerian shell has to be strong enough to take the sting and the anger when she is slighted by his retreats. To her this is rejection, but they both fear losing.

CANCER WOMAN – SCORPIO MAN

This other Watery fatal attraction is not so disastrous as when the man is Cancer and the woman a Scorpio. There is, at the start, an obvious sexual magnetism. They both feel the same urgent responses towards one another. The Scorpio will be able to see right through the Cancer's shell. To him it is as translucent as mother of pearl and, to a Scorpio, a shell is no barrier to the one he desires. Emotionally and sexually he will immediately be able to respond exactly to the Moon girl's subtle and mysterious sexuality. Crab girls really do want someone who can understand their silence, their sensual and gentle modesty. The Crab's shy inner self will be upturned once the Scorpio man begins to penetrate her normally tough waxing. Because he is so aware of her needs she will instinctively let go of her outer Crab-like pincers and she will feel secure in his intensely hungry soul, perhaps more than with anyone else. It won't be a sensitive relationship, however, more a battle of wills, passionate and sometimes a doomed affair. Scorpios have always the problem of their destructive nature, which works alongside their constructive one. And he will demand power in the relationship, emotionally and sexually.

What Scorpio wants to believe in a woman is that she will be as fanatical about him as he is about her. A Cancerian girl does get obsessive about love. It may only be the whole of her life for that moment, the next she may suffer the pangs of disillusion: she is a creature of changing moods, remember. Both have shells that need cracking, and maybe the Cancer girl, once opened up, will show the Scorpion that it's not so bad being exposed after all. They both suffer from pain and instability, but the Scorpio is more of an extremist than the Crab. For all her depressive lows and manic highs, he will be the one really to suffer if she ever rejects him.

CANCER MAN – SAGITTARIUS WOMAN

It's not easy for the freedom-loving Sagittarian woman to accept the gentle but demonstrative leadership of the Cancer man in her life. She would rather be doing a different kind of head-hunting than the career kind, and, for any girl Archer to admit to be turned on by domesticity and routine, she would have to held down and tortured first. The Cancer man will find her very extrovert spirit of adventure a headier version of his own manic side. For the Archer girl is the most blithe spirit of them all. She may have her faults, she may be land-locked in honest self-expression and the need to move on to another challenge, but, basically, she doesn't worry about emotion and finds it a tad stifling in her irrepressible and easy-going lifestyle. The Cancer man wants to possess and cherish, to be treated with gentleness, for his shell to be opened daily and be cleaned out spick and span with housewifely devotion. This woman will rarely even imagine being someone else's groom, but she might enjoy leading him astray for a while. She is Fire and he is Water, and usually the firework is put out quickly by this man's emotional puddles. He can turn her on sexually and induce sensuality and a little refinement to her rather casual love-making. But the passion she feels won't be enough to enliven her twenty-four hours a day. She needs a mental and physical equal, not a secretive, wound-up Crab with a nasty chip on his shoulder about his mum. If, for a while, he seems an escapist and a lunatic, both of which she admires and is attracted to in a man, then maybe she will hang on to the extrovert side of his nature, until the Moon comes back to shadow him in melancholy. Yet he will adore her frankness, at least she doesn't criticise, only tells the truth, however painful it is. She will want to travel the world, he would rather avoid anything which requires coming out of his shell, and whether he can cope with her free love is questionable.

CANCER WOMAN – SAGITTARIUS MAN

The deep-seated devotion of the Cancerian girl can make a Sagittarian male almost retch with the thought of all those nasty words in his dictionary like chains and ties. Not that a Sagittarian is ever nasty, he is always honest, a bit of a scoundrel, and basically so happy-go-lucky that most women want to capture him. Unfortunately he is not the catching type. A Crab out on one of her sideways walks may come across such a vibrant, sparkling Archer and decide that she can't stop herself falling in love, so she might as well sit it out in her Crabby shell until he comes begging at her door. Her determination is admirable, but the Archer, in all fairness, really loves all the world, and lots of women. He prefers the company of extroverted, funny, charming, beautiful girls, to the more introverted damsel-in-distress types, but he has a very soft heart and will defend any woman in trouble, or any girl who needs a friend and a shoulder to cry on. When friendship is mentioned he's frank, forthright and blunt. He will play with the Crab girl's apparent lunatic fringe character and not realise that, in the background, her emotions are flowing towards a very deep river of sorrow, when he finally says some outrageous, cutting remark that he didn't actually mean.

The Crab will always listen to an Archer. He can go on for hours in a rather optimistic and self-centred way. He changes the subject as quickly as a Gemini though, and if the Crab touches on emotion or commitment too soon, he will change tack more quickly than he can change his ideals. In sexual intimacy the Archer is quick to please and fired spontaneously. He would rather have sex when he feels like it. She would rather it were a routine sensual experience where true feelings were expressed, both physically and mentally.

Jealousy will be the catalyst for their arguments and, eventually, for their separation, for this man is profoundly freedom-loving and this woman is deeply possessive.

CANCER MAN – CAPRICORN WOMAN

The simple fact of the matter is that most opposition signs of the zodiac have a great affinity for each other. It is something they can both sense but are often not sure why, and, least of all, are able to communicate. Both the Cancer man and the Goat woman are the least likely of all the zodiac to communicate verbally anyway, which makes it doubly hard for them to verbalise their feelings and desires when they first meet.

They both need power within a relationship, and this can cause a sticky beginning. The Crab is motivated by his own lack of confidence and fear of rejection: he needs to enrol a tender leadership, a sideways attack, rather than full-frontal recklessness.

The Goat lady appears on the surface a veritable kid glove, rather than a Goat, but beneath her calm and thoughtful exterior, beats a hard and sometimes mercenary ambition to run every show on earth.

Her efficiency is what makes the Crab's heart flutter with desire. Here is a woman who loves stability, is quietly romantic when she chooses and doesn't have stinging arrows to throw at his emotional side. Well, not at the outset anyway. The problem is that the Goat lady will, of course, love the initial fling of any romance, she is charmingly feminine and will provide him with the reassurances he needs. He will also provide her with the solid rock and desire for success that he would like to believe he is capable of and often dare not test out. Together they make a formidable pair, a good partnership, if they can rationalise the fact that the Cancer male will often have to play the mother figure, while the Goat girl takes the lead and ensures her climb to the top of the mountain. After the romance has faded they should still be able to satisfy each other sexually, although the Cancerian man is more likely to suffer from frigidity brought on by her apparent lack of interest. Her life is serious, and she takes sex seriously too. But she won't be pressured into false sentiment and unreal emotion. She will warm to the sexual thrill between them, and even the Crab will come out his shell. If he does the Goat may climb down from that mountain, just for a while.

CANCER WOMAN – CAPRICORN MAN

The secret desire of most Cancer girls is either ambitions for their career or their ambitions to find the man of their dreams. The driving force behind the Capricorn man's motivation is either for a strong and equally ambitious woman, for his powerful need to be on top, or for winning consistently until he proves his place in the domination stakes. Both these opposite signs share the need to lead, to be on top. But the Cancer girl is always ready to take on the support of an equal, as long as he doesn't dominate her. The Goat's hardiness, his ugliness, are actually quite appealing to the gentle Cancerian waters. She wants to build a solid home for him, to be there and support him, as long as she has her own way and as long as he is also able to accept her own ambitions. The Crab won't be that keen on the way the Goat runs their relationship like a business association. His initial romantic inclination is well rehearsed, not the plot of an actor, but the speech of a politician. He is also a grim comedian, the taskmaster, the ordered man who will only allow chaos in his life if he is in control of it. When the rather loony Moon girl enters his domain, full of conflicting emotions, sensitive and inconstant whims, he will be put to the test. To order her might be to lose her.

Both these signs need stability in their life, and their sex life will be a permanent fixture. For once the Goat may well choose to experiment, he may not 'feel' with the same depth as the Crab, but he will always be there, aware, determined to be the one to rock her bed, fascinated by the power she can exert over his hard-edged sexuality. The Crab can melt the stern face of the Goat's father-figure ways, and the beautiful Moon girl will reflect only the bright light of success in his eyes.

CANCER MAN – AQUARIUS WOMAN

The lunatic in the corner will not obviously show his intentions towards any girl. He is a flippant impressionist at times, and at others the cynical blues player. These extremes of behaviour remind the Aquarian woman that she might like to quiz this man about his inner nature when she begins to suss him out, and she will become more fascinated by his antics when he poses no threat to her quirkiness. Aquarians believe everyone should be their friends, and the constant struggle to keep all their present and past relationships going is part of their stubborn need to be different. The Aquarian woman is nosy, not with the inquisitive curiosity of a Gemini, but because she wants to bare the facts, the sordid details of life, and then, if a man lives up to her analysis, he might find a place in her social calendar. Unpredictable as ever, she is more likely to instigate a meeting with a Crab. The independent spirit and genuine friendliness of this girl will make the Crab feel comfortable and at home (which is where he likes to be immediately). He may step out of that shell just for a while and agree to ridiculous and alien behaviour. To the Crab, any behaviour which is unconventional has got to be attractive. He is often the most conventional and passive of signs when it comes to love, and this girl isn't. Sooner or later the Crab will begin to resent her blunt speech, and her inquiring mind. He has secrets that he desperately wants to keep, even from himself. To be strung up like an intellectual and emotional corpse will make him retreat fast. Cancerians really like their love and their partner's love to be exclusive – Aquarians don't. The other problem is that Aquarian women aren't too bothered about sex. They like it, sure, but it has nothing to do with love. Love is between friends, good friends; being in love is about romance, and sex, well sex is somewhere in the middle. It's fun, and fun with a Crab is a matter of luck and the Moon. Of course, she might laugh at his conventional ideas, put him into a black mood of rejection, and the termination of their relationship will seem inevitable. It usually is, unless they can appreciate each other's very different qualities.

CANCER WOMAN – AQUARIUS MAN

The more a Crab girl attempts to circumnavigate this cranky man with her ideals about home life, permanence and stability, about emotional input and sexual fulfilment, the more the Aquarian will run for his independence and resort to his full and varied circle of friends. If he met her, was fascinated by her ability to keep every secret back from him, he will be determined (for they are awfully stubborn) to find out everything he can before he can attempt to analyse forming a relationship with her. His rather aloof glamour will have attracted her initially, she can appear very aloof too. She loves his sense of fun and his rather strange behaviour which is always fighting against tradition. This is where his fixed attitude lies: not to change and rebel inwardly against the normal constraints of society but to see society and those around him change with the world. He has the conversion of others at heart, not his own. The Cancerian girl is very adaptable, she has to be because of that shifting Moon, but she is not fond of change. If the Aquarian man digs deep enough and finds her emotional responses too intense, he may expect her to give up her secrets and be as crazy about living as he is. She is serious about everything, he is serious only about his effect on abstraction. The Moon girl needs to take a position of control in their relationship, and he will certainly find this unacceptable. He needs freedom and a lot of choice in his friendships and he certainly won't be tied to commitment.

Sex is something he's always enjoyed as any other pleasure in life. He can over-analyse, and is not exactly filled with deep feelings, but he can provide the passion, for she instils in him a need to find out exactly what is going on in her private little head. Her secretiveness is her magnetism for this man, and he won't rest until he finds out what all this love and tenderness is about.

CANCER MAN – PISCES WOMAN

The perception of a Fish woman is dazzling, it's almost like the sensitivity of the Cancerian man. Both are immediately attracted to one another and will flow into each other's hearts before they even have time to think. Mind you, neither of these two does much thinking, they live in their emotions and their intuitions. The Fish girl will feel secure and comfortable in the Crab's company. He may have his swings of mood, from depressive to manic, but if anyone can understand and tolerate them, a Mermaid can. Her insight can be a shock even to herself and, though the Crab won't want anyone to penetrate his inner self, he won't be able to resist the Fish lady and her innocent sense of knowing him, without even asking!

The Crab will love her sometimes helpless, child-like appeal, and her gregarious charm. The quiet way she can let him feel in charge is actually rather soothing to both of them, because she needs his strength, although sometimes she could do without his weaker, more depressive moments. She can soak up his emotions so easily that she can turn into a rather melancholic dreamer with him, but she lives for the moment, and does not indulge herself as much as most people would imagine.

The Crabby claws may cling a little too much at times for this very independent girl, but she loves to be needed, and her compassionate nature will hold him close to her, if he feels alone and unwanted. They both live in their hearts, and they both are quietly private together. Sexually they can find much inspiration, although the Crab may feel the Fish is sometimes too far away and too lost in her world of dreams. But then the Crab never really believes enough in anyone. His suspicious soul is an eternal battle within himself.

CANCER WOMAN – PISCES MAN

If the Pisces man surfaces for one moment he might glimpse across the ocean a strange Moon, one that rises quite slowly over the horizon. It isn't full, it's a new Moon, glinting soft light on the darkness of the black sea. When a Pisces man first meets a Crab girl he will find her own shimmering and spooky light an encompassing magnet. He will know intuitively that she will fulfil all those dreams in which he lives. Reality is something to escape from, and with this woman he can both escape and find a true and delightful relationship. She will be a little possessive, but he shines in the attention, and the need to drift like the tides of his Moon. He is restless and changeable, for he is a dual sign, and she is adaptable and driven by the moods of her loony tunes. He admires her ability to save money, and collect the material of life so that she is secure and comfortable, while he is actually hopeless with finances, and can get frustrated by her need always to keep an eye on every penny. But he trusts her judgment. He would rather let her lead than any other woman.

Their romance will be long-lived. Both escapists, both dreamers, although she can wail buckets of self-pity, the Fish will prefer to retreat into the water and avoid confrontation. He hates scenes, hates emotional conflict and, if she does drop into one of her more forbidding moods, he will escape to the bath tub, or go for a long walk, or play music until he's sure she'll come back out of her shell. But he is equally vulnerable to his own mood changes. It's not so much that he broods, or breeds resentment, for a Piscean is incapable of bitterness, but he will turn silent. He prefers his own company and turns often to solitude as his true companion.

CANCER MAN – ARIES WOMAN

Another doomed but potentially explosive relationship! The Aries girl has a direct, no-nonsense approach to love. Her feelings are aroused instantly not latently or later after the flush of passion has subsided. She'll want immediate love, to receive immediate attention.

The Ram girl may be overwhelmed by the Cancerian man's love of her strength and the pure Fire burning in her soul. They both have, believe it or not, the same goals in a relationship, but neither of them is remotely able to perceive the similarities, only the differences. They both want success, both hunger after a secure relationship and both want to motivate others to love as intensely as they do. Sounds like the perfect formula? Well it's not.

The Aries girl's aim for success is a sunny, bright, optimistic motivation, and the Cancerian man's is fuddled by the Moon, always melancholic, pessimistic, sadly lacking in confidence in any relationship. If the Crab is too cautious, then the Ram is too self-confident. If the Crab plays the extrovert when he first meets the Aries girl (which he usually does quite unconsciously), she will fall desperately in love with the image that he projects so well but refuses to believe he can live up to. He will fall instantly in love with her charm and her impetuous nature. They are both outrageously jealous. The Aries girl won't cope with his smothering possessiveness, and he won't be able to understand her anger if he so much as winks his Crab-like gaze at a distant Moon girl. He will brood, she will lose her Fiery temper. Yet his need for sensationalism may draw her constantly back to his side. Aries women don't forgive easily, nor forget, but the Cancer man is such a mad, sad clown, that she might, just for once, return.

CANCER WOMAN – ARIES MAN

The Moon girl's initial attraction to this incredibly arrogant man will probably be because of his daring, independent spirit and his extremely good looks. Water and Fire don't mix awfully well, and Fire signs don't like being smothered by anything, particularly a dousing of water; it turns their red-hot passion into a sizzling black ember of bitterness. The Aries man may admit to finding the Cancerian girl's sensuality a temptation of the flesh. He may not at first care about her deep inner self that she cherishes so guardedly, nor her emotional need for a long-term relationship with a protective, dominant male. He is dominant, but not awfully good at protecting, unless he's in the middle of a risk-taking enterprise or adventure, and then he will spring to action like Tarzan. However, the Aries man is basically too reckless with money and too reckless with most things for a Cancer girl to stay around long. And equally, his honest, enterprising spirit won't have the patience or strength to play moods with the loony Moon. He may be fascinated for a while by her intensity of feeling and touch, and her deeper secrets may unlock themselves for an Aries man, but a Cancer girl's possessiveness will send him running for the first flight out of commitment. There is always a dangerous battle brewing between sensitivity and arrogance here and he will retreat quickly if he feels those Crabby pincers anywhere near him. The last thing he really wants is someone else to worry about his pennies when he'd like to go out and spend them on anything, as long as it's flash! Sexually, he'll be enlightened by her cool sensuality, but she may not be able to put up with his passion and impulsive, hot-headed love-making. Cancer women often end up hurt because they pop back into their shells when self-pity takes them out of the frontline. And, unless she is a masochist, it is often wiser for the Crab sensibly to retreat from this relationship before she gets stuck in her shell forever.

CANCER MAN – TAURUS WOMAN

The hub of a Crab man's sexuality is his need, secretly, to be mothered. Cancerian men take great delight in lying back and letting someone else take the lead, particularly if the woman they are with is beautiful, strong-minded and willing to be the boss. The Taurean woman will quite easily fall into this role. The major problem between them is they both hate making rash and impulsive decisions. In fact, any kind of decision is to be avoided and they won't want to rush headlong into commitment. It can take a Taurean woman years finally to admit she loves a man, and it can make a Crab suffer endless emotional torment to try to admit that the girl he loves is worth taking a sidestep for around his mother's apron strings.

Cancerian men can have hang-ups about their mother which

carry on until they marry someone like her. Most get out of this obsession in their teens, but there are a few old ones with a mummy problem. Taurean women have all the mothering characteristics and, if a Crab can just swallow his introverted pride and communicate how he feels, then he'll be rewarded. However, sexually they are well matched – she loves sensual, warm sex and he loves emotional warm sex – there will be trouble when they both retreat over an upset. She goes off and stubbornly sits in her field and waits, he'll pop back in his shell and won't be coming out until the tide turns.

CANCER WOMAN – TAURUS MAN

The Cancerian woman will love to cook food, and the Taurus man will love to eat it. The only trouble is Mr Bull loves solid, honest simple food. Meat, chips, eggs and beans will keep most Taureans happy. The Cancer girl, meanwhile, will be into the latest fashion in food, down the delicatessen after quails' eggs and mung beans. Those weren't really the kind the Bull had in mind and insect-sized portions just don't do much for his image. Yet she could keep this affable soul quite happy if she began to understand his very basic needs. Cancerian girls are notoriously jealous, a very different scenario from being possessive. For a while these two will appear to have the same emotions, gradually the Bull's possessiveness will cause more damage than the Cancerian girl's jealous nature. The Crab girl will imagine more than is true and will often use a man's sexual performance as proof of his love. But to the Earthy Taurus, sex isn't proof of anything, let alone love. Sex is good and natural, body language lives and love is to do with stability and ownership. The Cancer girl can fall in with this line of thought for a while, but her moody, introverted side will fill with imaginary fears. Taurus doesn't really have the energy to listen to emotional wallowing. He cares, but he won't budge from his opinions without a fight. But the Cancer girl will love this man for his solidity, and he can keep her balanced when her emotions can't handle the real world.

Taureans usually respect the Cancerian girl's sensitivity, and frankly he will be impressed that she instinctively understands every need of his body. Sexually, Cancer girls usually have a need to be dominated (women's lib or not!). But a Bull is more of an affable, idle and able conqueror with an open-ended gift for inertia. His kind of domination is gentle and caring, more like a sleeping- pill than a pick-me-up. Man on top mostly, woman underneath after all, his body is doing the work, isn't that enough?

CANCER MAN – GEMINI WOMAN

Fantasising about an ideal is something the Twin girl will constantly try to enact. It stays with her as she restlessly moves through life attempting to find out who she really is. When the dreamy Cancerian, extrovert and so like her (Look, he's even flirting!), suddenly turns into this emotional and highly sensitive Crab who lies in wait for her, one day pretending indifference, the next passionate love, she might change her mind about ideals. The Gemini girl will find this all quite romantic, and possibly enchanting. The Crab might stay up all night with her discussing the latest world news, then offer to play tennis with her at dawn which, of course, is as much fun to her as spending the night in bed with him. His reason for this is to avoid making the first move towards bed, yet she will probably assume he's as detached about sex as she is. She will find his arrogance less apparent than an Aries', less infuriating than a Leo's and thus more acceptable. She hates arrogance, and she hates egotists. The Cancer man will think he has caught himself a harem. The Gemini girl can be all things to all men, if she wants to, and while she wants to. But this doesn't last long if she gets bored with your routine first.

The truth of the matter comes when the Cancerian finally puts out his grabbing pincers and tries to possess the Twins: she will immediately feel a walkabout coming on. The Cancerian will usually pout, feel desperately sorry for himself and sink into a mood of indescribable self-pity. He only asks for it if she tells him she never really fancied him anyway. It was just a game wasn't it? Geminis are honest, so are Cancerians, but the Gemini is amoral when it comes to emotion, and the Crab can only play by the depressing rules of his introverted habits.

CANCER WOMAN – GEMINI MAN

When a Gemini man spontaneously suggests dinner with the Cancer woman he's just met at a party she will, of course, be instantly flattered, but will wonder instinctively if he really can winkle out all her secrets. The Crab girl is mysterious and he will like to solve any mental or intriguing puzzle that occurs to him. It's not so much that he has fallen in love with a Cancer girl because of her emotional content, but because she poses the sort of mental challenge that he likes to meet. This may sound cold and heartless, but Geminis live in their heads not their hearts. The Gemini man does have one, but he doesn't loan it out until he finds someone who can read its Twin desires and a Cancer girl is probably one of the least likely to do so.

They will be drawn sexually to one another quite easily. Geminis are usually youthful in appearance and exciting in bed. Twins like to have fun and to communicate their sexual habits quite openly. The Cancer girl is an extrovert on the surface and so the Gemini might think that he has latched on to a fun-loving Air sign, until he comes across the weaker, emotional wreck that sometimes hides behind this charade of gregarious living.

The Crab girl will take her time to get involved with this up-front, speedy man who may zoom in and out of her life when she least expects it. She needs stability and seriousness in her life; she wants to feel comfortable with the future and with the past. She wants to belong, and the Gemini man doesn't want to belong to anyone. He is the drifter of the zodiac, the nomad of love. If commitment throws its ugly head in hearing distance of his own radar, he'll pack his bags quite happily. Sex isn't important to him, not physically, nor emotionally, only in his head. Unfortunately it can be the very existence for a Moon girl.

Leo

COMPATIBILITIES

LEO MAN – LEO WOMAN

The Cat family is known for killer instincts. Cats are also known for their soft purrs, their need for warmth and a good bowl of milk from their owner to prove their love and affection. They will sit on your lap and warm you, rub up against your legs in a provocative way, and then irritate you with their arrogant, boasting frolics. Bet you can't climb that tree like I can! Leos are very similar, except they are human and have emotions that are extravagant, rather than the claws. They both need worship and adoration. They both need to be the glamour puss, or the glitzy one, or the big-spender or the showman. Together they make a formidable pair, but the problem they share is that they are so willing to put their egos on the line, they really can't stand being topped by the other.

Both will want their space to be 'mine'. And also want proudly to show off their other half as if they invented relationships. If the Leo girl gets in first with this act, then the Leo man may quite easily feel heated about where she got that idea from: it was his! They never like to be made to look small, and the man with the golden heart's worst fear is not to be the life and soul of the party.

This nerve-racking relationship can get out of control if the Leo lady is already making big money and has the sort of career and status that the Leo man would only consider fit for himself. As much as he realises she is a Leo too, he will make it immediately obvious that if she wants to hang around with the Big Cat then she has to let him be boss. This competitive spirit is

OK for a while, but it can lead to terrible rows and blazing exits, especially if the stubborn Leo woman really won't budge her career an inch to satisfy the Leo man's pride. And why should she? If they can accept they both have to be number one, and that maybe together is better than being alone (and Leos secretly fear being alone), then they may stay together to fight another day. Sex is great fun for both of them, and their Fiery passion will make earthquakes seem like wormcasts. But Leos will even fight beneath the sheets to decide who's turn it is to be on top, and that is when their claws really come out!

LEO MAN – VIRGO WOMAN

Virgos are for ever trying to improve on what they have, to perfect their own high standards. If they get involved with a Lion along the way, then that might just as well involve improving the Lion to their own meticulous flow-chart. The problem for the delicate pedantry of the Virgo romantic is that Leos don't usually fit into any improvement programme. For a start they are already better than anyone in bed, around the house, intellectually, and with money. In relationships they convince themselves that they know how to make it work, and a Leo man will certainly not listen to a woman who thinks she knows best. He would rather show the Virgo how to enjoy life, living for each moment, rather than running around worrying about it. She might go along with this idea, for a while, but she won't tolerate his terrible untidiness and his constant need either to work like it's the last day he's got on earth, or to play every game until he's won.

His loyalty will impress her, but her attempts to clean the ring round the bath every time he has one will hurt his pride. He doesn't like to be reminded he's left his books all over the house, and really can't see what it's got to do with her anyway.

The chances of their getting this far in their relationship are slim. The Virgo will at the outset play her feminine charm, her quiet side, quite naturally. But she will want to criticise, and she will want to instil her ideals on this rather bold presumptuous and prattling man. He's just the type to listen isn't he?

Unfortunately, Leos only listen to themselves, and can get hard-of-hearing quite easily if they feel their dignity is threatened. She will inspire him to tenderness in bed though, albeit not quite the passion he needs to ignite his full attention. Mentally she'll be challenging, but once she begins to clock him into the house and out of it, he may well begin to wonder what happened to his Cat-flap.

LEO WOMAN – VIRGO MAN

Practicalities are the same as perfection to the Virgo man. He needs order and neatness, he needs to feel in control, and he needs a conservative and simple lifestyle. He may hang his pyjamas over the chair every night and brush his teeth for exactly two minutes. He may keep a digital clock and a mechanical one, just in case one is fast. If he gets into a conversation with a Leo lady, he may surprise himself that he finds her gushing and flamboyant chatter quite entertaining. He is rather serious in life and here is a ravishing, fun-loving girl who is ready to flirt everyone under the table. Their attraction will emanate from curiosity: his because she is so ridiculous, and hers because he is so staid and neat. The likelihood that she will fall in love with him is slim; it could happen because he was playing the perfect-lover role, which is his only role, and a good one at that and because his head is full of the most incredible things, not the sort of things a Leo will necessarily need in her own ostentatious brain, but different, concise, like a concise dictionary rather than the compendium of life with which the Leo lady believes she is blessed. She thinks she knows everything, but she needs warmth too. The Virgo man is cold and really knows everything. That is what they have in common. He is sensitive, for all his apparent coldness. Unless she gets her pride hurt, she may never be aware of this side of his nature. Her attempt at playing the leading-lady in his life might set him with an interesting mental spiral, but it will quickly make him dizzy. She won't want to be the wife with the grace he expected, nor will she want to time his egg, nor be punctual for their dinner-parties.

Sexually she'll surprise him often. She has passion, is full of passion and he will still be looking up the next position in the Kama Sutra if she hasn't left him first. He is dexterous and believes he has mastered the art of sex like a true technician. But Leo ladies don't want technicians in their beds, they want a star act.

LEO MAN – LIBRA WOMAN

When a lovely Libran lady gazes straight into the eyes of a languid Cat, he will be instantly enchanted, knowing that this beautiful woman could perhaps be the ideal lover. With magnanimous pride and a will only matched by Hercules, he will attempt every trick he knows to entice her into his lair. Actually she won't be that hard to entice. It's not that she's a pushover, and she doesn't have the time of day for chauvinists, but a Libran girl always knows what she wants and will be attracted both to his romantic dazzle and to his quite boastful air. She can see through this, and beyond it, which is why she doesn't get put off by the way he tramps around thinking he knows what is best, while she really knows that she does.

Normally girls fall at his feet, listen to every word as if he were a guru, and believe him to be the best thing in bed since it was invented. However, the Libran girl is mentally alert to this kind of nonsense. She will love him for what he is, but it's certainly not because he has more love-affairs notched up on his bedpost than most men, and not because he puts on a pretty good impression of a pretentious peacock. The male Lion will provide all the right romance in her life. She has extremes of energy, sometimes wild and passionate, sometimes languid and cosy. He will respond quite well to both these, although he may find her distant Airiness a bit hard to comprehend when he'd rather be battling out who will sort out the socks. They may stick together through many a battle of wills, but he needs her fairness and sense of justice occasionally to remind him the red carpet is not just for him.

LEO WOMAN – LIBRA MAN

Now Libran men like to get out and about and adorn themselves with pretty friends and pretty things. They can prefer crowds and parties to company with only one woman but, if they are pushed, they will accept that a permanent relationship has to involve living with their partner. Some Librans would do better living alone, but Librans really do need a partner whether they can convince themselves it is right or not. A Leo woman seems the perfect answer, on the surface. She is genuinely outgoing too, cherishes adoration, and needs to be in the company of men. She is also warm-hearted, romantic and not fluffy. She is bossy and uncompromising and won't have to rely on someone as vague and indecisive as a Libran man. However, she will be more likely to want to know where he was all night, than he will want to know where *she* is. The Libran can find himself partying a bit too much and not staying at home. But the Leo lady, when she gets an idea in her hot head, usually keeps it there, and she might decide that her knight in shining armour is not as naive as he seems. Charming is one thing but that he cannot commit himself, stay at home and adore her, are another. Libran men aren't jealous, and they can't see the point of it. Emotions are thin in the Libran's heart, but he does care, and he does love. He may well have to spend more time proving it to the Leo woman than he thought. She needs presents, physical expressions of love, not words on the phone, mind-games and idealistic ramblings. Hers is a world of brash and glittering honesty, passionate life and living for every minute. Closeness in bed is essential, and they will both find that the Libran loves making love and the Leo woman loves both giving and receiving it.

LEO MAN – SCORPIO WOMAN

There is an instinctive rapport between these two when they first encounter each other, perhaps because they know that they have met their match: the Leo because the Scorpio girl is so serious about life and love; the Scorpio girl because she realises that the Leo lives on a different planet.

His planet is that of pleasure, movement, and extremes, of living on the edge, of winning and achieving. Her planet is filled with imaginary fears, of dark secrets, heavy emotions and love, endless love. The hidden power of the Scorpio can come as quite a surprise to the very brazen and generous Leo. The Cat may well play his own games, boast, impress and generally live on a high but, when the dark Snake slips out of her mysterious coil to take over, he will feel the sting of a very powerful tail indeed. Her animosity towards him will be because he is so confident, so sure of himself and so ego-driven. This is not unlike her own motives, but hers must be kept hidden at all costs. If he should realise that she is governed by darker, obsessive undercurrents he would surely run.

This could be a very sexual relationship, before it becomes any other kind. The male and female forces will turn on and off at their command. He will want rhetorical fun, she will want passion, but the sexual passion she stirs has to be taken deadly seriously. For a rampant Lion, this can be a little too emotional. He loves with all his heart, but he won't want to be taken over by her tumultuous feelings. She lives in her feelings, he lives in his actions. If they can manage to overcome her jealousy and his pride, then they could survive. But the Scorpio girl will never forgive him when he flirts, and, for the Leo, enjoying the company of others, whether he means to flirt or not, is more important than any Scorpio's obsessive tail.

LEO WOMAN – SCORPIO MAN

Secret weapons or not, this is when Scorpio's infallibility with women comes to a grave and dangerous test. Making a drama out of a crisis is what the Leo girl and the Watery man are good at achieving together. The Scorpio man won't be able to resist trying to bring down the Leo pride. He likes to delve into mysteries, to wound and hurt in a truly sadistic manner to see how far he can go without causing his own pain.

He is motivated by his inability to cope with the Leo girl's

Fiery and unabashed temperament, so different from his own withheld, destructive one. However, Leos are proud, fiercely loyal to themselves, and won't let a Scorpio get the better of them. If she feels he's come too close, has placed a dangerous rather than a glitzy ring upon her finger, she'll retaliate, like only a Cat knows how. As much as she will be attracted to his dark sexuality she won't like the incessant probing of her mind, and eventually his tactics might become too obsessive. Leo ladies need warmth and loyalty, security and generous shows of affection and verbal expressions of love. The Water in which the Snake lives is murky and crusted with cold dangers. His will is generated by sexual completeness, and the thrill of the chase and the catch. He can roll love in his jaws like a crocodile rolls a dead man to the bottom of the river, and he has to win, or to die.

It could prove to be a great battle of wills, but the Leo lady will always want to be *with* the world, not hidden from it, and, inevitably, the Scorpio's insistent jealousy will no longer be able to control her extrovert nature and he will, unconsciously, destroy their love.

LEO MAN – SAGITTARIUS WOMAN

Both Fire signs, both in need of affirmation of their strength and of much support from each other. They are extravagant and live on the danger line, always wanting to find another, more exciting edge to their relationship. This can lead to quarrels: he will be fired by her independent spirit and wish he could tame it. However, the Leo, for all his vanity and his own roaring self-importance, finds it hard to pin this lady down. She needs her independence and freedom in a relationship. But she also needs to feel loved. The Leo man could provide this in his own self-centred way. The universe was born for Leos, and the Lion will only want to ensure his path through life is not tainted by inferior emotion or shrewish criticism. And the Archer girl will do neither of these. Both of these Fire signs are extrovert and need the company of other people. (To feel uncomfortable alone is a sign of being an extrovert, and to fear company is a sign of being introvert.) If he flirts she will find her jealousy at times too emotional for her lifestyle, and he will begin to feel hurt and betrayed if she sarcastically bites back at his innocent bragging. She has so much honesty and a frank tongue that the Lion will be unnerved at times, but he needs her insults to bring him down to earth occasionally. She has to say what she really feels and, if the Lion can't stomach it, then she'll move on. They will feel the same heat of passions, the same energy of purpose, but sometimes they will lose sight of one another when the tests of loyalty and devotion become less of a game and more of power of will.

LEO WOMAN – SAGITTARIUS MAN

When the Archer stumbles across the lady with the glamorous lifestyle and the charming sincerity of her magnanimous and generous character, he may be numbed into thinking this is the sort of woman with whom he would like to dance in life.

He thinks grandly, has ideals that outwit being trodden upon, and his standards are higher than his brisk, flippant chat-up lines seem to imply. He is essentially an idealist and a free man, the lonely pirate who travels the world in search of a ship of dreams. Sometimes he will find her, then, for reasons best known to himself, he will mutiny, scuttle her and sailor on for another ideal, another dream. The Leo lady may have the courage and the strength of a battleship to hang on to him. She is not possessive, and she is not likely to boss him around in the way she might try to organise a Water sign, or an Earth sign. She loves his dashing, cavalier approach to life, as Fiery as her own but subtly more gregarious and more instinctive. He has Jupiter as his pal, and he likes pals, female ones particularly. If the Leo girl can accept that when he openly and candidly talks about his past lovers, or his platonic girlfriends, because he believes he can share everything with the one he loves, then she must realise that it is she whom he loves most of all. He cares deeply about her pride, he's got a bit of it himself, but he also cares if he hurts. He can open his big mouth too often with a Leo girl and she's easily hurt.

When they are apart he will miss her, when they are together he will think of the lonely road and miss that too. He needs both, his freedom and the lovely loyalty of a strong woman, and maybe he can share his pirate dreams with her.

LEO MAN – CAPRICORN WOMAN

The enthusiasm of the Leo man can get almost literally buried beneath the mound of dominating compost the Capricorn woman needs to pile into her relationships. As much as she is a quiet, gentle soul, her power is driven by real, practical forces and her ambition is paramount to her existence. It may take her a long time to like this man but they are linked by their need to be top in everything. The only difference is that while Leo can do it nicely, warmly, and with a certain amount of humour, the Goat lady just gets on and climbs impassively. She doesn't get led astray by love, beauty or fun, and would rather wait until she's sure, absolutely dead-pan sure, that a man is worthy of her strength. To a Leo man this can quash his enthusiastic love-making with an impotence he had never believed, and occasionally it can turn to frigidity unless he finds the warmth and love he deserves.

They do have their moments though, a few of them. Littered with a past that he would love to share with a woman, not to cajole nor to incite jealousy, but just because his method is part of his madness, he flows through a Goat woman's life and comes out the other end without touching down on her compost heap. If he does, he may have to face life at the bottom, and that for a Leo man is like being dead.

LEO WOMAN – CAPRICORN MAN

The battle for dominance here might rage for weeks, even years, if it's given the chance. Meeting a Leo woman gives the Goat a big thrill. Here is someone quite outstanding. She is glamorous, sophisticated and full of an expression and lust for life which is far removed from his own lacklustre corner. But can she stand the dull pace of his controlled and ordered lifestyle? Frankly, he may wonder if her mouth is as big as her cheque book. Goats quite honestly are known to fritter away their wives' money for their own ends and to use glamorous, exciting women in their climb to fame or power. If she's sharp, which she may not be initially (it takes a while for the Leo enthusiasm to settle down in the first pangs of passion), she might notice that the over-nice and abnormally sensitive Capricorn is actually meeting her head on in his own quiet taciturn way. He can dominate without appearing to which, for the Leo girl, is probably the best bet. She needs to feel that she is organising his life, and is in charge of the relationship, and the Goat is fairly sensible and capable of appearing as if he is organised when in fact his cool determination is the pulse behind the beat of their partnership.

The major problem they face is that she needs an extravagant and exciting lifestyle, to get out and about. He won't be too happy about her enthusiasm for other men, and her rather self-centred approach to love-making. He is wise to the world and grows cynical as he ages, and she grows ever more ingenious which means their power struggle will always be real, if they can face it.

LEO MAN – AQUARIUS WOMAN

The girl who breaks all the rules will seem a prey of a delectable new species to be tasted by a Lion. Her unpredictable nature, her rather strange analytical approach to life, are things that get the Lion's mane slightly ruffled when he first meets her. He is used to women who listen to him with very open ears, and nod a lot, which makes him feel smug. Leos need to feel smug, and this enhances his image of himself. This Aquarian girl won't ever make him feel smug, she's more likely to knock him over with her extraordinary and quite challenging rebellion. His Fiery emotions are vulnerable with this carefree and very independent spirit. She is not tameable, and he won't even dare try. She will find him quite vain, and wonder what he has got to feel so haughty about. His generosity will intrigue her and his enthusiasm for everything will actually provide the spark for her own inquisitive nature. There is more to their emotional relationship than appears on the surface. The Aquarian stubbornness will resist any obvious signs of emotion, and the Leo will spend most of his time trying to impress her to avoid her ever really knowing how belittled he can feel in her company,

There will be times when her need to rise against the norms of society will infuriate him. Leos like to feel that they are above everybody, and that includes even a dissident Aquarian. Their sexual relationship can be passionate, but often tainted by the Aquarian girl's coldness. Sex isn't a big thing for an Aquarian girl, but it is for a Leo. If he can understand that their friendship is more important than love, she can provide him with the sort of experiences in bed that are wildly entertaining, and certainly unconventional!

LEO WOMAN – AQUARIUS MAN

The Aquarian man will immediately want to unravel the secrets of the Leo woman's character. She is so full of up-front insolence and so full of passion he can hardly believe he is so attracted to her. The Lion lady will not be particularly surprised by his aloof interest in her. Most men are interested in Leo ladies, and she really can pick and choose most of the time. But this rather Bohemian man resembling a mad scientist or an anarchist is not so much fascinated by her image, and her shining, regal appearance but by something inside her. He will analyse her quickly, more quickly than anyone he has ever met, and he will find it hard to resist the magnetic pull of her sexual attraction. Opposite signs are always attracted by the physical chemistry of the other sign immediately. Once an Aquarian man realises that this Leo lady is so different from him, he will want to know more, to test her out, see if she comes up to scratch. Sexually the Leo girl will find this man doubly attractive because he is so aloof. Cold men are a challenge, and she likes to prove her strength. But emotionally the Uranian man is an out-of-space man, and the chances that he will be able to fulfil her need for warmth, compliments and much admiration are slim. He may initially find this an amusing pastime, he does love his pastimes, but he will eventually tire of the game, as he tires of a worn-out jumper, and revert to his social life. For the Leo lady, whose pride is the mistletoe of her sexuality, she can turn frigid very quickly and look for a greater deal of comfort and warmth.

LEO MAN – PISCES WOMAN

When, like a Lion man, you're a burning inferno of passion, sunlight and romantic combustion, to find a woman who is romantic, dreamy and feminine can turn your whiskers up and make you sharpen your claws on the nearest sofa. The Leo's enthusiasm for love and a warm, eternal relationship can be easily highlighted by the soft gentle rhythms of this Sea lady. He is also rather fond of the way she's not pushy, not bossy and listens to him as if she really means it, as if she might actually believe in him, and that his words are of value. Dramatic Cats enjoy the initial romance of any relationship. It means they can play the lead role without anyone knowing about their vulnerability. It's only later in a relationship that any wise woman will begin to sense the Cat needs a good deal of stroking. But the Piscean girl will immediately feel this when she first meets the Pussy Cat. She will find him at once delightful, for, although she is of water, drifting through life with misty eyes in search of an ideal, here is an equally idealistic man but one who is fired by ambition, and is full of genuine altruism.

The Leo will always fear that the rather placid and laid-back Fish will drown him in his own sense of rejection. She may reject him, however, if he becomes too vain and arrogant, too loud and over-protective. For this is when she will need to return to the depths of the sea to escape the onslaught of the sometimes over-bombastic lectures of the flashy Leo. The passion of the Lion might also wash over her rather faraway and distant love-making. She needs mystical love, spiritual awareness between two souls, and the Leo needs human flesh, to feel the blood pounding in his loins and real affection in his partner's arms. Unfortunately the Fish girl can turn from this over-dramatised man to seek a deeper freedom.

LEO WOMAN – PISCES MAN

The vague and rather elusive quality of the Pisces man can set the seeds of being in love in the Leo woman very quickly. The Fish will generate in her heart pangs of affection for the rather lost and forlorn act that she doesn't often come across. The Leo lady is dominant and haughty, and also rather loud about herself, which can initially make the Pisces man hesitate about getting involved with such an arrogant girl. His feelings may churn and send him back down his whirlpool of retreat unless, of course, the Leo softens, becomes the tragic figure and listens for a moment. Intuitively they should get on as friends first, and then maybe she will begin to be less overpowering. Somehow he knows that her inner nature is fraught with fears similar to his own. He will not have a power struggle with her, because he doesn't feel any need for anyone to be in charge. If she can let him escape from her Cat-like claws occasionally, she will find that he is more likely to hang around longer. He needs solitude, a lazy languid trip through life's impossible waters. She will need company, lots of company and a Force Ten gale to keep her on a trip of dramas. She would prefer life to be like the *Complete Works of Shakespeare*, and he would like it be a slowboat down a muddy river, time to dream, time to write those words instead of play them.

At first he may seem the ideal lover, always feeling and intuitively knowing what she needs. But he is too ephemeral, too intangible, for her feral passion, and the more demanding she is, the more likely he will return to that slowboat and find himself alone.

LEO MAN – ARIES WOMAN

The independent Aries woman will get a shock when she first meets a Lion in an extravagant and conceited mood. For the first time in her life she'll be confronted with a man who can give as good as she does, and won't take no for an answer. Her own bossiness will be burnt away by the Lion's attack (always from behind because he's less likely to get hurt that way), to find herself mysteriously carried away by the manner in which he tells her he knows all the answers, and really how could she ever doubt him if he's decided he has chosen her? His superior and rather condescending approach to women won't unnerve her. Although she may get angry when he tries to explain to her the meaning of life, Leos have the knack of thinking no one except they know the answer to it. Her Martian impulse will rile him frequently, and they are sure to have blazing rows at all times of day and night. Aries and Leos are both Fire signs and they have the same passionate need for a wild and careless sexual relationship. Once they have fallen breathless between the sheets they are more likely than most couples to forget their differences. Unfortunately, it will be the Lion who may on occasion find his pride is hurt more than he can bear and he'll withdraw and become icy. He can inflict pain without thinking and will often quite innocently make frequent comparisons and references to past love-affairs, because he really does believe he is God's gift to women. If she can accept that his arrogance stems from fear of making a fool of himself, and that, like the Lion he is, the bravery is all a front for a warm and loving heart, she might just learn to forgive him in time.

LEO WOMAN – ARIES MAN

A thrilling contest of egos battling out for the leading role, and the competition to be the centre of the universe! Who comes first? Leo women believe they have to be in charge, and Aries men believe they should be in control in everything, including bed, from day one. The best bet for these two optimists of the zodiac is to take it in turns to be on top. The Leo woman is less likely to burn herself out if she lets Aries take the dominating role. Actually if she realises that she is organising his stardom, then that to her is the battle already won!

Emotionally they will tumble together like loaded dice. They burn fire with fire and will both love the high they get from this exhausting and frantic relationship full of blazing rows and hurt pride, especially the big Cat's.

The Aries man's troubles may arise from his lack of discretion. He has a rather honest and open way with words, and may open his big mouth when he should be mumbling words of love or adoration to the Leo girl, as she does need a lot of stroking. He might reveal his Leo lady's favourite colour underwear to his mother, when he should have been discreetly suggesting they elope instead. In a blaze of passionate impulse he may turn up on the Ram's doorstep at four in the morning and expect her to share a bath. Of course this youthful energy will keep them both acting like a couple of kids, but there will be moments when Leo will want more affection, and more emotional strength from him than he is actually capable of giving. They both love a glamorous and fast lifestyle, would rather live for today than plan too much for tomorrow. Seeking an intense and dramatic involvement will keep them both on their toes, and this could be a loving and permanent relationship if they've both got the energy to survive.

LEO MAN – TAURUS WOMAN

Leo men love flattery and to know they are the king. Unfortunately Taurus girls don't take kindly to compliments and very rarely want to get into heated debates or flowery speeches. Yet these two complement each other in ways that may just produce a warm affinity. With the Leo's love of everything big, everything dramatic and glitzy and the Bull's innate desire for a calm passive down-to-earth world, their very different motivations can actually benefit one another, if they have the time to communicate. This happens infrequently, because Leo is vainly jousting with every possible event that he can organise and Taurus is generally determined to succeed in a quiet and patient lethargy. Thus their chances for actually sitting down and working out their relationship is about as risky as was its beginning in the first place. He may have been attracted by her sensuality, her very beauty and cool poise, and she may have been infatuated with his haughty energy and his flamboyant extravagance.

Between the sheets a Leo will find the Taurean girl's sensuality and talent for enhancing his ego more than a delight. He loves sex passionately and, sexually, their compatibility will outweigh all their differences . She will understand his pride can be hurt by indifference in the day-to-day humdrum of life but, once in bed or wherever they feel comfortable together, they can both make one another feel sexually unique.

LEO WOMAN – TAURUS MAN

The Lioness will probably chat up the Bull even before he's realised how glamorous and exciting a woman she is. Leo women are drama queens but they are also determined and loyal and, if there's something a Bull respects and admires, it is determination and loyalty! Both Bulls and Lions are very conscious of being dominant types, and the chances are that their relationship could turn into a power-struggle and a tug-of-war contest in bed, rather than the simple basic Earthy relationship that the Bull really wanted all the time. Leo ladies like to be the boss and, quite honestly, placid Taurus can get a mite fed up with being bossed around, particularly where his sexual satisfaction, and sensual pleasures are concerned. He believes he is passionate, not in the roaring, extravaganza way of Leo, but in his sensual and erotic version. She wants action, as well as passion. A Taurean won't actually be very active, although he can seem so to begin with. He won't want a wrestling match in bed every time she takes the lead. Warning! Wrestling in bed uses up a lot of energy, and this man is an artist of sleep, not of activity.

Apart from the other Earth signs, a Leo woman is probably the only one who could get away teasing a Bull, while she humours him by gently stroking his back. Mentally a Leo needs a lot of stimulation, which the Bull might find hard to provide. His lack of verbal diarrhoea can also infuriate the more precocious Leo, who loves talking about everything under the sun and knowing the answer to every question. But her bossy, warm air will make him relax and laugh and there will be an easy harmony between them. He can't bear any woman being in control, but somehow the Leo lady might, as usual, get away with it!

LEO MAN – GEMINI WOMAN

The Gemini woman has learnt the art of flattery. Communication is big business to her, and so is flirting, because it really does get her moving through life and gives her the best possible chance of finding the man of her childhood dreams. She loves men very much, like they should be loved, as big brothers, fathers and lovers. But the love is ephemeral, and her cold heart can sometimes turn a big-hearted, forgiving Leo to stone. They both share the same optimism for living. They will drink their way through the night and postpone love for another day. She will strike a harmonious note on his ego if she wants to and, although he'll constantly remind her that he knows best about everything, it will be to his advantage if he occasionally lets her have her way. He needs a lot of affection, physical as well as mental. Gemini women are pretty hot on mental affection, but they do let the side down with a rather distant, cold approach to anything sensual.

The Gemini girl's mind might well be somewhere else when they are in bed, like writing her next film script, or going through the motions of a well-loved fantasy. Sex is not all passion and ecstasy for the faint-hearted Leo with a Gemini. He will have to learn that she will never give the whole of herself to him, or to love, and she will have to learn that he requires more than a cold shoulder on which to rest awhile, otherwise he will quite quickly find another. He is very proud, and very vain, and she is too devious and inconstant for the Fire to stay lit for long.

LEO WOMAN – GEMINI MAN

Don't ever tell a Leo woman that her hair is a disaster and her clothes are outdated, unless you are a Gemini man with a little-boy-lost look, an artful creator of the perfect tease. Somehow the Twins will always get away with it. Leo loves trying to tame this rather fickle and glib beast who, she believes, should really have a home and not roam so freely. But Geminis are in need of change and they need their heads to be full of Air and ideas, or they become more restless and more liable to promiscuity. A Leo lady can solve this problem if she's got the guts (which she normally has) to show the Gemini cheek that you can have a lovely loyal and true relationship with one person as long as it is with her royal highness, the Leo Cat. The reason she manages to convince the Twins is because she believes she is God's gift to men. Men have to want her, have to chase her, have to find her, and the Gemini man who isn't particularly interested in all that preliminary catching will soon find that if he doesn't keep up with her own Pussy-Cat behaviour, then he'll be suddenly and awkwardly dumped.

Keeping him keen is not as difficult as she might imagine: it comes down to proving that she will always be interesting, will never tire of his changeability and will never try to pin him down. This last bit could prove tricky because she does like the idea of permanence. Sexually, the Lion will want more warmth than he can ever give and he won't be as passionate as she would like. But they can keep each other alive and alert, and they both share the need for extravagant living and wild and ridiculous loving. He will live in his head, and she will live in her heart. But the Gemini man can play any role she wants to create for him. As long as she is centre-stage, she will create the best parts that give him the most freedom.

LEO MAN – CANCER WOMAN

The ego of a Leo man in search of a relationship is usually the first thing that confronts a Cancerian girl, alone and vulnerable. She will play a game of elusive interest, and probably be fascinated enough by his proud boasting to realise that, actually, he may not be so bad when he calms down. He is arrogant, and he is definitely convinced he knows the answer to every subject under the stars, including the deep secrets of the Crab girl. But she will remember in her deepest fears that he's forgotten to mention himself in this scenario. And what she fears most is getting tangled up and then being rejected. She'll play a challenging game to seduce him, though. And because a Moon girl senses the heat that scorches the Lion's ego, she knows that he might just be the sort of man she needs. A Cancer girl wants a strong, protective Fire around her, not wishy-washy dreamers who may sink her further into her depths of despair. She wants to admire a man for his abilities, for his energy, for things that are very much part of her own strength, but often sublimated by the moods of the Moon.

He will find her feminine, sensitive mystique instantly lovable, and his natural protective instinct and his masculine pride will find an easy scapegoat for his boasting vanity, because he knows he will be pampered in the kitchen and in the bedroom.

Back in the bedroom the Leo can be over-demanding and too impulsive in his love-making and the Crab lady can be too passive and emotionally wound up. If she's in one of her moods and retreats to the kitchen for solace in a Crab sandwich, then the Leo's pride can be deeply hurt. He is vulnerable, actually a lot more vulnerable than he appears. The secret is that his is a stubborn belief that he is right, always right, and, like the Lion, his bravery is only as courageous as the prey he is chasing. The Crab has a very tough shell of protection; the Lion doesn't.

LEO WOMAN – CANCER MAN

Leo women are renowned for their bossiness and their need to organise everyone else's life. When a Lion lady meets a sensitive Cancerian man, she usually thinks that here is a kind, weary soul who needs organising, will be affectionate, loving and just the kind of man to have around her to boost her ego. Yet she may find out to her horror that actually a Crab, for all his sulky moods and rather side-saddle enthusiasm, wants to be the leader in their relationship. The shock for both of them is that while Leo can still do the organising, Cancer will instinctively let her get on with it, convinced secretly that he is in charge. The Crab knows that the Lioness must feel that she is in control, even if he is actually running the show. The Crab man will be instantly attracted to this woman's Fiery, proud and intensely loyal goodness. For all her know-it-all attitude, she actually means well and has a generous heart with a real warmth that can liberate even a Crab in a deep depressive sulk. She will be the one who can lift him out of depression, and coax him into an optimism that is her true spirit. The Sun and the Moon are classic in their differences, the Moon moody and silent, sensitive and emotional, the Sun passionate, vibrant and glitzy.

A Leo woman needs someone who can understand her deep sexual desires, and a Crab man does because he has the intuition and the emotional strength to reflect it right back at her. One of their major set-backs can be that he is liable to smother himself in self-pity if the Leo lady rejects him, and the Leo can sulk and proudly turn frigid, like the Sun has been eclipsed by the Moon, for very long periods if she thinks his retreat into his shell is a snub. It usually isn't, and there is enough warmth in this relationship to make sure that the Crab and the Lion both feel secure in the truth.

Virgo

COMPATIBILITIES

VIRGO MAN – VIRGO WOMAN

For the precise and methodical Virgo to meet a girl so incredibly in tune and in time with his own lifestyle is probably the most enchanting, perfect moment he has ever experienced. Here is a girl who loves punctuality, admires his quiet and cool poise and is fascinated by his mental sharpness. Equally, when the Virgo girl climbs into bed the first time with the Virgo man, she is dumbfounded by the way he has mastered the art of lovemaking in the same manner as she's mastered the art of dissecting the turkey for Christmas. Liking the same method of living, and thinking the same in life is essentially a brilliant start for any relationship. But because they are so alike, they must learn to analyse their own faults which are clearly mirrored in each other.

Although these two are able to perfect their routine without interference, they actually stimulate one another's usually rigid mentality into becoming a more vibrant and lively one. In fact two Virgos chatter as much as two Geminis, the difference being Virgos are more analytical and critical; the Geminis, however, are actually communicating.

As both are uniquely gifted with tact, meticulous, and practical knowledge, they can support each other mentally and emotionally. They may get upset if they both worry about the same things.

Virgo men are likely to rise early and jog round the park, appear precisely at eight a.m., expecting the Virgo girl to have timed the eggs in the poacher. This kind of simple mental arithmetic causes few headaches. Virgos don't like scenes and emotions, and they don't like headaches. It might be the first sign of brain damage and they are awfully fond of their brains!

Although the Virgo man has perfected love-making for his own satisfaction, and the Virgo girl will at first be impressed by this, it's not because of the quality of his art and the pedantry of his style; in fact both are more fascinated by each other's minds than each other's bodies, and sexually they may both have a fairly cold relationship.

VIRGO MAN – LIBRA WOMAN

What these two have in common is that Libra rather admires Virgo's ability for self-discipline, and Virgo admires the Libran's fair play in everything. Admiration is a mutual stimulation for an otherwise fairly stark relationship. The Virgo Man is not particularly interested in the high life, in socialising, nor in charming the world and enjoying it. He also prefers predictability and would rather share his life with a placid, easy-going girl. This is how the Libran girl appears to be when he first meets her. He will fall in love easily with her bright, sparkling, Airy chatter and, mentally, she will provide him with a fascinating and constant strength of purpose. The Virgo doesn't want to be bossed, and he needs a companion rather than a lover. He doesn't like laziness, nor untidiness and, although he enjoys sex, he doesn't go wild about it. Now a Libran girl may find all this sharp, rather austere attitude a little mind-bending. She likes to have her brain well used, but she also loves to get out and about and enjoy herself. She may find the uncluttered existence of the Virgo rather cold and unwelcoming, his punctuality will irritate her and, as fair as she tries to be, she cannot quite justify in her head why she has to stay put, get up to catch the same train every day, and make decisions when she would rather avoid them.

If she does get as far as spending the night with him, it could initially seem a magical experience. She is not in need of passion and hot steaming beds and nor is he. But she does need warmth and affection and to feel really loved. The Virgo tends to criticise, not flatter, and the barrier of ice can build up around her quicker than he intended.

VIRGO WOMAN – LIBRA MAN

The Libran man is charmed by mental brightness and sparkling, romantic eyes. His ideals are driven by dreams and beautiful women and, when he meets a gentle, rather sweet and feminine Virgo girl, he will immediately, and quite thoughtlessly, plunge into an affair with love. It's easy for him, and it happens often, but really this time he should have known better. The Virgo woman is usually very careful about who she allows into her space, and the easy-going and rather romantic man who walks through her door will enchant her with his abstract mind, and considerate judgments of the world. The Virgo woman, however, can sense that he prevaricates more than he thinks. He is an extrovert, and demands the security of people around him, which she doesn't. He will begin to grumble when she nit-picks at and criticises his friends, and when she says she would rather he stayed at home more and not play the romantic with every girl he meets. To be so charming is fine when she is on the other end of the flirt, but to see him playing the same tune to other women is, for a Virgo, the shortest route to total frigidity.

The Libran man believes that the Virgo girl is happy with her lot, while he wanders off to socialise. But these girls are not quite as home-loving as they seem, and would rather build a career than actually go and do the shopping. They both enjoy a pleasant, comfortable lifestyle with no heavy scenes, but the Libran doesn't take easily to commitments, any choice implies rejecting the alternative. And if it's a toss up between freedom and the Virgo lady, it will be a decision that he will probably never make. But she will!

VIRGO MAN – SCORPIO WOMAN

The inquiring nature of the Virgo man can seem trifling in comparison with the penetrating, all-power-seeking probing of the Scorpio woman. The Virgo man lives to find a woman who can provide him with mental stimulation and practical support. He is strong, but he needs to feel strength around him so that it is real. The Scorpio woman will immediately love the Virgo man's level-headed and analytical mind. She will be attracted both to his romantic nature and to his practical one. Scorpio women are emotional and determined. Their strength is their character, and the whole of their life is lived with purpose, both for love and for life. The Virgo man may find this hard to live with. He doesn't exactly enjoy emotional scenes of any kind, and he certainly can't cope with the pressures that a Water sign like Scorpio can turn on him in her most passionate moments.

He would like to be enlightened by her tremendous power to inject all kinds of feeling into her love-making but somehow he is never quite there with her. He will be dexterous, agile and know every position under the sun, but he won't be able to provide her with the solution to love, and the universe, which is essentially what this woman wants from her sex life. Virgo believes sex to be pure. It is an art to be perfected, it does not have any deeper meaning to his life. Sadly, this involves not a jot of the emotional content that a Scorpio woman reads into every move he makes. They can quite easily misunderstand one another, even while they enjoy being together but, after a while, she will become too demanding, and the Virgo is more likely to suffer with headaches, turn on the cold shower too often, and resort to a high-powered fault-finding mission to recuperate.

VIRGO WOMAN – SCORPIO MAN

Now the Virgo woman does enjoy submission at times; not often, because she is a very proud and careful practitioner and won't be made a fool of easily. But there's something rather sensational about the soulful way the Scorpio waits to move in.

A Virgo is not overtly a 'feeling' person, but this man can send shudders down her spine, and melt her poise before she's even felt the sting of his tail. They may meet and spend a long time being attracted to each other without either of them summoning up the courage to do anything about it. For all his womanising, the Scorpio prefers the waiting, the lingering and the anticipation of the moment. He is drawn to mystery and darkness. And if he can keep the light out on her inner self for a long time, the more charged his sexual energy will be when it is time to release it. He will be suspicious of her intentions at first – he is suspicious of daylight too. Virgo women are pretty good at mental sharpness and, like barbed wire, a Scorpio can become caught up in her mind. Usually he moves in and wipes out his victims with vows and promises of passion and fulfilment. This may tempt her, but her Earthy, practical nature will always keep clarity in her visions. Both have an ability to appear cold and unfeeling. Hers is to avoid emotion and his is because he feels so intensely that it's easier to keep the true depth of his love hidden, even from himself. If the Virgo girl turns sexually cold on him, which she will do if she suspects he is gathering his strength to form an onslaught on another unsuspecting female, then he will end their relationship with sadistic pleasure.

VIRGO MAN – SAGITTARIUS WOMAN

The communication is good between these two rather oddly matched signs. The Sagittarius girl seeks freedom and love. Finding the paradox is her quest in life, and the Virgo man can understand this mentality, because it is a thinking process he can analyse and act upon. To a poised, unruffled Virgo man, the wild and extremist behaviour of Fire signs usually fascinates him to begin with and then, after a while, irritates him. It's always easier to find fault in strength rather than in weakness. The Archer girl is incredibly adaptable, and so is Virgo. She may think him pedantic and rather too steady for her clattering lifestyle. She will insist on having fun, playing jokes on the man she loves, and generally misbehaving.

Full of surprises, the Archer girl likes to outwit even a Virgo intellectually. This is not something he will get a buzz from, and he will have to prepare himself for the mental red-alert she presents. But the Archer girl's independence and spirit needs a firm shoulder to lean on at times. She has insecurities, but her strength is intuitively knowing what goes on in a Virgo man's head. He may not have much of a heart, but she can stretch it out into the world of romance with extraordinary talent.

Virgos aren't exactly balls of fire in bed. He may not even stir her the way she really wants to be stirred, but he will be romantic and willing to be led on sexual adventures that he never knew existed. He wants to understand her egalitarian and clowning behaviour, and she finds his old-fashioned and stuffy mind an easy prey for her outspoken and blunt humour. They could find an easy rapport in time, but it will be based on friendship, rather than any sexual intimacy.

VIRGO WOMAN – SAGITTARIUS MAN

The sensible and sometimes tight-fisted Virgo girl will find that the Archer's extraordinary generosity and rather lax approach to finances make her squirm with disapproval. She will want more than anything to organise him, and hope that his expansive attitude to money is not the same as it is to women. Unfortunately her hopes may be dashed. The Sagittarius needs to open up his life and take everyone into it, and give it all to the world if he can. And in this respect he really does want to be friends with everyone he meets. Other men are suspicious of such honest and open carelessness and women, of course, are usually convinced that they are the true love of his life. They should beware, especially Virgo women. She may well fall instantly in love with the rogue of the zodiac. It's easy. He is so child-like, so lovable and funny. He's a bit clumsy with his heart, and can be rather big-mouthed and coarse, but he is also honest. And a Virgo girl really gets high on honesty. At first he'll be impressed with her intellect, as bouncy and easy as his own. To a

Sagittarian man falling in love is often as sudden as the arrow he's just fired, but another arrow can come angling along and split the first, and the Archer is vulnerable to his own need for freedom. Another woman is freedom from the first, and, although he never means to hurt anyone, he can throw relationships around without thinking, as if they were sharp stones on the road to happiness. He is thoughtless rather than harmful, and the Virgo woman can end up the temporary stop-over on his quest for the ideal woman. And a Sagittarius always has one of those!

VIRGO MAN – CAPRICORN WOMAN

This sensible pair is well matched for any partnership, but essentially it will be a partnership in the style of a business arrangement rather than a love-affair. Both the Virgo Man and the Goat girl are after stability and firm foundations on which to build their mutual need for success. The Capricorn girl can often be more ambitious than her Virgo mate, and this could work very well to her advantage. She has no contest over who leads, and there will be sensible meetings between them, ready to face the boardroom and take the consequences of their actions. However, both are stubborn to varying degrees. She because Goats really are rigid and reserved in their opinions and won't budge if they are goaded. A Virgo will mentally attempt to budge as he enjoys mind-games, but he doesn't like to disagree, nor argue. He likes to put things in their place and let them stay there, unless he feels they may be changed. The Goat girl will find him a bit chilly in the bedroom, but her own desire for privacy and her more important need for a dependable and reliable service (she may treat him rather like a bus timetable) outweigh basic sexuality and love. The Goat may tire of the rather purist tactics the Virgo Man attributes to her success.

Neither is interested in emotion and they will find their rapport will be built on belief in commitment and sharing the good and pleasant things in life. As they grow older together, their bond will be usually unbreakable.

VIRGO WOMAN – CAPRICORN MAN

If a Goat has reached the top of his own special mountain, he might be glad of the respect and admiration that the Virgo girl can give him. He never actually gets too excited about anything apart from personal hard-lining. If this includes making a permanent fixture of the Virgo girl, then he may find he has chosen the best course of action. The road to his success is littered with women who can be useful, carry him up the golden stairway, or leave him cold and bitter. He is a cynic, but the Virgo girl is equally able to understand he's had a few rough and tumble relationships before he met her. But she is convinced that he will find her the perfect, trusting and sensible partner. She won't necessarily want to be his prop, more like his companion. Both strong characters will find much stability in this well-balanced and sensible relationship. She needs to communicate in her own strident way, and he rather likes her fine and highly critical mind. It does enhance his mountain top. She will occasionally unnerve him with her hypercritical nit-picking over breakfast, or the importance of getting to the train on time when he was actually planning a very important take-over bid for the next-door neighbour's building plot. She might have to be wary of his habit as he grows older to play the genial youth. The need for order and for control in his relationship might occasionally be undermined by her pig-headed affront at being treated that way. She is a feminine but strong woman, and he is a very powerful man who needs her.

VIRGO MAN – AQUARIUS WOMAN

The Virgo man is essentially a loner, and the Aquarian girl is mostly everybody's friend. She needs people around as if they are part of her very being. However, the Virgo man, who has taken a keen interest in her extraordinary and unpredictable behaviour, at first might be able to understand her humanitarian and extrovert nature. Aquarian girls like analysing and subjecting people to bold and frank inquiry. It's interesting for her to see how they tick, and whether they get upset by her form of character analysis. Funnily enough, the Virgo man can get quite happy on criticism and analysis too, but on a fussier level. Mentally they have much in common, but their differences can cause friction and tensions which may never get them further than a first encounter.

Being an Air sign makes the Aquarian girl fairly immune to emotion and also fairly uninterested in sex. She insists on maintaining an awful lot of freedom in her relationships, mostly so that her rebellious and lawless attitude is never subjected to restraint. The Virgo will attempt to let her have free rein, but he won't enjoy the company of friends in the kitchen and on the telephone, or hanging round their flat all hours of the night. He has his routine, and he has his order. She has no routine, the less routine the better, and she loves her chaos.

This can make them either become inextricably fascinated with each other, or separate them quickly. Sex is not something either of them find the core of their lives, so if friendship and partnership are handled carefully they may stick it out. Not an exciting romance, but the chance of a lasting partnership.

VIRGO WOMAN – AQUARIUS MAN

The first thing an Aquarius Man must do is respect that the Virgo girl he's become fascinated by is as independent as he is, but not interested in his friends. This may come as a shock to him, because he really dotes on his friends, more than he possibly would a dog. Why can't she just be another friend? Why does she insist on being someone special? Aquarians don't like to think anyone is more special in their life than themselves. Friends, relatives, spouses, business partners share his equality rule. He will give pleasure to the world with the same amount of attention, and will hope that those around him benefit from his ability to change them. The Virgo woman might not enjoy this at all. She can adapt to anything with great ease, but she won't want to be changed for the sake of change. He will stubbornly exert his contrary opinions upon her most of the time, and she will attempt to remind herself that she saw in him a dreamer, a visionary who could make the world a better place. But he does keep trying so

190

hard to be difficult, and different, and turning a relationship upside down for the sake of it is the kind of tactic to alienate even a Virgo girl.

She is difficult to please too, so there will be times when he will slump off with his friends and ignore any conflict. He can get angry with her nit-picking and the way she has to clean up his chaos. He likes a rather obscure orderliness, one that he has designed. He will choose the most austere furniture, or the most way-out central heating system, refuse to have animals around because he gets allergic to dust and hairs, and stubbornly believes she would be a better woman for his cranky habits. If she can resist criticising his friends and accept that she will never be the only woman in his unorthodox life, then he might just agree to try eating toast in the morning instead of a piece of lettuce.

VIRGO MAN - PISCES WOMAN

The Fish girl is by nature sensitive, sweet and gentle, but she also has a certain Watery deviousness which often pops to the surface like the bubbles from her Fishy gills. The times that these slippery and spicier facets of this woman arise is usually when she's met a Virgo man. Virgo men have this uncanny ability either to bring out the worst in a girl (usually if she's one the Water signs) or the best (another Earth). Of course what happens to the Air and Fire signs is up to them! The Piscean girl meeting the rather mean and uncompromising Virgo with a wad of cash and no one to spend it on, can become masochistically infatuated with his very tight personality. The Virgo hangs out his role of perfect lover as a Daz advert exposes the whiteness that it claims is unique to Daz. But the Fish can see right through this charade. Beneath that perfect- gentleman act is a man who is an idealist and one who is in love with purity. He will immediately believe she is the purest form of woman. Not only is she a dreamer, wistful and difficult to catch, she is not interested in his robotic seduction. He hasn't, of course, the intuition or sixth sense that she has to realise she is being the rather slippery character that often mermaids are.

When he finally beavers in to claim her, to seduce her with words which have a finer chance of working than just male lust, he might just find that their sexual encounter will bring the true purity that he needs, and the idealistic love that she always feels is waiting. He may find her gregarious nature clashes with his rather lonely one, but she feels deeply, and will usually come back to listen to him with an open heart.

VIRGO WOMAN – PISCES MAN

For a while, when he comes dripping out of the ocean in search of romance on solid ground, the Fish will realise that there are very few true and pure women, very few ideals are ever better than the ones you can dream. But as he slithers on to the shoreline of the Virgo girl's quite sharp and bright-eyed affection, he will begin to wonder if maybe dreams can be made on dry land.

He will be wary of her rather private, solitary way of life. His own is friendly and humane and, although he is renowned for his disappearances into lonely woods and solitary seashores, he actually needs people very much. There will be arguments between Virgo and her Fish because the Piscean is basically a ditherer, always vague and not quite ready to make a definite commitment, either verbally, or emotionally. Virgo on the other hand wants to know the truth and will pull him to pieces with her caustic mouth, if he messes around too long.

But she faces another nagging problem. She really hates spending money, and he loves spending it. When she realises that his extravagance can lead him to be addictive in many of the more escapist pleasures of life, she will try desperately to stop him. But the Fish can turn cold and unresponsive if anyone throws too many demands on his sensitive scales.

She can be the seductress in his bed, and the restrictive force in his life. He will enjoy her romantic side but will have to tolerate the restraints she imposes on his natural freedom. And Fish are better at tolerating than Virgos. She will need his gentle sexuality. His dreamy, always mystical and faraway love-making. They may be mutually fulfilled if they learn to see in one another what is lacking within themselves.

VIRGO MAN – ARIES WOMAN

The outgoing and tactless Ram girl can seem quite a viable proposition for the Virgo idealist looking for perfection. To be able to control this headstrong woman would seem to him a rather invigorating and mentally challenging business, as long as she doesn't attempt to wash his socks, because he always does it *his* way, and makes sure she cleans up every crumb from the bed before he gets into it.

The Virgo man is sometimes unsure of what his ideal is. When he meets an Aries he is, of course, initially infatuated with her very opposite fantasy to his own. But her mystery, however enticing it is to him, can crumble into truth and become an irritant rather like those breadcrumbs between the sheets.

An Aries woman will find his cold, unyielding purity not at first an attraction. But he could be the sort of man she might recklessly have a frantic love-affair with, or just forget him all together. Yet there is something rather strangely magnetic between these two, and often an Aries girl will push back the frontiers of the Antarctic and storm into his heart to try to find if the ice is meltable on her own very high temperature gauge. The Virgo may find her irresistible, while the romantic perfectionist is working overtime. His performance in bed will win her over for a while but once the initial sexual encounter has diminished between them, there is very little left for them to salvage except her independence and his digestive problems.

VIRGO WOMAN – ARIES MAN

Now we all know that Virgos have a thing about perfection. Not the heady, sensitive perfection of a Piscean dreamer, but a practical, down-to-earth belief that there is someone out there who can provide a Virgo with her heart's desire. Now an Aries out for an entanglement, sexual or otherwise, turning on his favourite virility lesson, can seem the kind of hedonistic turn-on that a Virgo will find both alluring and repellent. The Aries Ram will pick her up for her femininity, think he can save her from a life of dull routine, and is sure she must find him the most beautiful creature. (Fire signs have a rather naïve vanity.) He won't be fond of her cold and rational resentment, although he's got his own jealousy to contend with too. The Aries man will be amused by the Virgo woman's sharp, subtle mentality, and he'll get infatuated with the apparent Earthiness of her sexuality. But don't believe that it will keep him coming back for more unless she can inspire him with a bit more heady passion than financial considerations or whether she defrosted the fridge and left the door open. The Virgo girl will want to organise him from day one, and this man really doesn't like anything to be organised, let alone himself!

The coldness of her passion won't be their only obstacle to success. She has this awful ability to appear to disapprove of all the Aries man's most genuine and child-like qualities. He is chaotic, fun-loving, impetuous and risky. She is ordered, a worrier, sensible and concerned with purity, not passion. She is a lover of romance but, once the romance has gone, she is happy to work hard for a good solid relationship based on how she sees a perfect marriage. Never mind what the Aries man thinks, as far as she is concerned he doesn't think, he merely acts. And the Ram's actions don't usually speak loud enough for her analytical and precise mind.

VIRGO MAN – TAURUS WOMAN

The Virgo man is hypercritical of most women, but there's something very pleasant and comforting about the Taurean girl. It's as if she's as perfect as a woman could possibly be, and that's a standard he rarely believes he'll find. These two usually meet at work, rather than at play. The Virgo man does little playing and that which he does won't usually involve places where he can be tempted by women.

His hunt for perfection will often lead him to question the Bull's placid nature and strength of purpose and, when he realises that he can't pick many holes in her character, he will decide, meticulously, and analytically that therefore she must be the most suitable candidate available. He is known to fall in love, but it's a quiet, emotionless experience. Romance is easy for him, because it involves no thread of emotion, only lines from a book. The Taurus girl will think this man a prig at first, conceited, over-obsessive and the plaintive for cold and unresponsive pedantry. Yet when she realises he's got the same motivation and determination, that in fact he is quite resilient and is happy to clarify every situation with analysis, she might even uncover a subtle depth to the sensible way he folds his pyjamas. (A lot of Virgo men do still wear pyjamas, and like them to be ironed.) A domestic-minded Taurus will get on better with him than a career girl but, if she can show enterprise and initiative, not cause emotional scenes, stamp her feet, or leave too many pairs of tights round the bathroom, he might just feel content with her.

Sexually he can seem cold, and she might take a while to warm him up. But if anyone can, a Taurean's basic sensuality will get him off on a different planet than he's ever known. Could she be the perfection he's been looking for?

VIRGO WOMAN – TAURUS MAN

So you've heard that two Earth signs together makes one big heap of volatile compost? Well, in some respects you're right.

Taurus and Virgo have the same approach to life. Unfortunately the difference is that the Virgo girl has a discriminating approach to sex and love, and Taurus doesn't. The Bull is down-to-earth, but probably too hedonistic for the Virgo girl when it comes to all the Earthy pleasures he needs to indulge in. Virgo girls like to analyse sex. Perfection between the sheets is what they want, not the snore of a Bull at dawn and smelly socks on the pillow. The basic raw attitude to life of a Bull is actually not very satisfactory to a Virgo, unless she can control him, and organise him without his even noticing that she is! Taurus isn't a fusspot and doesn't care if the duvet cover wasn't washed since Sunday as long as the bed is comfortable and he gets enough sleep. He can be intolerably untidy, and a Virgo is incredibly tidy-minded. She may actually like the Bull's mess, and choose to clear it up or ignore it, as long as it is ordered chaos, then it's OK. He could actually provide the Virgo girl with her delight for cleaning up and worrying about his dirty collars, and she could be the answer to his sloppy living.

Virgo girls need romance, pretty linen sheets, flowers on their birthday and champagne, which sometimes the Bull forgets, and finds her desires hard to cope with. If their relationship isn't a purely physical one, then it would be better for them both. In fact these two Earth signs make an excellent marriage and then, at least, the Virgo will have something more to criticise than just the Bull's slobbing in bed till noon.

VIRGO MAN – GEMINI WOMAN

The precision-timer of the zodiac will get quickly frustrated when he meets a Gemini woman, mainly because her time-keeping is her own law. If she says she will meet him at eight she will usually bump into an old friend and chat for an hour before she remembers to call him. Her ability to go off at tangents and attempt the impossible and be in two places at once is part of her Mercurial charm.

The Virgo man has little Mercurial charm, he has all the prac-ticalities it imposes on life. Of course, he is a perfectionist, requires a normal amount of affection and a large amount of logic in his love-affairs, but really can't waste his precious time with a girl who changes her personality and her job more frequently than a kaleidoscope changes colour.

Virgo men are quite adept at the first inklings of romance. They like to believe they are better at picking up a girl than any other sign. However, because they secretly yearn for a wife, rather than a lover, the Gemini girl will not be awfully good at this kind of partnership. They have little in common, and sexu-ally they will probably flounder fairly soon after any initial infat-uation has subsided. The Twins hate to be cornered, and the Virgo man is essentially quite keen on cornering and then dissecting the female of his attention. She may fall for this the first few times, but eventually even the lightness of a Virgo sexual encounter can bore her.

VIRGO WOMAN – GEMINI MAN

Not a relationship on which dreams are made. The Gemini man certainly won't want to enrich his life with hyper- criticism and meticulous analysis of why he didn't arrive dead on nine o'clock when he was supposed to. The Virgo girl will find herself constantly suspicious, and probably on red-alert if he so much as decides to travel anywhere without her. She will also find it hard to understand why he is so casual and so laid-back about life. At first when they meet romantically it might be all birds and bees. They share the same mutability, the same restless desire for knowledge, except the Gemini will actively seek change and love change and the Virgo would rather sit down and dwell on it, and then organise it within the compartments she's chosen. Her orderly mind gets the Gemini man reaching for his suitcase pretty quickly. He hates to be told what to do and the Virgo girl loves telling people what to do. He also won't want to take the future or their relationship too seriously. Romance is all very well, it has an ending in sight, but a future with a paradigm of virtue sounds to him like the sweetest icing on the biggest wedding-cake. And you know how he hates weddings!

Sexually they have little in common. He is cool, and can fluctuate between sex in his head and no sex. She is in need of romance, of affection, and an Earthy lightness, rather than a mental one. Their Mercury ruler may give them the same ability to analyse and dissect, but the Virgo will turn it to fault-finding and the Gemini will turn it to wondering what he is doing in bed with this serious woman in the first place.

VIRGO MAN – CANCER WOMAN

The Virgo man seeks perfection in a woman. Occasionally he comes across a woman who, he thinks, may be answer to this niggling problem, but very rarely. The Crab lady certainly appears the sweetest, most charming, feminine and deeply emotional woman he has ever met, but there is something he can't quite reason about her. And he does love to reason everything. The Crab girl has the same approach to life and money as the Virgo in many ways. They both like to look after their money, and they both need to maintain a certain privacy in their personal lives. The Virgo man, however, is cold emotionally and, although the Moon girl has her frigid moments, she needs a warmth that might not be returned from this rather old-fashioned and hyper-critical man. He worries too much about his health, and the Moon woman will know every cure in the book, intuitively she will be able to sense his headache coming on, will reach for the aspirins before he's even noticed and be at his side with a port and brandy when he's got a sneeze. They both are very attentive towards each other, but the Virgo's perfection-seeking might begin to niggle her. The Crab won't be able to take his caustic comments for long, and she certainly won't like to be organised like a telephone directory. There will be many breakdowns in their sexual communication. For although the Crab is perceptive, the Virgo can get mighty restless about being in the same bed as anyone, even the one who he thought was so perfect. He does like his crisp white sheets, and the window open in the winter. The Crab will quickly retreat and the Virgo will cool down, and the sexual perfectionist might even turn to celibacy if he feels that the Moon girl has abandoned his ice-box.

VIRGO WOMAN – CANCER MAN

Modesty and refinement walk hand-in-hand usually. One will support the other and they both will work hard to carry and share the load. With a Crab man and a Virgo girl there is a lot of modesty on both sides, and mostly refinement from the Virgo tastes in life. They may first meet through a third party. Cancer men don't often pick up girls, and Virgo women are very fussy about who they talk to. A Crab will, as usual, be extremely cautious about revealing the darker side of his nature. He will flirt his extrovert side around quite casually and the Virgo girl can be genuinely infatuated by the bright, strong leadership quality of this sensitive and genuine man. She likes genuine people, honesty and truth. The Virgo girl will then settle down to analyse the Cancerian man. After much deliberation, she reaches a decision that he may actually suffer from emotional trauma, he is affected by the Moon, but she can understand why his behaviour can change with his moods. She will suggest a relationship that can be assured permanence. He will admire her for her mental and highly intellectual reasoning power. It seems she's the sort of girl he needs, a woman who can remind him of the logic behind his deep and complicated search for truth, and someone who can keep him secure and contented. He may find after a while that her analysing turns to criticism, and that her bright and fresh intellect is too crisp and clear-cut for his more emotional swaying one. Sexually they will complement each other unless her Virgo criticism extends to the bedroom and then the Cancer will turn as frigid and cold as the Moon.

VIRGO MAN – LEO WOMAN

Practicalities are the same as perfection to the Virgo man. He needs order and neatness, he needs to feel in control, and he needs a conservative and simple lifestyle. He may hang his pyjamas over the chair every night and brush his teeth for exactly two minutes. He may keep a digital clock and a mechanical one, just in case one is fast. If he gets into a conversation with a Leo lady, he may surprise himself that he finds her gushing and flamboyant chatter quite entertaining. He is rather serious in life and here is a ravishing, fun-loving girl who is ready to flirt everyone under the table. Their attraction will emanate from curiosity. His because she is so ridiculous, and hers because he is so staid and neat. The likelihood that she will fall in love with him is slim, it could happen because he was playing the perfect-lover role, which is his only role and a good one at that. And also because his head is full of the most incredible things, not the sort of things a Leo will necessarily need in her own ostentatious brain, but different, concise, like a concise dictionary rather than the compendium of life with which the Leo lady believes she is blessed. She thinks she knows everything, but she needs warmth too. The Virgo man is cold and *really* knows everything. That is what they have in common. He is sensitive, for all his apparent coldness. Unless she gets her pride hurt, she may never be aware of this side of his nature. Her attempt at playing the leading-lady in his life might set him with an interesting mental spiral but it will quickly make him dizzy. She won't want to be the wife with the grace he expected, nor will she want to time his egg, nor be punctual for their dinner parties.

Sexually she'll surprise him often. She has passion, is full of passion, and he will still be looking up the next position in the *Kama Sutra* if she hasn't left him first. He is dexterous and believes he has mastered the art of sex like a true technician. But Leo ladies don't want technicians in their beds, they want a star act.

VIRGO WOMAN – LEO MAN

Virgos are for ever trying to improve on what they have, to perfect their own high standards. If they get involved with a Lion along the way, then that might just as well involve improving the Lion to their own meticulous flow-chart. The problem for the delicate pedantry of the Virgo romantic is that Leos don't usually fit into any improvement programme. For a start they are already better than anyone in bed, around the house, intellectually, and with money. In relationships they convince themselves that they know how to make it work, and a Leo man will certainly not listen to a woman who thinks she knows best. He would rather show the Virgo how to enjoy life, living for each moment, rather than running around worrying about it. She might go along with this idea, for a while, but she won't tolerate his terrible untidiness and his constant need to work either like it's the last day he has on earth, or play every game until he's won. His loyalty will impress her, but her attempts to clean the ring round the bath every time he has one, will hurt his pride. He doesn't like to be reminded he's left his books all over the house, and really can't see what it's got to do with her anyway. The chances of them getting this far in their relationship are slim. The Virgo will, at the outset, play her feminine charm, her quiet side, quite naturally. But she will want to criticise, and she will want to instil her ideals on this rather bold presumptuous and prattling man. He's just the type to listen isn't he? Unfortunately, Leos only listen to themselves, and can get hard-of-hearing quite easily if they feel their dignity is threatened. She will inspire him to tenderness in bed though, albeit not quite the passion he needs to ignite his full attention. Mentally she'll be challenging, but once she begins to clock him into the house and out of it, he may well begin to wonder what happened to his Cat-flap.

♎♎
Libra

COMPATIBILITIES

LIBRA MAN – LIBRA WOMAN

Tasteful people actually seem to create a good deal of love and pleasantness wherever they go. There's something nice and well balanced about their charming friendliness, and constant chatter. When Librans first meet one another they may gaze quite strangely into what seems like their own eyes. Reflective at times, but mostly ready to compromise, they will accept without question any faults that the other half will have. They usually complement each other, share the love of conversation and romantic nights out, and generally behave with the style and optimism that most couples would love to emulate. But all is not perfect under that tinsel dressing. The discrepancy occurs because they both like parties, both like the other sex, over-indulgence in the good things of life, which can also include a wild amount of flirting. Both are convinced they need to be the dominant partner, which can also lead to a lot of indecision about who is going to make the bed, or who is not going to drink at the party and drive home. Librans want to have a good time and let their hair down, and to be the boring sod in the corner, all pleasure withdrawn for a safe ride home, doesn't encourage a strong bond.

They both love romance, and they both need a strong partnership. But there are times when they are easily led astray by attraction. Life is attractive, and it's safer staying on the surface. Digging too deep is dangerous and the Libran really doesn't want to get involved in making any decisions that require dredging the depths of emotion. However, being led astray by beauty in any form can certainly damage this relationship on a level whose existence they both refuse to acknowledge. If they can keep a light and Airy breeze blowing through sexual relationship, keep romance for themselves rather than spread it around, then they will ensure the balance and harmony in their life.

LIBRA MAN – SCORPIO WOMAN

There is a force and intensity to this woman that a Libran man can find a trifle alarming. His is a nature of symmetry and conciliation: the laid-back lover with a lazy, languid trust in most human beings, particularly women. He loves women a lot and feels safe in their company most of the time, they are less likely to expose him to conflict and dissension. Then along comes the Scorpio, out for involvement of the deepest and most sensitive kind. She has her cool, magical eyes fixed most definitely on him. He will be flattered, as any Libran is, by the attention of a beautiful woman, and will probably fall immediately into his usual trap of being in love with love. The Scorpio woman falls for his rather lax attitude to life, hers is so serious, and she yearns for more sweetness and fun. He can provide this, as long as she doesn't overrun him with the tensions and emotional struggles for which he is not cut out. But Libra can cope quite well with her dark and hidden forces because he lets it flow over him and around him, and is usually willing to give way a little for the sake of harmony.

He will want to get involved with this woman as long as he can have his freedom. Unfortunately the jealous and deep emotional anger of a Scorpio woman will sear his heart if he so much looks at another woman. This is where their disparate characters can cause a lot of flak. Sex is the meaning of life to this girl and the Libran's rather fickle approach to romance will begin to empty her heart of any imaginary future they had. His capricious flirtations with another beautiful woman could mean the end of any commitment he might have given an inkling of sharing. He wants desperately to form a special relationship with someone, but he still really believes that his ideal is out there, and if he doesn't carry on searching, he might miss the true love of his life. Scorpio may see this fair judgment merely as an excuse, and she won't play fulcrum for his alternating thoughts on whether to take the risk with her, or to lose it all on another chance.

LIBRA WOMAN – SCORPIO MAN

A Libran girl can fill the Scorpio male with a vengeance that will storm through her life, and end her idea of romance with him. She is a chatterbox, loves people and desperately wants a permanent relationship, when *she's* made her mind up, and not before. Along comes the Scorpio with lodestar sexuality and a compulsive personality. He exudes sex and he spouts poetry like a romantic, keeps hidden secrets to lure her into believing he must be the answer to the universe. Of course his mystery is just that he likes mystery. He takes life so seriously, and the Libran girl takes life so lightly. If the Snake will let her be the life and soul of the party, then she might make the sun shine for him too. But, as is often the case, the jealous and torrid intensity of the Scorpio's sting will break their relationship before she has had time to convince him, let alone herself, that this could be good. The Scorpio is also a very stubborn and egotistic person. Fire signs' egos are easily inspected, open to the world and almost comfortable to put up with compared to this Plutonian darkness, the almost satanic ego of a stranger. He will always be a stranger to this woman; even though she feels in control of their relationship, she can never really understand the intense depths of feelings this man rarely admits even to himself.

He fears rejection more strongly than she, oddly enough. When she is floundering in her head, and he would rather she were floundering on the bed with him, he will sense that potent sexuality may not be as ideal for her as he first imagined.

The one thing that he ought to learn, but it is unlikely because Scorpios are usually convinced they have nothing left to learn, is that she needs open communication. He can make powerful and compelling love, but when the Air girl is in her head and tangled in another mental harmony act, it will need the idealism that she first saw in him to get her back into his arms with real tenderness.

LIBRA MAN – SAGITTARIUS WOMAN

There's something rather circus-like about Air and Fire signs together, a lot of singing and dancing happens, and they can really bring out the best in each other. For the Libran man, falling in love with the freedom-loving Sagittarian can be the best thing that happens to him. Not only will his usually wishy-washy nature take on a new and perhaps lightning speed to reach decisions, but he will begin to feel that beauty and cheery lightness in his life is actually benefiting the world. For the Archer girl, possessed of a strong and extrovert character, the Libran man who charms his way through life, avoiding conflict and managing always to appear as if he's dressed specially for every occasion, will seem like the only man who can possibly fulfil her own ideals. Both these signs are idealists in their own way. The Sagittarian girl seeks to fill the world with love, and the Libran merely to dress it with love. But both want to enjoy it. He can be a little too self-indulgent and irritate the Archer girl when he attempts to hold court to his social gathering. She is equally able to do so and they might try to better one another with verbal attacks, but it will always be with a gentle heart.

There's nothing morose or bitter about these two: they suffer as a partnership only because they are both not practical about life. They are party-goers, not party-givers. Love for them is not necessarily built on the stability of life. They don't need routine and don't encourage commitment.

Both these partners want to feel secure, but they can never quite make up their minds if they should. For the Sagittarian girl it would mean giving up her very precious freedom, and for the Libran it just means making a decision! Sexually he will be the most romantic lover; she doesn't need emotion and feeling, she needs action, and communication. He will love her passionate, rather self-conscious moments in bed, but they will have a lot of laughs, a great empathy and sense of fair play. And how they love to play !

LIBRA WOMAN – SAGITTARIUS MAN

The half-horse man is secretively rather more romantic than he appears on the surface. He'll ride recklessly around showering happiness and optimism on people's lives and play the wild boy when he gets the chance, but actually he would quite like to believe that there exists a woman who will let him be free, love him for being free, and always be there when he comes back, without resentment and without giving him a hard time. Not many women can come up with this ideal, but a Libran is one of them. She would love to make a commitment with this horse-man, who is the most romantic and Fiery lover, bedazzling himself and her with his opportunist rush through life. He doesn't stop very easily and a Libran girl would be better off going on any travelling adventures with him. That way she can enjoy the fun and games, and ensure he doesn't disappear on some moment's impulse in search of a different freedom.

She is strong, good fun, and sexually the kind of woman he likes. The Archer doesn't like soppy girls, and needs romantic pals with a head on their shoulders, not tears. She won't criticise him, and will laugh about the girl he nearly picked up at the bus stop in the rain for a joke. She will inspire him with her sparkling smile, but he can hurt her with his blunt truths and unintentional remarks. Like the Archer, she is mentally alert and quick-witted and, although she is considerably more lazy about life, she has the adaptability to get up and go when he calls on the spur of the moment from some faraway place.

The Archer has to win, and has to make his ideals come true. For someone like a Libran girl with the same sort of attitude about how she fits into the scheme of things, he can seem a very viable partner. He can be over-enthusiastic about sex. He is a Fire sign and, however free-ranging and dual his personality, he needs to boost his ego as much as he can. Handling his inquisitive and suddenly changing mind can thrill her. He is often quicker at changing the subject than a Gemini, but he'll never have a problem delighting the Libran's own fast-paced and often garrulous personality.

LIBRA MAN – CAPRICORN WOMAN

There are some notorious and difficult differences between these two signs that might make relationships between them more intriguing than any other pair. For a start, Libran men are gregarious mixers who actually like people and need harmony and peace and fun in their lives. The Goat lady is ambitious for herself, would rather not expose her private life to passing strangers, and, as much as she is peace-loving, it will be because she is controlling her temper: she has the power to cause war if she wants. Frightening as she can seem to the fairly laid-back and affable Libran, he might actually find that her cautious and taciturn personality has a few faulty chinks he might be able improve on. He likes to share his optimism, and also likes to prove he's irresistible to women. In the nicest possible way, of course, which is why he often falls in love with love first and then gets caught out in sticky affairs with women who really aren't his type. He never looks before he leaps, but the Capricorn girl always does. She is a Goat, she's learnt wisely and, through many travels up that rocky ledge to the top of the mountain, she knows what it's like to slip and fall down the precipice of love. But the Libran never learns, and never really wants to. Whatever life brings to him, even in the form of a quiet, dominating and power-mad woman, he believes he will be able shrug off when, and if, he has to.

This unnerving faith in his own ability to fall in and out of love is one of his charms. And for the Goat, the Libran's amicable *détente* is the kind of ground she can build her ambitions upon, without involving the usual annoyances that go with love. They could combine positive, energy, the force that both have and use so differently. The Goat will see this, but the Libran will probably abandon it. He would prefer to live in romance and the party spirit a bit longer. Sadly he can become involved with and sometimes used by the Goat, who will then decide she was justified in her belief that too much of a good thing is not all it's cracked up to be.

LIBRA WOMAN – CAPRICORN MAN

The great and overwhelming self-opinionated Goat is quite frankly
the sort of man a Libran girl won't fall in love with easily. In fact,
to begin with, she may quite genuinely detest him. Goat men
have this absurd notion that if they dress up in their glad-rags,
appear charming, fun and willing to let laughter enter their lives,
and can keep a glamorous image on permanent hold, it will bring
all the gentle-natured, quick-witted, funny women rushing to
their sides. Actually Goats aren't good at deception, and they aren't
capable of passing themselves off as a Fire sign or a charmer like
one of the Air signs. The Libran girl, whose wits are as finely
tuned as her brain cells, may be amused by the Goat's antics, but
can see right through his deception. Down the pub he may appear
as if he could have fun at parties, and enjoy the romance of making
love in the woods, or the attic, but somehow, for this pretend
eccentricity, she can see quite clearly that he is restrained, grumpy,
and a prig beneath that clever guise. Now, being unfair about a
Goat is actually the only time a Libran girl will make a biased
judgment. In fact, it's because he is so taciturn, so imposing, so
powerful that she actually would rather not get involved. He might
just turn into a handsome prince and prove her wrong.

The Goat will, however, be enchanted by her smile and her
charm. He desperately would like to escape into her romantic
dreamland, but he has a slightly martyrish attitude about the
lifestyle he has chosen and, being power-driven, and old from
the day he was born, he can only carry through what he has set
out to do. This kind of ambitious Goat may well strike a more
interesting vocal chord for the Libran girl, but she needs fun in
her life more than solidity. Sure, she would love to have a partnership, needs to have a permanent relationship and still maintain
her social ramblings. This man will be very unlikely to allow her
either. He wants his relationship to be like his business: ordered,
prudent and winning. He lives with too much self-discipline for
this girl to understand and, although he might try to let go of the
rope he has tethered to himself, romance and floating dreams are
not the answer.

LIBRA MAN – AQUARIUS WOMAN

The trouble with Air signs is that they need fresh intellectual inspiration around them for life's rather tousling affair with their jumbled heads. The Libran man could fall desperately in love with this rather mad and rebellious Air sign, and she could quite easily find that his fair and lovely charm will instil in her the right sort of air that she needs to breathe. The mental fencing that these two play in their relationship can be more fun than the Olympic Games. Libra is quite bossy when he wants to be, and once the initial infatuation has worn from his Airy head, he might find he's tempted to goad the wilder side of the Aquarian girl's unpredictability into livening up the office party. She is incredibly stubborn, and insists on being awkward just for the sake of it. She is more likely to have decided he was charming enough to be one of her friends to begin with, rather than a lover. She is not usually the sort of female who goes around actively searching for a mate. The Aquarian female is in need of friends, friends and mostly friends! One day she will like the Libran's soft smile, and the next she won't. She's not fickle like Gemini, but just wants to be different. The more unconventional and crazy she is, the more the Libran will be forced to admit he can't keep control. But he has to accept that the Uranus girl has to trust him first before she even thinks about letting him into her private life. If his romantic notions include sex (which is inevitable with a Libran), he might have to be prepared for some pretty cold nights warming up the bed alone, while she's out spreading the news about him, and analysing his friends.

The Aquarian woman can be one of the most independent women of the zodiac. If the Libran man is forced to find solace in drink and women while she's trying to understand what happened to their friendship, he may come back to a lonely bed and a lonely heart. However cantankerous she appears, she won't tolerate infidelity, unless it's her own. He needs love and affection more than she does, and he needs to feel the solidarity of team spirit. She needs harmony in her life too, but it can be exhausting for a Libran man to have to be the Aquarian girl's friend rather than her lover, she can be too cold with his very special heart.

LIBRA WOMAN – AQUARIUS MAN

The tactless and rather eccentric behaviour of the Aquarian man will usually make the Libran girl smile quite charmingly, and ask questions later. She is nosy, and would like to know why he is so fanatical about being different, and why he has to have so many friends. She loves people too, but she loves love as well, and the Aquarian seems to be about the coldest man she has met. His aloof and rather glamorous appeal will often seem a challenge at first to this quite strong and mentally fair girl. She will quite calmly seduce him, with her usual easy-going and apparent harmless charm. The Aquarian will be naturally suspicious, will put on a cold confrontation to protect himself from her undoubtable attraction, and may even show her how terratorial he is, either by planning her life before he's even got her to the bedroom, or by getting her to the bedroom before he even knows her name.

This touching girl won't be touched for long by his law-unto-himself behaviour. And this is where they can suffer most in what could be a rather challenging and exciting relationship.

What's fair to an Aquarian is not necessarily fair to a Libran girl. Actually she likes fairness, but it's on the surface fairness, the closeness of it to her own life and love. The Aquarian will make generalisations, wrongly or rightly, and the only fairness to him is that the world should be a better place and everyone in it should be treated fairly. The Libran girl hates conflict, hates ugliness in her own world, but the Aquarian would rather take on the whole of life and change it on behalf of change. He will love her loveliness, very much like his own idealistic truth. But she will find times when even their sexual compatibility, a rare thing for an Aquarian, will remind him that harmony is important in his own life, and the only way sometimes is, perhaps, to accept one person as more special than the rest.

LIBRA MAN – PISCES WOMAN

The Pisces girl is invariably drawn to men who are either independent and spirited, to complement their own self-expressive style, or to those who are gregarious, idealistic and possibly more dithery than she is. The Libran man is all these things, and very often they will be drawn to one another by an intense physical attraction. The Libran's ideal of beauty will often materialise in the seductive and sympathetic Fish, a catalyst of visions. She soothes, he entices, and together they can make a harmonious and sensitive partnership. Their problems arise because her perceptiveness and the way she takes on every trouble of the world can, to the Libran, be partial and not really fair at all. He believes that everyone's opinion is valid, that to take sides, or to be judgmental has little to do with pacification. The Pisces woman often comforts those in the middle of disastrous love-affairs and the Libran man often interrupts to speak up for the defence. He will defend the Fish to the hilt if she *is* fair and not judgmental, but being able to bend in the directions of an argument could upset their own balance.

Their very different approach to living can end the initial and physical attraction very quickly. But they do share the need to escape. The Libran man can lead the Fish astray into party-land, nightclubbing and general hedonistic delights, which he has the strength to handle, and she often does not. She can become addicted to love as to any other pursuit and, if the charm of the lovely Libran keeps her emotional and intuitive side happy, then she will accept his rather cold and rational mentality that precludes most of their disagreements. This is a good romantic association, rather than a highly sexed one. But they can provide each other with lighthearted dreaming if he stops balancing logic with every moment of feeling.

LIBRA WOMAN – PISCES MAN

Firmness, tact and reality are not easy for the Piscean man to attempt with much success in his life. If a Libran woman should dance past his eyes while he is in one of his escapist moments, he will be as easily deceived by her as by most beautiful things. He has vision, and his intuition is so natural that he rarely realises that he uses it. But if a flirtatious, gregarious girl should flit through the waves and give that enigmatic smile, he can be swept into the tide of love without a moment's consideration, with no rational thought as to whether this could be a wise move.

Surprisingly this couple has a good chance of a firm, romantic and quite lengthy sexual relationship. But she is logical, cool and poised, not ready for emotional depth, and would prefer to fly through life, rather than swim through it. He will drift quite happily beside her while the going is good, but if her compassion and her common-sense take over, if the practicalities of their relationship begin to outweigh the dreamy quality that they first discovered, then he will have trouble adapting himself to rational discussions like who should be earning the money, and how it should be spent. If the Libran woman handles this alone, and she is very adept at doing so, then the Fish can carry on drifting with romance and unreality. She is more likely to be out earning the pennies while he still lies in the bath, but she will find his similar laid-back lethargy easy to live with.

However hard a Libran works, she makes sure she has time for his languid moments and her own. The Fish will be attracted to her spiritually first, and she physically to him. Yet they will be able to ensure a passionate and affectionate sexual harmony, which can hold them together better than any commitment they may both feel uncertain of making.

LIBRA MAN – ARIES WOMAN

The Female Ram is devoted to carnal and passionate pleasures. When she is attracted by a beautiful, charming and apparently expert lover like a Libran man, she will think immediately (because she always thinks impulsively) that this man could be the love of her life. She desperately wants someone to understand that beneath her quite frank, bossy and organising nature, she is a really gentle, kind and loving woman.

The Libran man will find her, at first, rather awkward to handle. Used to seducing females with fewer masculine, up-front expectations, he may make a bosh of it and turn her physical attraction for him into an optimism that, maybe tomorrow, she'll meet the man of her life, not just this minute, thank you all the same. Yet because they are opposite signs, these two should find that the instantaneous attraction (which stems mostly from the Aries woman) will spark into the Libran's loins the kind of idealistic romance that he had never believed possible. Used to charming his way through life, he will admire her challenging and sometimes naïve self-confidence. She has a way of locking into his Airy ether and reminding him that love is about more than just romance. Sexually they are matched quite beautifully. But she will occasionally feel that he is somewhere else apart from the bed, and he will find her overpowering, burning arms can get a little too wrapped around his aesthetic need for dreaming. The Libran needs freedom, and he needs a companion who can understand his social wanderings. She's a burner, he's a dreamer, and their attitudes to life and what it means are very different.

LIBRA WOMAN – ARIES MAN

Dreamers dream and Aries man puts the whole lot into action, if he really believes he can! And usually he does. Like any Fire-Air relationship, the Libran girl will provide the dreams and fuel for his Fire and, because they are opposite signs of the zodiac, the attraction will be immediate, sexual and intensely concentrated. Love grows in this kind of swirl of emotion and physical involvement. The passion will be real and one that neither of these two fun-loving signs will be able to resist in one another.

Libran ladies aren't too keen on making decisions and Aries men are. The impulsive nature of the Arien's rush to reach a quick answer won't always suit the gentle, lovely, Libran lady. He believes he is always right, sometimes she won't be too convinced, only because, after he's boldly made his leap into the dark, she really won't be sure if he was fair in his impetuous and hasty move. On the other hand, if the Libran girl doesn't agree with the Arien's opinions, which can be downright self-centred and unfair, then she will find it hard to convince him that, as much as she cares what he thinks, other opinions matter too. But like all opposition partnerships, this could be a knock-out relationship. Both Aries and Libra will always have a lot to say, a lot to do and places to go. As long as she lets his confidence shine, and his passion pour into her sunshine heart, then he will always be there for her.

LIBRA MAN – TAURUS WOMAN

Now a Libra man oozes romance, and so does the Bull lady, in similar quantities, but with dissimilar qualities. Yet they will both agree to differ, which is startling in the first place because the Libran finds it difficult to agree about anything, in case it means rejecting the alternative, and secondly because a Taurean girl usually wants to have the last say and make sure hers is the correct one. The Bull girl's fixed attitude complements his driven one, and their initial relationship will be full of a secret dimension. They could be locked in a lift together and the Libran will want to make romantic love while they wait for the engineer to turn up. The Bull lady will find it a challenging experience, enlightened by the Libran's sense of love for her wherever he is. The only problems occur when the Libran man decides it was about time he started activating his social life a bit more. As much as he would love to stay at home with the Bull, he would prefer to get out and about, and this can cause much resentment at best and a stampeding Bull at worst.

His charm can delight her, his fatal attraction is his beauty for, although it is only skin-deep, to the Taurean girl it's as deep as she wants to believe it. But the Bull will want decisions about their future, a slow commitment, but a definite one. She will wait patiently for him to choose her as a permanent partner, and yet the Libran man really would rather not make this sort of decision at all. In some ways, he thinks, it wouldn't be fair to rush into any commitment, as much as he wants a partner, because maybe she will regret it. He is, after all, only being fair.

LIBRA WOMAN – TAURUS MAN

On reflection, and she'll need a lot of it because a Libran girl likes to spend a lot of time deliberating, she could get that Taurean out of his rutting phase quicker than any other sign. She has the charm and all the Airiness that appeals to the strong sense of ownership with which the Bull would like to smother her. Underneath, of course, she is also a woman of the world, and very capable. In fact, if she seduces the Taurean first, she has the guile and the charm to let him believe that he was the one to do the seducing and will thus avoid hurting his sexual vanity. He has a lot to offer a Libran and she has a lot to offer a Taurean both sexually and in love. She might find his habits of too much self-indulgence, although not far removed from her own, a little too down-to-earth and not much like her more ephemeral and fantasy pleasure-seeking. Libran women are quite adept at getting what they want and, with their natural beauty and their innate, restless search for an ideal, they seem dream-like to the more pragmatic Bull.

Physical compatibility will probably enhance their relationship. She will appeal to his masculine ego, which demands a very feminine attachment and he will appeal to her own rather languid approach to life. They are both hard workers but, once they are out of hours, they'll drop everything for sleep, food, or sex. Actually the poor Bull is often fatally drawn to Airy types, because he cannot quite resist their very ephemeral qualities. But the Libran can get bored with the routines that Taurus likes to impose, and also with the fact that he will not communicate unless forced out of his field. This can mar their relationship and a Libran will often prove fickle in the eyes of the Bull and he'll retreat stubbornly to his grazing when, if he'd fought a bit harder, he might have got her to change her mind.

LIBRA MAN – GEMINI WOMAN

The flirtatious, spontaneous, witty girl Gemini will be the first to admit that the romantic noises that the Libran man makes are probably the only way she'll be seduced. Usually Gemini girls like to do the seducing, which often leads them up paths they wished they'd never chosen. But, with a lovely Libra, she will often fall hopelessly in love. (For now anyway.) The Libran is a charmer, like her. Both have the ability to realise that the Air they breathe is the love they make. But she has a restless soul, and he doesn't. His Airiness is based on finding an aesthetic way through life, to impress, to lead and to attempt to bring fairness and serenity into the world.

This is crucial for the Gemini girl because, here at last, is someone who really understands her, who can love her without possessing, who can let her go without jealousy and who could well be her mental saviour. (She finds it hard to find intellectual equals.) The Libran male knows too that, sexually, they will make starlight together, rather than loud shouts of ecstasy and emotional torrents of tears if you leave a kiss behind. He needs romance as much as she does, but they both need to hide behind their masks. Sexually, they can take turns on top, and they will both be fascinated by each other as far as they only want to see. She will have fallen for him because of his hair; if he cuts it off she may fall out of love just as quickly as she fell into it. If she tries to make him grow it again, he may begin to find her surface attraction as shallow as his own.

LIBRA WOMAN – GEMINI MAN

An unpredictable and quite wild relationship. Two Air signs can cause a lot of wind, blowing away the dust of boredom, the puddles of emotional indulgence and generally behaving like a Force Nine gale through a stick house. When the wolf blew down the piggies' house, he must have been an Air sign, and he could well have been a Gemini actually searching for a Venus girl. Being in love is something that both these signs do equally well and they find they fall into it with frequent ease. When it's with one another, there's a good chance that the Gemini will understand the beauty and the charm of the Libran woman and accept her need to be right, even when she does find it hard to choose. She will realise that his conman act is only because he's not sure who he is. Instinctively they will share a wonderful rapport for each other's rather Airy and lighthearted sexual needs.

Neither of them wishes to be tied by restrictions imposed by a partner, and neither will allow their personal freedom to be jeopardised by love. Because they are both adept at tricks of love, wizardry in the art of charming, it won't take them long to laugh about it, rather than carry on playing magic games.

Sexually they will keep the romance and forget the passion. They both need a light, intellectual sex life, and would rather flit around the country on a bed crawl, than stay in some cosy nest for their fornication. Their interest will be in the different places they visit, the change and the newness of the bed, rather than what goes on in it! It will be easier for them both to remember that she takes a long time to make up her mind if she wants a permanent relationship, and to understand that he won't be too fond of the decision either.

LIBRA MAN – CANCER WOMAN

On the surface a harmonious and gentle relationship that, with time, can turn into peaceful contentment. Learning to compromise is the greatest challenge for this strangely matched pair. The Cancer woman is eternally pessimistic, and the Libran man is always optimistic. However, they can both bring each other to a realistic approach about their day-to-day affairs, because extremists are linked by the Air in the middle of their differences.

The Libran falls in love instantly and really believes (each time) that it will be for ever. The born romantic will swerve through life, in a charming and sometimes arrogant manner, convinced that all women will fall at his feet in a swoon at the twinkle of his eye. They often do. But the Crab lady will be the first to be seduced quickly back into her shell by a Libran. She will retreat instinctively because she can intuitively sense that the Libran man has done this before, can fall head over heels with the surface attraction and then give up when the harmony ends and the bitterness begins.

But why should it with a Cancer girl? For a start she is a home-lover, not a day-tripper. She doesn't dampen personal freedom and, for her, commitment is security. The Libran needs warmth and stability, but he also needs to venture forth, to play the romantic whenever he can or he becomes stifled and resentful towards his partner. If the Crab can let him go when he wants, doesn't question him or get emotionally possessive, then they have a chance. Essentially they are both kind and peace-loving. Arguments would only be caused by the Cancerian girl's frigidity or the Libran's rather tactless self-opinions and lack of direction. Sentimentalists can share the past but, unless the Crab can steer clear of suspicious and possessive emotion, and the Libran man can try to let her share his social wandering so that she has no cause for grouching, they will have little nostalgia together.

LIBRA WOMAN – CANCER MAN

The social Libran girl doesn't have much trouble finding men to enchant her, nor a partner among all the choices who would like to have her as their lover. As the life and soul of the party, her charm and her wit draw all sorts of signs to her, and particularly the Cancer man, who does love beauty. Again, he can be as light and flirtatious as she, and, when he first meets her, will throw in those wise-cracks and loony humour for which he is better known. The balanced and harmonious girl has the gentleness and strength of the Cardinal Air sign she is. The Crab is a Cardinal Water sign and together they can blend the right amount of companionship and understanding to stay together. Emotionally the Libran is well suited to the ups and downs of the Crab's temperament. She won't judge and she won't ever criticise him when he's down. He will be impressed, and he does need to be impressed, by her level head. He never thought someone so charming and lovely could actually be so tough and so clear-thinking, so full of life and not screwed up!

The Cancer man will never rush into anything, particularly a love-affair, or a commitment, unless he first makes very sure deep inside that he is right. (Some Crab men will ring their mother to check with her.) The only problem with the Libran is that she really is quite hasty about being in love with love. She won't dare make a commitment unless he makes it first, but then, if she does involve herself in a permanent relationship, what if she's missing out on her freedom? The Crab may get jealous and possessive because the Libran girl does need a lively social life, whether it's with men or women. This in turn will irritate her. He really doesn't have to be suspicious of anyone. Libra will always be honest and open. A Crab often finds it hard to express himself, because he really hasn't quite worked out if revealing his true feelings will lead him into deeper waters than he can handle.

Sexually they may not get on after the initial giddy infatuation. She can be lightheaded, and lighthearted about every night, and he can get too intense and emotional for her touch.

LIBRA MAN – LEO WOMAN

Now Libran men like to get out and about and adorn themselves with pretty friends and pretty things. They can prefer crowds and parties to company with only one woman but, if they are pushed, they will accept that a permanent relationship has to involve living with their partner. Some Librans would do better living alone, but Librans really do need a partner whether they can convince themselves it is right or not. A Leo woman seems the perfect answer, on the surface. She is genuinely outgoing too, cherishes adoration, and needs to be in the company of men. She is also warm-hearted, romantic and not fluffy. She is bossy and uncompromising and won't have to rely on someone as vague and indecisive as a Libran man. However, she will be more likely to want to know where he was all night, than he will want to know where *she* was. The Libran can find himself partying a bit too much and not staying at home. But the Leo lady, when she gets an idea in her hot head, usually keeps it there, and she might decide that her knight in shining armour is not as naïve as he seems. Charming is one thing but his inability to commit himself, or stay at home and adore her, are another. Libran men aren't jealous, and they can't see the point of it. Emotions are thin in the Libran's heart, but he does care, and he does love. He may well have to spend more time proving it to the Leo woman than he thought. She needs presents, physical expressions of love, not words on the phone, mind-games and idealistic ramblings. Hers is a world of brash and glittering honesty, passionate life and living for every minute. Closeness in bed is essential, and they will both find that the Libran loves making love and the Leo women loves both giving it and receiving it.

LIBRA WOMAN – LEO MAN

When a lovely Libran lady gazes straight into the eyes of a languid Cat, he will be instantly enchanted, knowing that this beautiful woman could perhaps be the ideal lover. With magnanimous pride and a will only matched by Hercules, he will attempt every trick he knows to entice her into his lair. Actually she won't be that hard to entice. It's not that she's a pushover, and she doesn't have the time of day for chauvinists, but a Libran girl always knows what she wants and will be attracted both to his romantic dazzle and to his quite boastful air. She can see through this, and beyond it, which is why she doesn't get put off by the way he tramps around thinking he knows what is best, while she really knows that she does. Normally girls fall at his feet, listen to every word as if he were a guru, and believe him to be the best thing in bed since it was invented. However, the Libran girl is mentally alert to this kind of nonsense. She will love him for what he is, but it's certainly not because he has more love-affairs notched up on his bedpost than most men, and not because he puts on a pretty good impression of a pretentious peacock. The male Lion will provide all the right romance in her life. She has extremes of energy, sometimes wild and passionate, sometimes languid and cosy. He will respond quite well to both these, although he may find her distant Airiness a bit hard to comprehend when he'd rather be battling out who will sort out the socks. They may stick together through many a battle of wills, but he needs her fairness and sense of justice occasionally to remind him the red carpet is not just for him.

LIBRA MAN – VIRGO WOMAN

The Libran man is charmed by mental brightness and sparkling, romantic eyes. His ideals are driven by dreams and beautiful women and, when he meets a gentle, rather sweet and feminine Virgo girl, he will immediately, and quite thoughtlessly, plunge into an affair with love. It's easy for him, and it happens often, but really this time he should have known better. The Virgo woman is usually very careful about who she allows into her space, and the easy-going and rather romantic man who walks through her door will enchant her with his abstract mind, and considerate judgments of the world. The Virgo woman, however, can sense that he prevaricates more than he thinks. He is an extrovert, and demands the security of people around him, which she doesn't. He will begin to grumble when she nit-picks at and criticises his friends, and when she says she would rather he stayed more at home, and not play the romantic with every girl he meets. To be so charming is fine when she is on the other end of the flirt, but to see him playing the same tune to other women is, for a Virgo, the shortest route to total frigidity.

The Libran man believes that the Virgo girl is happy with her lot, while he wanders off to socialise. But these girls are not quite as home-loving as they seem, and would rather build a career than actually go and do the shopping. They both enjoy a pleasant, comfortable lifestyle with no heavy scenes, but the Libran doesn't take easily to commitments; any choice implies rejecting the alternative. And if it's a toss-up between freedom and the Virgo lady, it will be a decision that he will probably never make. But she will!

LIBRA WOMAN – VIRGO MAN

What these two have in common is that Libra rather admires Virgo's ability for self-discipline, and Virgo admires the Libran's fair play in everything. Admiration is a mutual stimulation for an otherwise fairly stark relationship. The Virgo Man is not particularly interested in the high life, in socialising, nor in charming the world and enjoying it. He also prefers predictability and would rather share his life with a placid, easy-going girl. This is how the Libran girl appears to be when he first meets her. He will fall in love easily with her bright, sparkling, Airy chatter and, mentally, she will provide him with a fascinating and constant strength of purpose. The Virgo doesn't want to be bossed, and he needs a companion, rather than a lover. He doesn't like laziness, nor untidiness and although he enjoys sex, he doesn't go wild about it. Now a Libran girl may find all this sharp, rather austere attitude a little mind-bending. She likes to have her brain well used, but she also loves to get out and about and enjoy herself. She may find the uncluttered existence of the Virgo rather cold and unwelcoming, his punctuality will irritate her and, as fair as she tries to be, she cannot quite justify in her head why she has to stay put, get up to catch the same train every day, and make decisions when she would rather avoid them.

If she does get as far as spending the night with him, it could initially seem a magical experience. She is not in need of passion and hot steaming beds and nor is he. But she does need warmth and affection and to feel really loved. The Virgo tends to criticise, not flatter, and the barrier of ice can build up around her quicker than he intended.

Scorpio

COMPATIBILITIES

SCORPIO MAN – SCORPIO WOMAN

This is one of the fiercest, most intense relationships of the zodiac. It can be alarming to experience and to watch. It can be extraordinary to see what bubbles on the surface, when underneath the currents and depths of emotional and physical tension are omnipresent. Scorpio is the sign of intensity and determination and these are inherent in everything that a Scorpio does. When these two exo-skeletons first meet, each may immediately hate the other, intuitively aware that what they have met is a mirror-image, a very dark and menacing reflection of themselves. A Scorpio woman may appear on the surface lively, extrovert and Fiery. And yet, a Scorpio male will know exactly the calculations that are going on under that rather clever cover-up. They are both equivocal, and both fascinated by mystery. Their own obscurity is the channel to their hearts and they aren't fond of exposing it. But try hiding what you are from someone else who also hides what they are, then you are both connoisseurs of digging up dirt, and prying into the dark side of the Moon!

Pluto has a lot to answer for with these two when they begin to unfold the awful truth about one another. There will be a contest of wills, often fired off by sex and carried through every sexual move they make together. This can be the explosive part of their relationship. They can both use sex and the denying of it as a threatening and tension-building secret weapon. Trying to prove whose power is greater can also split them apart. Neither is good at forgiving or forgetting. Resentment can grow easily in the blackness of the Pluto night, and pain and bitterness can flourish in their vulnerable and deeply private souls. The Scorpio woman is less likely to hide her true feelings than he, but she has a sadder mask of indifference that can only make a Scorpio man feel impotent and betrayed.

This is a serious, deep and emotional relationship and, because of its strength, can be making up more than most other partnerships, unless it self-destructs first!

SCORPIO MAN – SAGITTARIUS WOMAN

The ruthless and quite deeply motivated Scorpio man can find the Archer girl so different and open to him that he might wonder if she really has any depth. That is why he will want to probe her, question her, seduce her and, most of all, possess her. Scorpios are very jealous and, for the Archer girl to get involved with a cryptomaniac, could be the end of freedom, the world and optimism as she knows them. An Archer is full of smiles, and wants to take life as it comes; she is convinced the sun will always shine the next day, and she rarely suffers from emotional traumas, or moods. Unfortunately the moody, serious Scorpio can lash at her with dreadful soulful loneliness. He needs solitude, spells of introversion where he can reinvest his vulnerable heart into more determined and voracious ambitions. Coming across the evasive, and quite honestly, brash thinking of an Archer can temporarily hold up his plans. Sexually, if she can't handle the meaning of life and fill him with emotional passion, he might give her reason to feel jealous too. He can be incredibly cold if he chooses. Cold is as acute as being hot, hating is as feeling as loving. He will do either, he minds not a jot which he does, as long as it is experienced with passion and honour. He will resent her freedom and may try to impose his very strong will upon her. As much as the Archer is seeking a partnership, a love that can move with the seasons, inflame passion and leave her mind and heart to itself, the Scorpio has neither the ideals nor the free-spirit to stay true to her. If he feels she is no longer worthy of his incredible devotion, he'll be the first to let her know. Unless, of course, she's already blown somewhere else on the flames of the wind.

SCORPIO WOMAN – SAGITTARIUS MAN

The Snake lady can wallow in hurt quite easily given half the chance. Both pain and happiness are real feelings, and either one will do. As long as she is feeling something intensely, the Scorpio woman is satisfied. When a bright, sparky Archer man comes galloping through her territory she will immediately feel uncomfortable because he is so incredibly unlike anyone she has ever met. He's open, frank, very warm-hearted and generous and seems careless about life and love. To entice him into the Scorpio's hole in the sand is a passion that she will find hard to resist. And the more a Scorpio woman draws on her clandestine determination, the more likely it is that she won't stop until she has got what she has set her eye on. Her obsession with a man like an Archer could be easily and quickly relieved. After all he loves women, is always waiting for an opportunity to seize, loves a challenge and flirts with any woman under the sun.

Of course, equally, if he should come across a beautiful, quite mysterious and magnetic woman he will more than likely fall temporarily in love. Temporary is the basis of Sagittarian love. Travelling through life means that relationships can be visited like countries, or fleeting glimpses of airports. Although he will never consciously hurt anyone, most of the women he meets aren't prepared to be a transit lounge while he refuels or changes flight. A Scorpio woman will want to be the whole world to him, and nothing less. He will, of course, enjoy a sexual relationship with her. But she wants completeness, expects a permanency to arise from sexual love, and won't be prepared for his lack of commitment. It's hard for a Scorpio woman to let go, unless it's for ever. But as much as she would love to suffer for this man, her possessiveness will eventually send him to the airport for the next flight out of her war-torn country.

SCORPIO MAN – CAPRICORN WOMAN

Both these signs live a sinister life behind a backdrop of a rather more lively act. The Scorpio is particularly good at pulling down the curtain and pretending he is an extrovert and a lively chatterbox with an open heart. The Capricorn woman is actually very shy, and can also play the interested, willing listener, when, actually, she finds most of life dull and, at its best, unnecessary. The Scorpio male immediately may drop his act to test out what it is this girl really wants. He is fascinated by everything under any surface: every stone will be turned and tossed until the problem is solved. The Capricorn girl on the other hand is neither curious nor interested in finding out the meaning of life, she just wants to get on with it. When he realises that, like him, she is also intensely power-mad and that she can live up to his very high expectations, not try to investigate his private self, and still be a wilful and able partner at his side, he might decide he's met the perfect woman. The Goat lady may be attracted to him physically at first. He is very self-willed, passionate and rather intense. And he has ambition. Although the Goat lady would prefer to be the controlling force in their relationship, she can realistically accept that she is the practical, driving force, and he is the emotive and sexual one. If the Scorpio also excels in business and family matters, then she will be impressed. They are both furtive people, and sense the loneliness within each other. Her restrained love-making can become more expressive in his bed, and they will certainly feel like they belong in the same environment. At first the Scorpio may find the Goat's rather stubborn and rigid lifestyle depressing. But the Snake is as fixed in his self-seclusion, as she is in her self-restriction. There may be a struggle for power of the mind, but the Goat will always leave the Scorpio's deeper psyche to himself, and he will, apparently, always let her win. He's good at that, because then he knows he really is in control!

SCORPIO WOMAN – CAPRICORN MAN

The witty and amusing Goat may prop up the bar down the local pub, be the business whizz-kid in the office driven by a wise power, but Goat men certainly have a problem when it comes to not being possessive. If anyone can get him out of his rather stuffy ways, a Scorpio woman can. Not only has she the strength and determination to soften his rigid views, turn havoc inside his usually reserved emotions, but she can turn him on like a Goat at stud once they pass the initial power-struggle of who is going to run this relationship.

The Goat treats his affairs with women on the same level as his business affairs. They need to be organised, ordered and mostly subject to his demands. He secretly longs to be a more wild and egalitarian type and, although he reserves his humour and imagination for the ears of men rather than women, he can find that a Scorpio woman will see right through his shy, gruff mask into his quite genuine love of the pleasures of life. He will be intrigued, and that's not often, because Goats are usually unaffected by subterfuge, they have enough of their own to digest. Being a brave Goat, if he's one who has climbed to the top rather than resigned himself to a circle of self-restraint, he will fearlessly suggest that they might have something in common apart from the desire to win. The Goat is possessive, so is the Scorpio, but the Goat also seeks permanence and security and is in need of less personal freedom. It's not that the Snake woman wants to dash madly around the world picking up men like pebbles on a beach, but she is proud of her very private and personal self, that needs to be away from even a reserved Goat at times. It is her regenerative process which, unless allowed to work, can only retaliate within their relationship. They will be comfortable with each other in bed, as much as they are out of it. Her passion will instil a bit more imagination into his rather practical and sometimes alarmingly rough sexual activities. This relationship grows with time and, once past the initial physical and sexual attraction, can turn into a solid partnership.

SCORPIO MAN – AQUARIUS WOMAN

The compelling antics of a Scorpio man in full attack and battle gear, ready to ride over any competitor and to win the object of his desire, can be daunting to the self-reliant and independent Aquarian girl. She might laugh at him initially, she does behave erratically, and unpredictably, and then she may find him fascinating. How can anyone be so mysterious, and yet so calculating about life? Scorpio by now will have already set his target high. The bigger the challenge, the longer it takes, the better. Yet he will be slightly confused by the Aquarian girl's very eccentric and determined sense of herself. It reminds him of his own personal integrity, but his is living life dangerously, it is being alive, and experiencing every feeling intensely. The Aquarian's is about analysing life, changing it theoretically and as awkwardly as she can. She may find him quite magnetic, a wonderful subject for dissection, mentally and even spiritually, and he, of course, will be thinking and feeling along very different lines, usually sexual ones.

It isn't that he wants to notch up another female spirit on his Ouija board, but he does find the enigma of this very individual and proud woman a compelling challenge.

For all her inquisitions the Aquarian girl only wants a sensible and intellectual equal, a companion who will be willing to inspire change, get on in life and look at it. Unfortunately, the possessive and emotional Scorpio will find it hard to bring out in her the depth of passion and strong sexual instinct that he lives for. She may seem cold when he is a living furnace of passion, she may seem contradictory when he wants to know where and who she is seeing. She needs friends, not lovers so much, and the Scorpio needs lovers rather than friends.

SCORPIO WOMAN – AQUARIUS MAN

The strong-willed and evasive nature of the Scorpio girl's emotional life is an instant hit with the Aquarian man. He is unconventional, eccentric, fascinated by the intellect, and prefers the company of disparate characters and oddballs to the normal beings that make up most of the population. (You may ask what star signs they are, and no doubt the population is not necessarily entirely made up of the other eleven signs of the zodiac. But normal people can be Aquarians and not be aware of their eccentricities.)

Meanwhile, back down the romantic path, the Scorpio girl will have found a man who will seem as full of surprises as she is. She can hide behind a range of masks to suit her mood, but the Uranian man will have already analysed, and poked deep enough to make his own judgments and theories. He will have concluded quickly that she is vulnerable and tender, whether she cares to admit it or not; and she usually won't.

If they get beyond the car door together he might have to remember that this woman needs sexual love with a big S. Being friends, and she is capable of having male platonic friends, is one thing but, if a relationship that involves love is ever to get off the ground, she needs to feel that passion is in his loins as well as in his head full of ideas. Aquarians, being a bit intellectual, can give the impression that sex is very much in their loins. But they will play that game to suit whoever it is they are experimenting on at the time. Sometimes a Scorpio girl can get the wrong message from his body language, and yet know intuitively that his heart and loins are not involved. She is possessive; he wants to get out and meet as many weirdos, as many women, as many of anything, as he can. She likes her personal freedom too, but his contempt for society, and his need to change the world and leave himself out of it, can be a small hint that actually the Scorpio girl is no more special than the man on the bus, which is where she may leave without a word, and jump off, before he really gets to know her deepest secrets!

SCORPIO MAN – PISCES WOMAN

Water signs together tend to generate their own deep-seated feelings and lock their experiences into floods of emotional ecstasy or agony. For the intensely passionate Scorpio to find an intuitive, understanding and compassionate girl like a Fish, can be the whole meaning of existence to him. Except that he might have rashly, in his egotistic way, forgotten that she is actually a good deal stronger than he at first noticed. His own acutely penetrating and compulsive nature will seem alarming to the girl Fish. Until she realises that he is so charmed and magnetised by her depth, a depth that even a Scorpio cannot possibly ever be able to discover, she begins to understand that she is actually the more powerful of the partnership. Her instincts and intuitions are more perceptive than his, and the floundering Scorpion's tail will miss its mark if it so much as attempts to sting the slithery Fish.

Scorpions have great wiles and are the great whales in the sea. Mermaids are Whale maids too, whose strength is often forgotten when they appear on the ocean surface with only their human form showing. The temptation to catch such a creature is irresistible to a Scorpion. He longs for her serenity, her elusive charisma and her often doubting self. She does make vague dreamy promises, and can change them at a whim, which will infuriate the Scorpio, who needs to know exactly where he is to feel in control. She may find he is over-possessive, and at times will retreat paradoxically to her gregarious lifestyle to avoid his over-demanding need of her. This can cause much jealousy from him. For the Fish to find a man she can share both her heart and maybe her soul with, and that sexually they have more to give one another than any other sign, should be pasted up on her noticeboard in big red letters! But she can stray from him just once too often, if he expects too much of her soul. He will retaliate like no other man but, if his high moral and egotistic standard has been threatened he will be lost, ready to sacrifice her for his integrity. With this woman a Scorpio can perhaps finally surrender himself. His passion, always held on the precipice of total fulfilment, could be released and exalted in the Fish girl and he has to remember that she holds the key to nurture his vulnerable soul.

SCORPIO WOMAN – PISCES MAN

As much as the Pisces man would like to resist, he cannot hold back from dreaming when he first meets this mysterious and enigmatic woman. They have in common a wonderful affinity for the deepest oceans of each other's hearts. Although the Scorpio woman is renowned for her jealousy, and this man will often incite hurt in her unthinkingly, the Fish is about the only man who can remind her that his secrets are as intense as her own. Scorpios need to know exactly where they are going, and how they are going to get there. Scorpios plan quite craftily if it involves attracting a Fish man, because a Fish is as devious as a Scorpio is menacing. The Fish is happy to drift, rather than to go on a crusade for emotional happiness. If a Scorpio girl appears too desperate in her love for him, he may retreat further to avoid being shaken by too much life. His fantasy land may not be able to escape her stinging tail. But the Fish is usually able to talk himself out of conflict and in-depth emotional scenes, neither of which he can stomach, because they drag him back to harsh reality. He has much tolerance, and he doesn't need to be a dominant force in anyone's life, let alone his own. If things go the way they go, then let them. It is not a weakness, and it can be his redeeming strength. If the Scorpio woman is determined for their relationship to survive, then it probably will. He cares, and he loves deeply, but sometimes he has to remember to face the Scorpion passion head-on, and not leave her suspicious and resentful because he is more elusive than she could ever be. Sexually, they will fulfil each other gently and quietly. Their passion will be one of quality, not quantity, as long as the Pisces keeps his freedom and Scorpio feels a rich and emotive bond.

SCORPIO MAN – ARIES WOMAN

On the surface a very sexual relationship, a Scorpio man will find the Aries girl's impulsive, carefree, untamed mentality a positive challenge, one that is opposite to his own. Emotionally they could drain each other dry with an intense passion for life. The Scorpio man will want to hit the Aries girl with big truths, deep confessions and expect her to stay in one piece. Scorpios like dangerous living, they thirst for the darkness and pain of it all. Aries like dangerous living because they don't think about what dangers are actually involved, the risk is what counts, the surface of the danger, not its depth.

The Aries girl may not be emotionally ready for the soul-searching of the Scorpio in the dead of night, but he could prove to be one of the best physical relationships she will ever have. Scorpios must control, and he won't like it when Aries won't be bossed around, can't be overpowered and won't be submissive. It's not in her nature, and she'll probably rebel against his dark and devious, broody moods. He will get het up about her Fiery spirit, and attempt to smother it in his Watery retaliation. Sex is the meaning of life and the meaning of existence to a Scorpio. It's the whole of life to him, and to an Aries woman it's only part of life. If Scorpio gets into his obsessive gear, then she will have to watch out; even a Ram can get stung by a Scorpion or bitten by a Snake!

SCORPIO WOMAN – ARIES MAN

The intangible mystery of a Scorpio girl is, without doubt, one of the most powerful attractions of any sign. The Aries man will respond to those dark sensual messages with true Fiery arousal. Sexual magnetism is a gift to the Arien hothead, his own impulses surge like flames through his heart and soul and to find such a whole, completely sexual woman is his heart's desire! An Aries man who bumps into this woman in one of her more intense and emotional moments may think she is the love of his life. But watch him begin to squirm. Thinking he can understand her every need, because Rams are convinced they are the only men in the universe to have this effect on a girl anyway, he'll get caught out by her sudden emotional and heavy involvement that he does not need dumped on his own superficial ego. Neither will he carry someone else's load for them, nor will he suffer deep-seated enigmas that can turn into a nest of bitter and twisted vipers. He is a dare-devil, she is fixed in her desires. But she will find him irresistible, and unable to let him go once he has entered her territory. The Scorpio woman is capable of making great sacrifices to hang on to the one she wants, and also of making great scenes of misery and despair in her all-or-nothing desperation. For the fairly straightforward Aries male this can all come as quite a shock if he's not prepared for the vengeance and spite that can turn in this woman's dangerous heart. Essentially this could be a very sexual relationship, but the Aries man may not be able to tolerate the secret torments for long.

SCORPIO MAN – TAURUS WOMAN

Taurus girls are known for their possessiveness, Scorpio men for their cruel jealousy. A girl Bull is also known for her sensuality and sexual awareness. It takes her time to fall in love with any man but, if a Scorpio is already out there with his hypnotic eyes fixed on her, she had better resolve herself to the ultimate sexual and emotional love-affair. Opposites in astrology usually provide what the other sign needs, or lacks, within themselves. For these two signs there will be instant chemical attraction: animal love, no boundaries; love and hate jelly-rolled all into one!

Scorpios have a reputation as lady-killers, but only because they take sex and love so seriously. It's the whole of life's mystery to a Scorpio so the Taurean girl will have to realise that giving herself to this man will involve her whole self and nothing but herself. The Taurus girl will love his passion but will find at times his emotional penetration of her soul too unnerving. Her temper can be roused more easily by a Scorpio, and they will either fight to the bed, or fight until she leaves. Her stubborn pride can win over his fixed purpose and, when a Scorpio has been challenged, he can kill the love within himself faster than a Scorpio can lash its tail. The Taurus girl has patience and the ability to keep her feet on the ground. And when he takes the trouble to look within himself with the same curiosity that he probes his Bull girl, he should find that she holds the real key to opening his heart.

SCORPIO WOMAN – TAURUS MAN

If a Scorpio girl wants passion, and usually they need an awful lot of it, then the Taurean man will provide more than enough for two. Opposite signs of the zodiac attract with a powerful magnetic force and these two opposites form one of the more potent and potentially disastrous of perfect matches. A Scorpio girl is never easy to live with, particularly emotionally, and a Taurean man isn't easy to live with at times because he doesn't look upon life with the same seriousness and intensity as the Scorpio girl. This relationship will always be a love-hate one which can end in love, or end in hate.

Scorpios never forgive anyone for a slight, or hurt, and neither do Taureans. They are both fixed in their opinions and like sleeping giants don't like to be disturbed. The Bull is the giant of indulgence, the Scorpio is the giantess of danger. They both enjoy deep, sensual sexual experiences, but the Scorpio will want it to be mysterious, sacred, as addictive as danger. This is where they may come unstuck because the Taurean has quite a bawdy sense of humour which he often takes to bed with him. He likes to tease, but Scorpios are really not awfully good at being made to look fools. The Scorpio girl has to learn that the Bull can get as ecstatic about the next meal in his life as he can about sex and, quite honestly, if you turn heavy on him, he'll turn his backside on you.

Love is living a placid life to a Bull, and love to a Scorpio is always intensively lived.

SCORPIO MAN – GEMINI WOMAN

This is an extremist relationship. She will hate his guts because he seems so arrogant, full of chauvinistic attitudes, and she will be unable to tolerate his secrecy, even though she may secretly admire it. The Scorpio will find her irresistible at first, amused by her charm and her butterfly mind, but don't Snakes and Scorpions eat butterflies?

The Gemini woman likes sex as much as any other of her million pastimes, and that is why Scorpio will find her such a delightful challenge. To teach a woman the secret of sex is the total fulfilment, it is life itself, and is what inspires the Scorpio to attempt to pull this girl together. But Geminis don't like being taught lessons, and change is in her nature like blood. She doesn't take easily to a concentration of sexual activity. Sure, it's part of the whole, but so is the wind on a summer's day. A lot goes on in a Gemini girl's head that a Scorpio will find hard to comprehend. He likes to unravel mysteries, and the mental gymnastics of the Gemini girl will amuse him for a long time. But he won't want her chatter in bed when he should be moving the earth for them both, and he will want to dominate her restless spirit, believing he can control it in his Serpent's mouth. This could be a successful sexual relationship, as long as she is prepared to drop all her friends, all her role-playing games and actually take him seriously. He's too jealous and she won't want to spend so much time having sex: it can make her short of Air.

SCORPIO WOMAN – GEMINI MAN

To a Scorpio woman feeling love is being love, is love. It is the whole of her existence, and every emotion and feeling displayed is the serious nature of her relationships. If, by chance, she should happen to be infatuated with the mental antics and agility of the Gemini man, she will want to consume him with passion first and talk about it later. Unfortunately the Gemini man doesn't like to be consumed with passion, and would rather talk. Neither does he relate very well to the incredible deep-seated emotion and rather serious way this lady looks at love. He might initially find her secretive, rather mysterious power to attract intellectually stimulating. She has hypnotic eyes and she draws you in like a Snake ready to strike. He is confident enough to try her out, but they can both become hopelessly entangled in a trial of love and hate, rather than the lightness and liberation of the kind of relationship a Gemini would rather have.

Physically they will be addicted to one another from the start. First meetings will either be full of his overwhelming attraction for her, or she will fix her mind and her emotions on him until he can't resist. This can be an excessively sexual relationship, which is of course odd for any self-respecting Gemini. His apparent coldness will make her even more responsive, even more determined to get to the heart and the soul of this butterfly man. But she never will, and that is often where they part company, she feeling betrayed, willing to destroy the love that has grown inside her, and he glancing across the room for another adventure.

SCORPIO MAN – CANCER WOMAN

This other Watery fatal attraction is not so difficult as when the man is Cancer and the woman a Scorpio. There is at the start an obvious sexual magnetism. They both feel the same urgent responses towards one another. The Scorpio will be able to see right through the Cancer's shell. To him it is as translucent as mother of pearl, and to a Scorpio a shell is no barrier to the one he desires. Emotionally and sexually he will immediately be able to respond exactly to the Moon girl's subtle and mysterious sexuality. Crab girls really do want someone who can understand their silence, their sensual and gentle modesty. The Crab's shy inner self will be upturned, once the Scorpio man begins to penetrate her normally tough waxing. Because he is so aware of her needs she will instinctively let go of her outer Crab-like pincers and she will feel secure in his intensely hungry soul, perhaps more than with anyone else. It won't be a sensitive relationship however, more a battle of wills, a passionate and sometimes doomed affair. Scorpios have always the problem of their destructive nature, which works alongside their constructive one. And he will demand power in the relationship, emotionally and sexually.

What Scorpio wants to believe in a woman is that she will be as fanatical about him as he is about her. A Cancerian girl does get obsessive about love. It may only be the whole of her life for that moment, the next she may suffer the pangs of disillusion; she is a creature of changing moods, remember. Both have shells that need cracking, and maybe the Cancer girl, once opened up, will show the Scorpion that it's not so bad being exposed after all. They both suffer from pain and instability, but the Scorpio is more of an extremist than the Crab. For all her depressive lows and manic highs, he will be the one really to suffer if she ever rejects him.

SCORPIO WOMAN - CANCER MAN

A highly charged magnetic and sexual attraction formed from basic empathy. The Scorpio woman may realise that the deep emotional caves of the Cancer man's inner psychology are the kind she can reach, and only she alone. Both are so emotionally tuned in to each other that it is possible that they can destroy one another too quickly. The Cancer man will find her powerful personality a little over-whelming at times. She will want to control him, and not be the one to follow. However, the Cancer man will want to be in charge and this can cause the Scorpio woman to lash out when she would be better trying to understand her own insecurities. Their differences are great, but their passion will override most of their day-to-day problems. Blackness is something a Cancerian man can sink into, as easily as he can lift the clouds of depression with his laughter and mad, loony humour. These moments of madness the Scorpio needs in her life. She is known for her gravity and her intensity in everything she feels and does. This makes the Cancerian begrudg-ing and melancholy at times because he really deserves more light-ness in his own mopish lamentations.

Sexually, she will melt his side-steps into a dance of ecstasy. Not many women can really get a Cancerian man going, but this one will, and it will be a buzz he will remember all his life. One of the reasons is that they are both secretive to the point of facing the firing-squad rather than admitting the truth. But neither of them will accept secrets being withheld. There could be a lot of interrogations from either side. He is possessive, she is innately jealous, and her tail can strike with alarming ease if she feels his aloof retreat from her could be anything to do with the suspicions she's cast upon him. He is equally suspicious, but her intense passion for him or her intense rejection of him, will either sever their relationship completely or create a deeper bond between them. Hers is a passionate and often a destructive love, and the Cancerian's shell has to be strong enough to take the sting and the anger when she is slighted by his retreats. To her, this is rejection, but they both fear losing.

SCORPIO MAN – LEO WOMAN

Secret weapons or not, this is when Scorpio's infallibility with women comes to a grave and dangerous test. Making a drama out of a crisis is what the Leo girl and the Watery man are good at achieving together. The Scorpio man won't be able to resist trying to bring down the Leo pride. He likes to delve into mysteries, to wound and hurt in a truly sadistic manner, to see how far he can go without causing his own pain.

He is motivated by his inability to cope with the Leo girl's Fiery and unabashed temperament, so different from his own withheld, destructive one. However, Leos are proud, fiercely loyal to themselves, and won't let a Scorpio get the better of them. If she feels he's come too close, has placed a dangerous rather than a glitzy ring upon her finger, she'll retaliate, like only a Cat knows how. As much as she will be attracted to his dark sexuality she won't like the incessant probing of her mind, and eventually his tactics might become too obsessive. Leo ladies need warmth and loyalty, security and generous shows of affection and verbal expressions of love. The Water in which the Snake lives is murky and crusted with cold dangers. His will is generated by sexual completeness, and the thrill of the chase, and the catch. He can roll love in his jaws like a crocodile rolls a dead man to the bottom of the river, and he has to win, or die.

It could prove to be a great battle of wills, but the Leo lady will always want to be *with* the world, not hidden from it, and inevitably the Scorpio's insistent jealousy will no longer be able to control her extrovert nature and he will, unconsciously, destroy their love.

SCORPIO WOMAN – LEO MAN

There is an instinctive rapport between these two when they first encounter each other, perhaps because they know that they have met their match. The Leo because the Scorpion girl is so serious about life and love, and the Scorpio girl because she realises that the Leo lives on a different planet. His planet is that of pleasure, movement, and extremes, of living on the edge, of winning and achieving. Her planet is filled with imaginary fears, of dark secrets, heavy emotions and love, endless love. The hidden power of the Scorpio can come as quite a surprise to the very brazen and generous Leo. The Cat may well play his own games, boast, impress and generally live on a high but, when the dark Snake slips out of her mysterious coil to take over he will feel the sting of a very powerful tail indeed. Her animosity towards him will be because he is so confident, so sure of himself and so ego-driven. This is not unlike her own motives, but hers must be kept hidden at all costs. If he should realise that she is governed by darker, obsessive undercurrents he would surely run.

This could be a very sexual relationship, before it becomes any other kind. The male and female forces will turn on and off at their command. He will want rhetorical fun, she will want passion, but the sexual passion she stirs has to be taken deadly seriously. For a rampant Lion, this can be a little too emotional. He loves with all his heart, but he won't want to be taken over by her tumultuous feelings. She lives in her feelings, he lives in his actions. If they can manage to overcome her jealousy and his pride, then they could survive. But the Scorpio girl will never forgive him when he flirts, and, for the Leo, enjoying the company of others, whether he means to flirt or not, is more important than any Scorpio's obsessive tail.

SCORPIO MAN – VIRGO WOMAN

Now the Virgo woman does enjoy submission at times; not often, because she is a very proud and careful practitioner, and won't be made a fool of easily. But there's something rather sensational about the soulful way the Scorpio waits to move in. A Virgo is not overtly a 'feeling' person, but this man can send shudders down her spine, and melt her poise before she's even felt the sting of his tail. They may meet and spend a long time being attracted to each other without either of them summing up the courage to do anything about it. For all his womanising, the Scorpio prefers the waiting, the lingering and the anticipation of the moment. He is drawn to mystery and darkness. And if he can keep the light out on her inner self for a long time, the more charged his sexual energy will be when it is time to release it. He will be suspicious of her intentions at first – he is suspicious of daylight too. Virgo women are pretty good at mental sharpness and, like barbed wire, a Scorpio can become caught up on her mind. Usually he moves in and wipes out his victims with vows and promises of passion and fulfilment. This may tempt her, but her Earthy, practical nature will always keep clarity in her visions. Both have an ability to appear cold and unfeeling. Hers is to avoid emotion, and his is because he feels so intensely that it's easier to keep the true depth of his love hidden, even from himself. If the Virgo girl turns sexually cold on him, which she will do if she suspects he is gathering his strength to form an onslaught on another unsuspecting female, then he will end their relationship with sadistic pleasure.

SCORPIO WOMAN – VIRGO MAN

The inquiring nature of the Virgo man can seem trifling in comparison with the penetrating, all-power-seeking probing of the Scorpio woman. The Virgo man lives to find a woman who can provide him with mental stimulation and practical support. He is strong, but he needs to feel strength around him so that it is real. The Scorpio woman will immediately love the Virgo man's level-headed and analytical mind. She will be attracted both to his romantic nature and to his practical one. Scorpio women are emotional and determined. Their strength is their character, and the whole of their life is lived with purpose, both for love and for life. The Virgo man may find this hard to live with. He doesn't exactly enjoy emotional scenes, and he certainly can't cope with the pressures that a Water sign like Scorpio can turn on him in her most passionate moments.

He would like to be enlightened by her tremendous power to inject all kinds of feeling into her love-making but somehow he is never quite there with her. He will be dexterous, agile and know every position under the sun, but he won't be able to provide her with the solution to love, and the universe, which is essentially what this woman wants from her sex life. Virgo believes sex to be pure. It is an art to be perfected, it does not have any deeper meaning to his life.

Sadly, this involves not a jot of the emotional content that a Scorpio woman reads into every move he makes. They can quite easily misunderstand one another, even while they enjoy being together but, after a while, she will become too demanding, and the Virgo is more likely to suffer with headaches, turn on the cold shower too often, and resort to a high-powered fault-finding mission to recuperate.

SCORPIO MAN – LIBRA WOMAN

A Libran girl can fill the Scorpio male with a vengeance that will storm through her life, and end her idea of romance with him. She is a chatterbox, loves people and desperately wants a permanent relationship, when *she's* made her mind up, and not before. Along comes the Scorpio with lodestar sexuality and a compulsive personality. He exudes sex and he spouts poetry like a romantic, keeps hidden secrets to lure her into believing he must be the answer to the universe. Of course his mystery is just that he likes mystery. He takes life so seriously, and the Libran girl takes life so lightly. If the Snake will let her be the life and soul of the party, then she might make the sun shine for him too. But, as is often the case, the jealous and torrid intensity of the Scorpio's sting will break their relationship before she has had time to convince him, let alone herself that this could be good. The Scorpio is also a very stubborn and egotistic person. Fire signs' egos are easily inspected, open to the world and almost comfortable to put up with compared to this Plutonian darkness, the almost satanic ego of a stranger. He will always be a stranger to this girl; even though she feels in control of their relationship, she can never really understand the intense depths of feelings this man rarely lets be known even to himself.

He fears rejection more strongly than she, oddly enough. When she is floundering in her head, and he would rather she were floundering on the bed with him, he will sense that potent sexuality may not be as ideal for her as he first imagined.

The one thing that he ought to learn, but it is unlikely because Scorpios are usually convinced they have nothing left to learn, is that she needs open communication. He can make powerful and compelling love but, when the Air girl is in her head and tangled in another mental harmony act, it will need the idealism that she first saw in him to get her back into his arms with real tenderness.

SCORPIO WOMAN – LIBRA MAN

There is a force and intensity to this woman that a Libran man can find a trifle alarming. His is a nature of symmetry and conciliation: the laid-back lover with a lazy, languid trust in most human beings, particularly women. He loves women a lot and feels safe in their company most of the time, they are less likely to expose him to conflict and dissension. Then along comes the Scorpio, out for the involvement of the most deep and sensitive kind. She has her cool, magical eyes fixed most definitely on him. He will be flattered, as any Libran is, by the attention of a beautiful woman, and will probably fall immediately into his usual trap of being in love with love. The Scorpio woman falls for his rather lax attitude to life, hers is so serious, and she yearns for more sweetness and fun. He can provide this, as long as she doesn't overrun him with the tensions and emotional struggles for which he is not cut out. But Libra can cope quite well with her dark and hidden forces because he lets it flow over him and around him, and is usually willing to give way a little for the sake of harmony.

He will want to get involved with this woman as long as he can have his freedom. Unfortunately the jealous and deep emotional anger of a Scorpio woman will sear his heart if he so much looks at another woman. This is where their disparate characters can cause a lot of flak. Sex is the meaning of life to this girl and the Libran's rather fickle approach to romance will begin to empty her heart of any imaginary future they had. His capricious flirtations with another beautiful woman could mean the end of any commitment he might have given an inkling of sharing. He wants desperately to form a special relationship with someone, but he still really believes that his ideal is out there, and if he doesn't carry on searching, he might miss the true love of his life. Scorpio may see this fair judgment merely as an excuse, and she won't play fulcrum for his alternating thoughts on whether to take the risk with her, or to lose it all on another chance.

Sagittarius
COMPATIBILITIES

SAGITTARIUS MAN – SAGITTARIUS WOMAN

The looseness of this relationship could be its undoing, rather like a very badly tied shoelace, or two bits of string that haven't quite been pulled tight. Sagittarians of both sexes need their freedom first and their friends second. They love having lovers but, usually, love implies commitment and they get awfully cynical about that as they grow older. Being mates is easier, it requires fewer responsibilities and it always leaves the door open for them when they want to breeze in and out, which Archers do, most of their lives. When a female Sagittarian meets a male Sagittarian, she'll be happily amused to find someone so like herself. Here is another extrovert, someone who likes to travel the world and someone who can get quite passionate if the mood takes him, and he will with her. She has the high ideals that he does, will chatter, change the subject and not get very serious about anything, or anyone. In fact the verbal gymnastics and the verbal games these two can play to outwit and outdate the other can be astounding, especially to anyone else who may be listening. They aren't very private about their lives, preferring to express feelings rather than repress them. Archers arm themselves with many mental rounds of ammunition and set out to enlighten the world. They mean it nicely, of course, but they can get unstuck when they bump into humourless people with tight and tidy minds.

Both have the ability to exaggerate and, when they become embroiled in a heated debate, there's a danger they will expand the truth a little too recklessly. Sexually they move through many different moods, from playful, teasing, sensual games, mental and always highly amusing tricks, and then back to total passion and energetic sparks. The only difficulty these Archers could have is the openness of their relationship. Their jealousy is quickly fired. They both have casual acquaintances and they both enjoy flirting quite openly, not meaning the other any harm. And yet, although both will insist on the right to have that freedom, they won't like it in the other half of the team. Free love is the Sagittarians' ideal and, as long as they don't spread it outside their own relationship, they could find they have the best of both worlds.

SAGITTARIUS MAN – CAPRICORN WOMAN

The truth of the matter is always what the Archer searches for, the ideals of life are always waiting to be sprung and, like the big bag of surprises he is, he wants to be the one to release the eject button on life. Because he meets so many characters the chances are that bumping into a Goat woman will be one of his more exciting adventures, but it may prove to be more than he bargained for. Goat ladies don't like casual acquaintances any more than casual relationships. And if the Capricorn girl thinks he's only interested in her to work off some Fiery energy, then she will give him the greatest run for his money he could ever imagine. Falling in love with her might seem the only route to forming a relationship with her and he is a connoisseur of falling in love, as he is at falling out of it. The resilient Goat will immediately pull over the cloak of calm poise and self-restraint to prevent any obvious challenge. He is all right, but he's a flirt, he's vain and he's a bit too cocksure. He has a boyish charm, and she can be quite easily flattered by his faith in her, but will she actually let him any closer than arm's length?

For the Sagittarian, it's not so much a question of getting any closer, its actually dragging her along for the ride. Archers don't need closeness in their frantic lives. He won't mind as long as she doesn't try and control him, order him about and generally throw mud on his Fire. He needs to feel free, and if she's clever enough and wise enough, which Goat girls usually are, especially as they grow older, she will be able to let him have as much distance and as much space between them as he wants. And she'll find, not with surprise, but with a smug satisfaction, that the Archer *does* want to come back. He needs a lot of affection, and trust, and a Capricorn girl can give it to him. She's learnt to be patient, to succeed. It's part of her reason for love. But she needs faithfulness and stability, and if she can hang on in and let him feel the power of freedom she could be assured of that faith.

SAGITTARIUS WOMAN – CAPRICORN MAN

The economics of any situation, whether it is to do with business or love, are what interests the Capricorn man. The first thing he may notice about the Archer girl is that she is uneconomical in the way she spends her money so quickly, and in the way she spreads herself around the world, in some vain attempt to bring ideals to every man. The Goat immediately would like to step in and organise her, order her life and in return (for there's always a return on a Goat's investment) take advantage of her very appealing and forthright charm. Capricorns are rigid and controlled, and Archers are not. The more discipline the Sagittarian girl feels around her the more she will attempt to escape, and so it goes on. The chances that she will pull herself together and accept the ambitious Goat's interest in her are very slim, unless she has spent too long on the road, and has finally given up her wild and changeable spirit. The Sagittarian girl can see a lot of faults in the Goat and will probably quite bluntly let him know about them. Whether she can actually love this man is another matter. She is inconsistent, whereas the Goat will always want to know where she stands and where she is. If it's out of range, he won't be unduly jealous; he fears emotion and very rarely lets it creep up on him, but he will feel out of control and, when a Goat is not in charge, he can resort to stern measures to keep the quo in his status. Being forced to do anything is against the Archer's natural habit of surprise. She won't mind giving him surprises, but not on demand. They are a very different pair, and that might be enough to send them into a brief ecstasy about each other for a while. Archers like the newness of love, and the romance of the first bites, and the Goat is always ready to try and make order out of anyone's chaos, especially if she's fast-moving, challenging and distinctly invigorating.

SAGITTARIUS MAN – AQUARIUS WOMAN

The honesty between these two is probably what first draws them together into a comfortable but spirited rapport. The Archer needs an 'honest injun' in his life, and he also needs to feel that she, like him, is free, independent and not likely to crack up emotionally at the change of the wind. An Aquarian girl provides a mental accessory to the normal high octaves of the Sagittarian train of thought. He will change subjects within seconds, and she will give him the fuel and fire to deal with it. She loves talking about every subject under the sun, and they both share the same need to have friends and oddballs in their life first, and lovers second. Who needs lovers when you can have friends? The Archer is probably more romantic at the beginning of any relationship with an Aquarian girl, and probably more willing to express his real feelings, but the Aquarian girl is also in need of an idealist, and one who has the sense and courage to spread that idealism. She isn't possessive, but Aquarians like Sagittarians are sometimes jealous. She can be stubborn about doing things her way. But because he has no need to be dominated, nor to dominate, he can accept her as an equal. When she sets her mind to some crazy scheme and becomes coolly distant, he is able to shrug it off with his usual adaptable carelessness. He avoids conflict with her, and that is the answer to their success. Passion runs deep through the Archer's sexuality, and at times she may seem too light and Airy, too interested in reading the next section of her book, when he would rather be looning around the bedroom. But both want similar amounts of freedom: the Aquarian for her friends, and he for his ideals. Both are optimistic about life and the future, and this can be a highly successful and mutually beneficial relationship.

SAGITTARIUS WOMAN – AQUARIUS MAN

The inventions of the Uranian man are often better in his head than let out on unsuspecting females whom he, at times, uses as part of his experiments. He is a genius of eccentricity and unpredictability, but he is not awfully good at being the lover of most girls' dreams. Aquarians are mentally fascinating, and physically often aloof and glamorous, poised with a feral instinct. And yet the fumblings of the Aquarian man can sometimes seem as distant as his heart. To the Sagittarian girl this man seems ideal. She needs romance, yes, but she adores his brain, gets off on his distance, because it keeps away from her own, and is intrigued by his cranky ideas and rather blunt admission to knowing that life is what you make it. He has ideals, and so does she, but he breaks rules and makes rules and puts up with her ridiculous forays into freedom. For this reason she may seriously consider forming a romantic attachment to him, but the problem arises when she finds that the Aquarian prefers to keep friends as friends, rather than engage in any special and distracting love-affair.

If the Aquarian man realises that this is the sort of woman who can put up with his mad-professor behaviour and his stubborn need to change those around him, he may slip into the relationship for its originality. She seems able to accept that he wants no ties, and also that he can't consider her more special than anyone else. She's also headstrong, open and honest, and has the guts to go where she wants to go and not to ask permission. Finally she may find his coldness doesn't always turn the pillow to ice. He may live on a different planet, but he is inventive in bed, and he does do some quite ridiculous things to make her laugh. This could be an ideal relationship if she has the patience to get past the lengthy friendship stage!

SAGITTARIUS MAN – PISCES WOMAN

If you have a problem the simplest thing to do about it is to forget it, then it goes away – usually the solution given by the Piscean woman, and also by the Sagittarian man. Their differences, however, are based on the fact that a Fish girl will evade conflict, and evade anything that suggests she may be put on a hook and dissected, and the Archer just doesn't really give a hoot and prefers to walk away because walking away might lead to another avenue of amusement for his ever-changing spirit. He is an honest man, and will ask direct questions and expect direct answers. On the other hand the Piscean girl is known for her elusive replies, and her ability to change the subject to avoid his ever knowing how she truly feels or what she really thinks. This can irritate the Archer. He does have a lot of anger if he's pushed, and getting rattled is something he would prefer not to do, even though he has the wilder passions of a Fire sign. If he gets angry with the Fish girl she may either take two courses of action, the first being quite cleverly to crumple into a heap of tears and hurt, or coldly to swim off to a different pool to be alone with the only one she can trust: herself.

Archers won't enjoy the tears very much. They care very much about people's feelings, and don't intentionally like to hurt anyone. They can't stand emotional scenes and recriminations. If the Fish escapes to shadowland, then he won't try to follow her.

He will always find the Piscean girl physically attractive, although sexually she is very different from him, and also because he admires strength in women who are his feminine ideals. He will be more impulsive about sex, preferring to make love when he feels like it. The Pisces girl sometimes prefers her solitude to sex, and this can shoot tremendous holes in his very delicate ego. They both need freedom, and they both need understanding, but she finds his bluntness too demanding, and he will probably think her secretiveness too closed.

SAGITTARIUS WOMAN – PISCES MAN

In time, if the Sagittarian girl is patient enough to wait, she may find that the dithery, dreamy quality of the man to whom she has been romantically attracted has an inner strength comparable to her own. On the surface, Pisces men often appear weak and wishy-washy. They seem sentimental dreamers, without thought for the reality of life, with no practical sense and ambition. But they are dual signs and, like their Gemini and Sagittarian friends, they are capable both of an adaptable nature and of a variety of guises to suit the weather. Geminis wear more hats than any of the other signs, but a Piscean will play better and the Sagittarian will enjoy the game and gamble more. When a Sagittarian woman gets it into her head that the Pisces man is a far more devious and slippery character than he first appeared, she might try to throw a few blunt and dangerous remarks to sort him out, and see who he really is.

However, if she is too blunt he may disappear to the seashore. He will find her free spirit and her generous nature attractive, but she will become frustrated by his dithery changeability. She is Fire and he is Water, and however hard she tries to stay open-minded and easy-going, it can be very hard with this man. He can drown her in his passivity, infuriate her because he takes so long to get up in the morning and never seems to get anything done. He walks round in a dream while she has already tackled ten jobs and made enough money to go and fritter it away on an impulse. She'll gamble on his love too, and he will respond with a great sexual intuition for what she needs.

Piscean men are always sensitive and sexually imaginative and will always want to give rather than take. 'But sometimes too much giving can be just as self-centred!' shrieks the Sagittarian girl in frustration as the Fish listens to the troubles of the world. But she is only teasing.

SAGITTARIUS MAN – ARIES WOMAN

The Archer looks for adventure, for opportunity, round every corner.

If he sees a challenge, a woman with strength and an honesty above his own, then he may find the irresistible urge to fall as impulsively in love as she can. He is drawn to lighthearted, independent romantics and would rather flirt than chat to the boys. His encounters with women are often platonic, but there is always an undercurrent of pure sexual masculinity, which he finds hard to cover up, for all his generous friendship and love of sharing his incorrigible charm.

The Aries girl won't be too careful responding to his undoubted charm, after all she is hasty in most things. But she's heard about the Don Juan of the zodiac and his cheeky, persuasive style. Somehow she can immediately feel vulnerable in this man's presence, perhaps because his values and ideals are matched against such high standards that even an Aries girl feels inferior to his desire. They have much in common, a liking for fun, adventure, an easy-going lightness in a relationship, where 'commitment' and 'for ever' are words hardly mentioned. But if they are it will be the Ram girl who first suggests permanence. The Archer rarely allows himself to be put into this position and, for any relationship with a Sagittarian, the Aries girl will have to make sure she never mentions the future, never makes plans, and constantly is unavailable and difficult to pin down herself.

They both have the same ideals in bed. He will be deeply passionate and funny, she will be intensely responsive and warm to his boy-like antics. Their egos may sometimes clash, but his is based on physical appearance, the way his works *through* the world, rather than the Arien ego which needs to feel confident in the world.

SAGITTARIUS WOMAN – ARIES MAN

A crazy relationship. Sagittarian women often have energetic and time-consuming careers, so that the chances are she'll probably meet a few of those fast impetuous Aries men along the same road. The Archer girls have a blunt and headstrong approach to sex and love and an equally passionate lifestyle. That's why the Aries man is often a good bet for understanding her expansive and altruistic nature. The Aries loves most women, and the Sagittarian girl loves most men. She's a humanitarian and may well have a host of platonic men-friends which, unfortunately, the Ram will find hard to accept. This relationship can be physically and mentally exhausting for both of these two Fire-eaters. She will want fun, to stay up all night and dance in the summer rain, to experience romance and live in the ideal world of free love as far away from commitment and traps as she can possibly manage. The Aries man may be able to give her most of this, but he really isn't awfully good at being the true romantic. His is the love of passion and the hunger of domination to trim his inflated ego. Hers is to be reminded that fantasy and fairy-tales might come true, even when the party is over. What he can offer her, though, is honesty and a reckless free-ranging independence. Sexually they orbit the same planet, and financially and mentally they can ride the same bus and remain friends even when they've both run out of cash and a joke. She'll put up with his egotistic chip on his shoulder; after all she's not power-driven, just lucky. There will be times when she feels she was unlucky to meet him when their Fiery tempers flare up, they both walk out in a temper and threaten never to speak again. But she'll probably be the first to say she's sorry, and that's what the Ram needs, someone who is true to herself.

SAGITTARIUS MAN – TAURUS WOMAN

A rock-solid relationship is what a Taurus woman wants, not a rocky one. Unfortunately, as much as she might fall in love with the Archer's uncanny ability to be optimistic, life's clown and the funniest friend any woman can ever have, she really wants him to be exclusively hers, which, to the honest and forthright Archer, is certainly not what life is all about.

Any attempt to curtail an Archer's freedom will make him disappear with alarming speed. He can love, and he wants to love, but freely, and with as many women as he can within human capacity, and he also needs spice and passion. Romance and love to him don't mean a trap, they don't mean commitment and they don't necessarily mean permanence, which of course they do to a straightforward, determined Bull lady. The Archer insists on a strong mental companionship as well as physical lust. He has fun sexually, but he needs a good pal to muck around with, to take on his travels, and would prefer to run in the surf than knit cuddly toys for the local toddler group. Emotionally he won't submit to possessive women, and certainly doesn't like being shunted into a hole of commitment. To him the Bull lady represents all these things, and he will shudder with fear if she seems to be pointing her horns in his direction. He needs to feel independent, and wants to show the world that his honesty is real. He hates domesticity, and is not very attached to family life, and would rather roam the world with as many pals as he can find. The Bull lady will find it hard to accept this very different man from herself and, sexually, her quiet, sensual approach may not be able to tolerate his open and frank expression of every physical contact they make.

SAGITTARIUS WOMAN – TAURUS MAN

There he goes again, fascinated by the Fire. As the caveman first discovered it, so does the Taurean heart yearn to trap Fire's secret and learn why it can burn and tear at hearts. The Bull will be attracted to the Archer girl because she is so wild, so blunt and honest, and full of optimism. If she doesn't mind giving up her freedom, roaming the world and collecting men friends, then she might just manage to stay an indulgence at the Taurean's banquet. But for all his fatal attraction to this Fire sign, he needs someone who will stay put in that messy bed, cook the fried mushrooms at dawn in the woods, and generally hang around with quiet contentment. The Archer girl hankers after adventure and challenges in life, and secretly she would like to have the sort of relationship a Taurean can offer her, but her mutability can be dampened by the Bull's possessiveness. Sex can be warm and affectionate and fun, but the Bull might bore her after a while, once she realises that he's not the headless horseman of her dreams. All Sagittarians have a fantasy lover – and Taurus seems at first to fit the role, until she begins to realise that he wants permanence and monotony. A wild, idealistic love-affair is not in his nature, he would rather settle in bed with those mushrooms and a Fire that he can tame. But that's where he can get hurt, for the Archer girl's Fire will never be put out.

SAGITTARIUS MAN – GEMINI WOMAN

These two opposites will adapt to each other from the word go. And they may well always be on the go, seeking new adventures together, travelling the world if they could and spending money as though it were free. Their child-like and capricious behaviour runs through every facet of their relationship together. If the Gemini girl is led astray by anyone it will be with a Sagittarian male. She is known for her wiles and guiles, but for every trick he plays on her (and Sagittarians love playing tricks and demonstrating their love with surprises and jokes), she will respond with something better. The challenge between them is intense and can provide amusement for onlookers too!

Outwitting each other is another game they will play, quite consistently. Sexually they are capable of finding a rare and perfect harmony, considering she lives in her head and his passion is a mixture of hitting the arrow where he intends and wishing occasionally he could try a new bull's-eye. In a way that is why the Gemini girl is probably the only one who can keep a Sagittarian man more or less a permanent fixture, not that either of them likes the word commitment. She'll learn pretty quickly that to make any kind of arrangement with a Sagittarian is like trying to arrange a marriage in his eyes. So she will have to wait for his phone calls, his surprises and this can sometimes be an infuriating aside in their truancy games. But they make a good partnership in everything and, if one of them does prefer the freedom of the road and wanders off one day into the sunset, they will always remain friends. They carry neither bitterness nor remorse in their open hearts.

SAGITTARIUS WOMAN – GEMINI MAN

An opposite attraction is a powerful, magnetic attraction between different sexes, and this is one of the most exciting and crazy relationships in the zodiac. The Gemini man is a genie of charm. He is astute and clever and witty enough to tempt the brave and honest Archer girl into his arms. They will both feel the magnetic pull of the zodiacal opposition instantly, across crowded rooms, very social gatherings where they are both likely to be. They may have fun to begin with, throw themselves around like a couple of kids and generally misbehave when they should be cautious. They have an irresponsible effect upon each other. But the Gemini man can at times be critical of the Sagittarian girl's big mouth, and she can turn her Fiery nature on him if he flirts more than she does. They both don't suffer from ego problems, so they will happily take turns at being the boss. She may at times wish he'd shut up so she could talk, but they both have trouble closing their minds, and closing their mouths. He has so much to say, and she has so much to do.

They both have a gregarious spirit and a fear of loneliness. Because they are essentially extroverts they will draw a wide circle of friends around them and, although the Gemini man isn't particularly jealous of the Archer's fondness for male company, she may get a little heated when he brings some female colleagues round for a drink. She needs more emotional support than he can frankly give her for, although she seeks freedom in relationships as much as he does, there is always a wistful part of her which longs to have a base, somewhere to start from, and somewhere to come back to. For the Gemini, beginnings and endings have no place in his life, unless they are temporary.

SAGITTARIUS MAN – CANCER WOMAN

The deep-seated devotion of the Cancerian girl can make a Sagittarian male almost retch with the thought of all those nasty words in his dictionary, like chains and ties. Not that a Sagittarian is ever nasty, he is always honest, a bit of a scoundrel, and basically so happy-go-lucky that most women want to capture him. Unfortunately he is not the catching type. A Crab out on one of her sideways walks may come across such a vibrant, sparkling Archer and decide that she can't stop herself falling in love, so she might as well sit it out in her Crabby shell until he comes begging at her door. Her determination is admirable, but the Archer, in all fairness, really loves all the world and lots of women. He prefers the company of extroverted, funny, charming, beautiful girls, to the more introverted damsel-in-distress types, but he has a very soft heart and will defend any woman in trouble, or any girl who needs a friend and a shoulder to cry on. When friendship is mentioned he's frank, forthright and blunt. He will play with the Crab girl's apparent lunatic-fringe character and not realise that her emotions are flowing in the background towards a very deep river of sorrow, when he finally says some outrageous, cutting remark that he didn't actually mean to be hurtful.

The Crab will always listen to an Archer. He can go on for hours in a rather optimistic and self-centred way. He changes the subject as quickly as a Gemini, though, if the Crab touches on emotion or commitment too soon, he will change tack more quickly than he can change his ideals. In sexual intimacy the Archer is quick to please, and fired spontaneously. He would rather have sex when he feels like it. She would rather it were a routine sensual experience where true feelings were expressed, both physically and mentally. Jealousy will be the catalyst for their arguments and eventually for their separation, for this man is profoundly freedom-loving and this woman is deeply possessive.

SAGITTARIUS WOMAN – CANCER MAN

It's not easy for the freedom-loving Sagittarian woman to accept the gentle but demonstrative leadership of the Cancer man in her life. She would rather be doing a different kind of head-hunting than the career kind and, for any girl Archer to admit to be turned on by domesticity and routine, she would have to be held down and tortured first. The Cancer man will find her very extrovert spirit of adventure a headier version of his own manic side. For the Archer girl is the most blithe spirit of them all. She may have her faults, she may be land-locked in honest self-expression and the need to move on to another challenge but basically she doesn't worry about emotion and finds it a tad stifling in her irrepressible and easy-going lifestyle. The Cancer man wants to possess and cherish, to be treated with gentleness, for his shell to be opened daily and be cleaned out spick and span with house-

COMPATIBILITIES – SAGITTARIUS

wifely devotion. This woman will rarely even imagine being someone else's groom, but she might enjoy leading him astray for a while.

She is Fire and he is Water, and usually the firework is put out quickly by this man's emotional puddles. He can turn her on sexually and induce sensuality and a little refinement to her rather casual love-making. But the passion she feels won't be enough to enliven her twenty-four hours of the day. She needs a mental and physical equal, not a secretive, wound up Crab with a nasty chip on his shoulder about his mum. If for a while he seems to be an escapist and a lunatic, both of which she admires and is attracted to in a man, then maybe she will hang on to the extrovert side of his nature, until the Moon comes back to shadow him in melancholy. Yet he will adore her frankness; at least she doesn't criticise, only tells the truth; however painful it is. She will want to travel the world, he would rather avoid anything which requires coming out of his shell, and whether he can cope with her wish for free love is questionable.

SAGITTARIUS MAN – LEO WOMAN

When the Archer stumbles across the lady with the glamorous lifestyle and the charming sincerity of her magnanimous and generous character, he may be numbed into thinking this is the sort of woman with whom he would like to dance in life. He thinks grandly, has ideals that outwit being trodden upon, and his standards are higher than his brisk, flippant chat-up line seems to imply. He is essentially an idealist and a free man: the lonely pirate who travels the world in search of a ship of dreams. Sometimes he will find her, then for reasons best known to himself he will mutiny, scuttle her and sailor on for another ideal, another dream. The Leo lady may have the courage and the strength of a battleship to hang on to him. She is not possessive, and she is not likely to boss him around in the way she might organise a Water sign, or an Earth sign. She loves his dashing, cavalier approach to life, as Fiery as her own, but subtly more gregarious, and more instinctive. He has Jupiter as his pal, and he

257

likes pals, female ones particularly. If the Leo girl can accept that when he openly and candidly talks about his past lovers, or his platonic girlfriends, because he believes he can share everything with the one he loves, then she must realise that it is she he loves most of all. He cares deeply about her pride, he's got a bit of it himself, but he also cares if he hurts. He can open his big mouth too often with a Leo girl and she's easily hurt.

When they are apart he will miss her, when they are together he will think of the lonely road and miss that too. He needs both, his freedom and the lovely loyalty of a strong woman, and maybe he can share his pirate dreams with her.

SAGITTARIUS WOMAN – LEO MAN

Both Fire signs, both in need of affirmation of their strength, and in need of much support from each other, they are extravagant and live on the danger line, always wanting to find another more exciting edge to their relationship. This can lead to quarrels, he will be fired by her independent spirit, and wish he could tame it. However, the Leo, for all his vanity and his own roaring self-importance, finds it hard to pin this lady down. She needs her independence and freedom in a relationship but she also needs to feel loved. The Leo man could provide this in his own self-centred way. The universe was born for Leos, and the Lion will only want to ensure his path is not tainted by inferior emotion or shrewish criticism. And the Archer girl will do neither of these. Both of these Fire signs are extrovert and need the company of other people. (To feel uncomfortable alone is a sign of being an extrovert, and to fear company is a sign of being introvert.) If he flirts, she will find her jealousy at times too emotional for her lifestyle, and he will begin to feel hurt and betrayed if she sarcastically bites back at his innocent bragging. She has so much honesty and a frank tongue that the Lion will be unnerved at times, but he needs her insults to bring him down to earth occasionally. She has to say what she really feels, and if the Lion can't stomach it, then she'll move on. They will feel the same heat of passions, the same energy of purpose, but sometimes they will lose sight of one another when the tests of loyalty and devotion become less of a game and more a power of will.

SAGITTARIUS MAN – VIRGO WOMAN

The sensible and sometimes tight-fisted Virgo girl will find the extraordinary generosity and rather lax approach to finances of the Archer make her squirm with disapproval. She will want more than anything to organise him, and hope that his expansive attitude to money is not the same as it is to women. Unfortunately her hopes may be dashed. The Sagittarius needs to open up his life and take everyone into it, and give it all to the world if he can. In this respect he really does want to be friends with everyone he meets. Other men are suspicious of such honest and open carelessness, and women, of course, are usually convinced that they are the true love of his life. They should beware, especially Virgo women. She may well fall instantly in love with the rogue of the zodiac. It's easy. He is so child-like, so lovable and funny. He's a bit clumsy with his heart, and can be rather big-mouthed and coarse, but he is also honest and a Virgo girl really gets high on honesty. At first he'll be impressed with her intellect, as bouncy and easy as his own. To a Sagittarian man falling in love is often as sudden as the arrow he's just fired, but another arrow can come angling along and split the first, and the Archer is vulnerable to his own need for freedom. Another woman is freedom from the first and, although he never means to hurt anyone, he can throw relationships around without thinking, as if they were sharp stones on the road to happiness. He is thoughtless rather than harmful, and the Virgo woman can end up the temporary stopover on his quest for the ideal woman. And a Sagittarius always has one of those!

SAGITTARIUS WOMAN – VIRGO MAN

The communication is good between these two rather oddly matched signs. The Sagittarius girl seeks freedom and love. Finding the paradox is her quest in life, and the Virgo man can understand this mentality, because it is a thinking process he can analyse and act upon. To a poised, unruffled Virgo man, the wild and extremist behaviour of Fire signs usually fascinates him to begin with and then, after a while, irritates him. It's always easier to find fault in strength rather than in weakness. The Archer girl is incredibly adaptable, and so is Virgo. She may think him pedantic and rather too steady for her clattering lifestyle. She will insist on having fun, playing jokes on the man she loves, and generally misbehaving. Full of surprises, the Archer girl likes to outwit even a Virgo intellectually. This is not something he will get a buzz from and he will have to prepare himself for the mental red-alert she presents. But the Archer girl's independence and spirit need a firm shoulder to lean on at times. She has insecurities, but her strength is in knowing intuitively what goes on in a Virgo man's head. He may not have much of a heart, but she can stretch it out into the world of romance with extraordinary talent.

Virgos aren't exactly balls of fire in bed. He may not even stir her the way she really wants to be stirred, but he will be romantic and be willing to be led on sexual adventures that he never knew existed. He wants to understand her egalitarian and clowning behaviour, and she finds his old-fashioned and stuffy mind an easy prey for her outspoken and blunt humour. They could find an easy rapport in time, but it will be based on friendship, rather than any sexual intimacy that they may share.

SAGITTARIUS MAN – LIBRA WOMAN

The half-Horse man is rather secretively more romantic than he appears on the surface. He'll ride recklessly around showering happiness and optimism in to people's lives and play the wild boy when he gets the chance, but actually he would quite like to believe that there is a woman out there who will let him be free, love him for being free, and always be there when he comes back without resentment, and without giving him a hard time. Not many women can come up with this ideal, but a Libran is one of them. She would love to make a commitment with this Horse man, who is the most romantic and Fiery lover, bedazzling himself and her with his opportunist rush through life. He doesn't stop very easily and a Libran girl would be better going on any travelling adventures with him. That way she can enjoy the fun and games, and ensure he doesn't go off on some moment's impulse in search of a different freedom.

She is strong, good fun, and sexually the kind of woman he likes. The Archer doesn't like soppy girls, and needs romantic pals with a head on their shoulders, not tears. She won't criticise him, and will laugh about the girl he nearly picked up at the bus stop in the rain for a joke. She will inspire him with her sparkling smile, but he can hurt her with his blunt truths and unintentional remarks. Like the Archer she is mentally alert and quick-witted and, although she is considerably lazier about life, she has the adaptability to get up and go when he calls on the spur on the moment from some faraway place.

The Archer has to win, and has to make his ideals come true. For someone like a Libran girl with the same sort of attitude about how she fits into the scheme of things he can seem a viable partner. He can be over-enthusiastic about sex. He is a Fire sign and, however free-ranging and dual his personality, he needs to boost his ego as much as he can. Handling his inquisitive and suddenly changing mind can thrill her. He is often quicker at changing the subject than a Gemini, but he'll never have a problem delighting the Libran's own fast-paced and often garrulous head.

SAGITTARIUS WOMAN – LIBRA MAN

There's something rather circus-like about Air and Fire signs together; a lot of singing and dancing happens, and they really can bring out the best in each other. The Libran man falling in love with the freedom-loving Sagittarian can be the best thing that happens to him. Not only will his usually wishy-washy nature take on a new and perhaps enlightening speed to reach decisions when she's around, but he will begin to feel that beauty and cheery lightness in his life is actually benefiting the world. For the Archer girl, possessed of a strong and extrovert character, the Libran man who charms his way through life, avoiding conflict and managing always to appear as if he's just got dressed specially for every occasion will seem like the only man who can possibly fulfil her own ideals. Both these signs are idealists in their own way. The Sagittarian girl seeks to fill the world with love, and the Libran merely to dress it with love. But both want to enjoy it. He can be a little too self-indulgent and irritate the Archer girl when he attempts to hold court to his social gathering. She is equally able to do so and they might try to better one another with verbal attacks, but it will always be with a gentle heart. There's nothing morose or bitter about these two; they suffer as a partnership only because they are both not practical about life. They are party-goers, not party-givers. Love for them is not necessarily built on the stability of life. They don't need routine and don't encourage commitment.

They want to feel secure, but they can never quite make up their minds if they should. For the Sagittarian girl it would mean giving up her very precious freedom, and for the Libran it just means making a decision! Sexually he will be the most romantic lover; she doesn't need emotion and feeling, she needs action and communication. He will love her passionate, rather self-conscious moments in bed, but they will have a lot of laughs, a great empathy and sense of fair play. And how they love to play!

SAGITTARIUS MAN – SCORPIO WOMAN

The Snake lady can wallow in hurt quite easily if given half the chance. Both pain and happiness are real feelings and either one will do. As long as she is feeling something intensely, the Scorpio woman is satisfied. When a bright, sparky Archer man comes galloping through her territory she will immediately feel uncomfortable because he is so incredibly unlike anyone she has ever met. He's open, frank, very warm-hearted and generous and seems careless about life and love. To entice him into the Scorpio's hole in the sand is a passion that she will find hard to resist. The more a Scorpio woman draws on her clandestine determination, the more likely it is that she won't stop until she has got what she has

COMPATIBILITIES – SAGITTARIUS

set her eye on. Her obsession with a man like an Archer could be easily and quickly relieved. After all, he loves women, is always waiting for an opportunity to seize, loves a challenge and flirts with any woman under the sun.

Of course, equally if he should come across a beautiful, quite mysterious and magnetic woman, he will more than likely fall temporarily in love. Temporary is the basis of Sagittarian love. Travelling through life means that relationships can be visited like countries, or fleeting glimpses of airports. Although he will never consciously hurt anyone, most of the women he meets aren't prepared to be a transit lounge while he refuels or changes flight. A Scorpio woman will want to be the whole world to him, and nothing less. He will, of course, enjoy a sexual relationship with her. But she wants complete wholeness, expects a permanency to arise from sexual love, and won't be prepared for his lack of commitment. It's hard for a Scorpio woman to let go, unless it's for ever. But as much as she would love to suffer for this man, her possessiveness will eventually send him to the airport for the next flight out of her war-torn country.

SAGITTARIUS WOMAN – SCORPIO MAN

The ruthless and quite deeply motivated Scorpio man can find the Archer girl so different and open to him that he might wonder if she really has any depth. That is why he will want to probe her, question her, seduce her and, most of all, possess her. Scorpios are very jealous and, for the Archer girl to get involved with a crypto-maniac, could be the end of freedom, the world and optimism as she knows it. An Archer is full of smiles, and wants to take life as it comes; she is convinced the sun will always shine, and she rarely suffers from emotional traumas, or bad moods. Unfortunately the moody, serious Scorpio can lash at her with dreadful, soulful lone-liness. He needs solitude, spells of introversion where he can rein-vest his vulnerable heart into more determined and voracious ambitions. Coming across the evasive and, quite honestly, brash thinking of an Archer can temporarily hold up his plans. Sexually, if she can't handle the meaning of life and fill him with emotional passion he might give her reason to feel jealous too. He can be incredibly cold if he chooses. Cold is as acute as being hot, hating is as feeling as loving. He will do either, he minds not a jot which he does, as long as it is experienced with passion and honour. He will resent her freedom and may try to impose his very strong will upon her. As much as the Archer is seeking a partnership, a love that can move with the seasons, inflame passion and leave her mind and heart to itself, the Scorpio has neither the ideals nor the free spirit to stay true to her. If he feels she is no longer worthy of his incredible devotion, he'll be the first to let her know, unless, of course, she's already blown somewhere else on the flames of the wind.

Capricorn

COMPATIBILITIES

CAPRICORN MAN – CAPRICORN WOMAN

Business is brisk in the Goat partnership. Both are ambitious and are happy to arrange the relationship within the rigid discipline of his stern and economical mind and her shy but uncompromising practical head. When they first meet these shy Goats may take for ever to get closer than a pint and a sandwich at lunchtime. Both are self-sufficient and conform to their individual rules. They don't take kindly to strangers, apart from throwing a few worn out gags to pass the time, and they won't be led out of routines and territory that isn't familiar to them. How then, can two such socially unenterprising people ever meet, let alone form some sort of bond, or relationship, that neither will be interested in instigating? Romance certainly is not something to be found on their mountains. Goats will scrabble around in their youth with other signs, get entangled with very different types who they find they can't control and give in to their own neutrality. But they are not neutral and meeting a counter-offensive from the only other person who will understand them, can provide them both with the stability they need.

Intangible affairs, like love, don't often appear in the Capricorns' diary. But after many meetings, they may decide that there is something they respond to within, they can't quite grasp it but, if the other Goat opened up a bit, if she were less shy, or he were less stuffy, then maybe, just maybe, they could both see the light together. It often happens that they do, but time is their lead-rein, and whoever gives in and appears to lose control, will always be the one who is less dominant in the partnership. The tough Goat woman, is just as likely to have a career and make sacrifices of love for her own power and glory but, with a Capricorn man, she can love *and* follow her path to success. The male Goat has genuine faith in her ability and may want her to be successful. But they can be cold to the world outside their private domain, and they can appear ruthless together in the face of love when what they both want is power and often fame.

CAPRICORN MAN – AQUARIUS WOMAN

These two are like the washers on a tap that's started to leak: one fits perfectly and never goes wrong, usually the cold tap, the other constantly needs mending, drips as soon as you change it, and then suddenly breaks, and it's hot. The first washer is the Capricorn man, and the second is the Aquarian girl who, although a cold and aloof star sign, can also get very heated about the injustices of life. Capricorn man will be reasonable about life, as long as he's in charge, and as long as it stays down-to-earth and tangible. The Aquarian girl will prefer the theory, the abstract qualities that make life work, and why we wonder why. This will seem nonsense to the taciturn Goat who will find her individuality too far removed from reality. He neither cares about why the universe began nor if there is a God, as long as it all works, and he's succeeding in where he wants to go. What is the point of skidding around trying to upset the balance, or telling the world it's going to end? The Uranian girl is not conservative-minded, she rebels for the sake of rebellion, and will incite total anarchy against the Goat and his conventional ways. One possible chance for this strange relationship is that they both have a very strong sense of integrity. If she can reasonably (which is part of her Airy nature) accept that the Goat needs to be shown that someone cares, then he may be able to communicate his feelings better. In the end the compromises will probably be hers alone. The Goat is rigid and unmovable, even though he admires her sense of purpose. This could be a very successful partnership, for a business-like marriage, but romantic love doesn't have much place here. They are not passionate by nature, her attitude to sex is detached and his is a basic instinct which he draws on as a reminder of power.

CAPRICORN WOMAN – AQUARIUS MAN

The relationship between an Aquarius and a Capricorn is better suited when the Goat is a woman. The Aquarian man will be quickly attracted to this rather shy, undemanding girl with the strength of a rock and the ability to support him in his wilder, more eccentric moments. If he would rather be building a computer in his garage, or riding a bicycle backwards, the Goat girl will be quite determined that he should succeed, as long as her own ambitions are rewarded. Goats live in reality, not in the abstract world of the Aquarian. But she can tolerate his need for non-conformity, as long as it doesn't threaten her own conventional way of life. The Aquarian rather admires the realism of the Goat, but he will be frustrated by her need for commitment, and promises of faithfulness. He can hardly promise himself what he's doing tomorrow, let alone commit himself to a woman for the rest of his life. He needs friends, lots of freedom and he needs to form new partnerships so that none is ever more special than any other. This humanitarian aspect may make the Goat lady shudder.

He will admire her practical common sense, and her quiet ambitions. She has calm and strength, and she is not excessive in anything. Both will enjoy sex together as they don't like to make a fuss about it, and they don't believe it to be the total meaning of their life. The Aquarian can be more variable about sex than she, but she has the understanding to accept his rather unpredictable behaviour when he goes off to spend the night with the chickens to see if they *really* go to sleep. She needs affirmation of her trust, but the Aquarian isn't awfully good at reliable words of love. But he can and he will attempt any challenge, and that includes the Goat he first saw at the top of that mountain.

CAPRICORN MAN – PISCES WOMAN

Lo and behold, the Mermaid has slipped into the room and quietly taken the Goat by surprise! She is enchanting, deep and lost in some ephemeral time warp. The more elusive she is, the more she will draw his attention. She slithered past him out by the front door as he cautiously checked his filofax for the next party on his list. Business and pleasure don't mix, he says easily, and when he smiles she knows she can slip perhaps a little further into his heart. Although the Fish is gregarious, she is actually quite introverted. Covering up her true feelings is not dissimilar to the introverted Goat's tendency to blot his out all together. With a bit of luck he will immediately sense in her a quite similar illusion, and it really is the only one: silence. His silence is not as golden as hers, though. She would rather trip off to dream land, but via the bank. She wastes money, plays with it and looks upon life as a game, a surface attraction that can be abandoned when she feels vulnerable to its reality. She hates male chauvinists and the Capricorn is the nearest thing to one when he's driven by the undercurrent of power that motivates his life. The Goat has to control and make sure that finances and practicalities are under his wing. Being with a spendthrift like a Mermaid is not going to make his life very easy. Her retreats and sensitivity will depress him and she will find there is little to lighten her mood when she is melancholic. He is funny, but only when it serves his purpose. He is not uncaring, but he is more interested in his own reputation, his own ambitions, and his own satisfaction. If a Fish girl wants to aid and abet him in life, then fine. But he won't tolerate her own struggle for success, and he won't put up with her flirtatious and gregarious lifestyle for long. Yet they both secretly envy one another: she his spartan detachment from love, his silent power, and he her dreamland ideals. They are both loners, but often two loners don't make it right.

CAPRICORN WOMAN – PISCES MAN

As the Piscean man cruises his way up the rungs of success in a profession that enhances his talent he often comes across a wealthy successful woman, an ambitious and uncompromising lady with her head firmly committed to power and glory and a lot of fame. Now Capricorn men are quite well known for their ability to sponge off successful women, to marry into money to achieve and gain advancement in their careers. Piscean men don't even think, let alone plot, along these lines, unless, of course, they happen to come across the Goat lady who is quick-stepping up the rocky path to the top, and is quite bedazzled by the talent and success in others. Her love of fame and fortune can be of benefit to the Piscean man. And the devious and often rather weak-willed side of the Fish may rise to make use of her expertise, direction and cash. The mercenary Goat will make use of his talent, his attractiveness to the world and his ideals. Even in other walks of life, these two can actually cash in on each other for their own advantage, but is there ever love involved in this rather cold and relentless partnership? She lacks romance and she lacks the thrill of the open road. He lacks commitment and would rather dream than go and sort out the neighbours' racket. The Goat can quite coldly accept that 'using' someone is just another relationship, not a particularly genuine reason, but it can improve her own trust. She really has to trust her own judgment, and she really has to believe that she can make it with this man to succeed.

The Piscean is often intuitive about character, and normally will make instant judgments. Finding a Goat lady who is resistant to his charm, unless he has something to offer her in return and thus make it a business arrangement, can be hard. She looks for romance at first, because it is so elusive in her own love. But when she looks more carefully and finds a man who will slip through her fingers, and cause her to feel she has lost control with every smile he makes at a passing fancy, it can turn her frigid overnight, unless, of course, he is the means to her own very determined ends.

CAPRICORN MAN – ARIES WOMAN

Unfortunately for the Goat man the Aries girl will only try so hard to get close to him and then, like the reactionary Fire sign she is, will give up trying just as she's within inches of his heart. He does have one, for all his apparent stuffy ways and the wheel-clamp of sacrifice to his business or his career. Finding a soul-mate is not particularly in his life baggage. He'd rather get to the top, stay manacled to a reserved existence or wait till he's older for the fun.

Aries girls like to have fun straight away, as soon as they can, sexually and emotionally. Capricorn men wait prudently and often become train-spotters or computer buffs in their youth to avoid having to face the games and chaos of love and sex. The Aries woman will turn his head, though. She has this knack of turning his Goaty fortitude into desire and, if she manages to catch the sort of Goat who is able to offer security, friendship and an easy sexual relationship, then he really can be almost, just almost, right for her. The trouble is he's not too hot on communication. That's why Goats are left on the top of their mountains with a trail of broken hearts down the hillside.

His inability to cope with her wild side might mean that they never reach one another. It's sad to see Pan rejected for his impassionate responses, but the Ram won't hang around for staid love. Those two words don't go together in her book, and she has neither the patience, nor the pride to hang around for a man who can't keep up with her zest for living.

CAPRICORN WOMAN – ARIES MAN

The logical incompatibility of these two is probably the only thing that will bring them together. A Capricorn girl prefers the stability of home or the solidity of her career and success. A settled existence either way, which means she really has little time for the antics of an Arien ego. But if she really should take a fancy to a red-hot Ram (he may be a colleague at work, or a long-standing friend who has recently returned to haunt her), she might take a trip out of her ordered existence. As long as she is acting within her own self-imposed restraint she may well allow herself to get involved with the ridiculous impulses of the Aries man.

She will find the impetuous and reckless lifestyle of this man contemptuous, and he won't exactly be nuts about her rather staid and cautious self-reliance. If she lets him into her heart then he might find a suppressed romantic trying to get out. But sexually she is likely to clam up with a man whose ego is bigger than her own. After all, he really is too irresponsible to remember the condoms, so what would it be like relying on him to sign the household cheques, or make financial decisions?

Her caution will always demoralise his love of spontaneity. Sexually he could awaken her latent passion, but she needs purpose of a different kind, a neater, perfected order in her life, not the fire and brimstone that can burn itself out when it reaches the top of the mountain, because that is where *she* is going first. An Aries wants to get there too, but he gets high on an awful lot of tangents that lead him off on adventures on the way.

CAPRICORN MAN – TAURUS WOMAN

The Goat man would rather like to consider himself a chauvinist at times. He believes that domination is an essential element of success and will provide him with self-approval in his private life. Finding a woman who can live up to his cartel of partnership values, rather than the sloshy sentiment of love and sexuality, is awfully hard. Usually Capricorn men find their best relationships are with other Earth signs, from them there is no threat to topple their male ego and power-driven motivations and they have much in common, practically and sexually.

A Taurus woman has very much the same Earthy drive as the Goat. They are both determined to succeed, both are usually financial wizards and both believe that caution and silence are better ways to success than impulse and passions. The one difference they must face is that the girl Bull is a sentimentalist and a sensualist, and the Goat is not. And she might require a lengthier love-affair, a more erotic sexual relationship than he prefers to offer. Basically he will play the robot lover with ease and his feelings, although somewhere lurking in his heart, won't be displayed very often, which most of the time is fine for the Bull woman, who would rather just get on with tactile fulfilment and not worry about emotion.

She will be more affectionate than him, which will suit this no-go area of his heart. But because he has put a curfew on warmth it might eventually turn her usual tenderness to coldness. He is not lacking in passion, but it's not subtle, Fiery sexuality, it can be cold and empty of love. If neither can communicate on this level then their sexual relationship will suffer, but they will have the strength of friendship and commitment and the security that they both need.

CAPRICORN WOMAN – TAURUS MAN

The ambitions of a Capricorn girl are usually grounded in her success in finding the perfect partner to reach the top of her particular emotionless mountain. The mountain may sometimes be a career, or other achievement, but if it involves a man, then he must be part of it too. The Bull man may appear to be the man she's been waiting for so cautiously. And her reservations about his suitability will, even to the normal pro-crastinating Bull, seem to take for ever to subside.

The Bull himself will be overpowered by her apparent sweetness, and charm, her quiet and cautious approach to life and love and, in a way, he will want to possess this Goat lady before he even has time to make up his own taciturn mind. Together they both have similar motives in life and in love, but the Bull will always have a more Earthy attitude to sex, which the Capricorn girl often finds rather barbaric. It's not that he's over-passionate. Sensuality is fine by her, in small doses, and the Taurean likes very large doses of every sensual experience possible, including sex. He gives and takes in equal proportions and seems as delighted with an Indian take-away as she does with the way she quietly expresses her enjoyment of sex. They are both practical and self-sufficient and, if they decide to form a permanent relationship, then the Capricorn girl is more likely to end the romantic side of their attachment more quickly, and turn it into a business and friendship arrangement. She can drop being in love, and turn it into a new agenda for partnership. She likes to be in control of any relationship, and a Taurean man is about the only man who doesn't mind too much what she does, because secretly he really likes her manacled devotion. She has no sentimental attachments but, underneath her rather cold detachment, she has a gentle refuge for the stampeding Bull. Silence can turn the Taurean man into the most considerate and no-nonsense lover: that is what she needs.

CAPRICORN MAN – GEMINI WOMAN

The newness of every experience, how it is, and how it works is how the adaptable Gemini girl responds to life. If she should meet a Capricorn man, which is usually not by chance but merely by introduction, or by working with him, then she will find his immediate response to her may appear to be love at first sight. Serious business, the ladder to success and a self-opinionated ego make this man appear incredibly chauvinist to a very male-minded woman like the Gemini. She will probably detest his strutting bigotry,when really he is only trying to convince her that flexibility is dangerous. The Goat is tethered to his own career stick, and finds love and sex a difficult motive for romping in the rain forests. He would rather end all that romantic trifling and get on with the real business, that is controlling her life, and controlling the relationship his way. Her changeable and unpredictable behaviour is a chaos he would like to order. As much as he appears to be in love, it is only his obsessive power-struggle to quash equivocation. And the Gemini girl represents exactly that.

Sexually they may be able to give each other a rather distant love, which they can both find rewarding. The Gemini girl hates emotion in bed, and Capricorn likes to make sure that sensuality is avoided. At a later date, when he's older and wiser, yet younger and spirited, released from his own self-denying chains, she may welcome his less pig-headed self and, as they both are capable of remaining friends, could find one another again, young at heart at a ripe old age.

CAPRICORN WOMAN – GEMINI MAN

When a Gemini man meets a Capricorn woman he will realise what it is like when an unstoppable force meets an immovable object. For the constant flit of the Gemini, a woman so quiet and solid, so inflexible and stable, seems like a positive millstone to avoid. There is calm in her heart, and practical common sense, and there is even power and ambition. The Goat lady will find the flippant ambiguity of the Gemini interesting to begin with but will, usually, with good common sense, retreat. She may find his smile and his charm irresistible, but she won't be conned for one minute. There might be a few sexual sparks flying but she is cold and so is he. The man who lives in the clouds may suit the cold romance of the Capricorn caution, but at the same time her need for an ambitious and reliable turn-on won't be forthcoming. A man who is succeeding, whether it is because of fanaticism or just good honest spunk, is more attractive as a partner than one who can fulfil her minor need for romantic love.

They will share the same need not to get too close physically, or emotionally, and thus, at times, this can be an harmonious relationship. She may find that he provides her with a chance to laugh and escape the inflexibility of her chosen lifestyle for a while. But the Gemini is unlikely to want a permanent fixture like a Goat on his own mental mountain, and she is quite incapable of accepting his woman-trotting escapades, and knight-errant insecurities.

CAPRICORN MAN – CANCER WOMAN

The secret desire of most Cancer girls is either ambitions for their career, or ambitions to find the man of their dreams. The driving force behind the Capricorn man's motivation is either a strong and equally ambitious woman, his powerful need to be on top, or that he can win consistently until he proves his place in the domination stakes. Both these opposite signs share the need to lead, but the Cancer girl is always ready to take on the support of an equal, as long as he doesn't dominate her. The Goat's hardiness, his ugliness, are actually quite appealing to the gentle Cancerian waters. She wants to build a solid home for him, to be there and support him, as long as she has her own way, and as long as he is also able to accept her own ambitions. The Crab won't be that keen on the way the Goat runs their relationship like a business association. His initial romantic inclination is well rehearsed, not the plot of an actor, but the speech of a politician. He is also a grim comedian, the taskmaster, the ordered man who will only allow chaos in his life if he is in control of it. When the rather loony Moon girl enters his domain, full of conflicting emotions, sensitive and inconstant whims, he will be put to the test. To order her might be to lose her.

Both these signs need stability in their life, and their sex life will be a permanent fixture. For once the Goat may well choose to experiment, he may not 'feel' with the same depth as the Crab, but he will always be there, aware, determined to be the one to rock her bed, fascinated by the power she can exert over his hard-edged sexuality. The Crab can melt the stern face of the Goat's father-figure ways, and the beautiful Moon girl will reflect only the bright light of success in his eyes.

CAPRICORN WOMAN – CANCER MAN

The simple fact of the matter is that most opposite signs of the zodiac have a great affinity for each other. It is something they can both sense, but are often not sure why, and least of all are able to communicate. Both the Cancer man and the Goat woman are the least likely of all the zodiac to communicate verbally anyway, which makes it doubly hard for them to verbalise their feelings and desires when they first meet.

They both need power within a relationship, and this can cause a sticky beginning. The Crab is motivated by his own lack of confidence and fear of rejection; he needs to enrol a tender leadership, a sideways attack, rather than full-frontal reckless-ness. The Goat lady appears on the surface a veritable kid glove, rather than a Goat, but beneath her calm and thoughtful exterior beats a hard and sometimes mercenary ambition to run every show on earth.

Her efficiency is what makes the Crab's heart flutter with desire. Here is a woman who loves stability, is quietly romantic when she chooses and doesn't have stinging arrows to throw at his emotional side. Well, not at the outset anyway. The problem is that the Goat lady will of course love the initial fling of any romance, she is charmingly feminine and will provide him with the reassurances he needs. He will also provide her with the solid rock and desire for success that he would like to believe he is capable of, and often dare not test out. Together they make a formidable pair, a good partnership, if they can rationalise the fact that the Cancer male will often have to play the mother figure, while the Goat girl takes the lead and ensures her climb to the top of the mountain. After the romance has faded they should still be able to satisfy each other sexually, although the Cancerian man is more likely to suffer from frigidity brought on by her apparent lack of interest. Her life is serious, and she takes sex seriously too. But she won't be pressured into false sentiment and unreal emotion. She will warm to the sexual thrill between them, and even the Crab will come out his shell. If he does the Goat may climb down from that mountain, just for a while.

CAPRICORN MAN – LEO WOMAN

The battle for dominance here might rage for weeks, even years, if it's given the chance. Meeting a Leo woman gives the Goat a big thrill. Here is someone quite outstanding. She is glamorous, sophisticated and full of an expression and lust for life which is far removed from his own lacklustre corner. But can she stand the dull pace of his controlled and ordered lifestyle? He may wonder quite frankly if her mouth is as big as her cheque book. Goats quite honestly are known to fritter away their wives' money, for their own ends, and to use glamorous, exciting women in their climb to fame or power. If she's sharp, which she may not initially be (it takes a while for the Leo enthusiasm to settle down in the first pangs of passion), she might notice that the over-nice and abnormally sensitive Capricorn is actually meeting her head-on in his own quiet taciturn way. He can dominate without appearing to which, for the Leo girl, is probably the best bet. She needs to feel that she is organising his life, and in charge of the relationship, and the Goat is fairly sensible and capable of appearing as if he is organised, when in fact his cool determination is the pulse behind the beat of their partnership.

The major problem they face is that she needs an extravagant and exciting lifestyle, to get out and about. He won't be too happy about her enthusiasm for other men, and her rather self-centred approach to love-making. He is wise to the world and grows cynical as he ages, and she grows ever more ingenious which means their power struggle will always be real, if they can face it.

CAPRICORN WOMAN – LEO MAN

The enthusiasm of the Leo man can get quite literally buried beneath the mound of dominating compost the Capricorn woman needs to pile into her relationships. As much as she is a quiet, gentle soul, her power is driven by real, practical forces and her ambition is paramount to her existence. It may take her a long time to like this man but they are linked by their need for being the top in everything. The only difference is Leo can do it nicely, warmly, and with a certain amount of humour; the Goat lady just gets on and impassively climbs. She doesn't get led astray by love, beauty or fun, and would rather wait until she's sure, absolutely dead-pan sure, that a man is worthy of her strength. To a Leo man this can quash his enthusiastic love-making with an impotence he had never believed, and occasionally it can turn to frigidity unless he finds the warmth and love he deserves.

They do have their moments, though, a few of them. Littered with a past that he would love to share with a woman, not to cajole nor to incite jealousy, but just because his method is part of his madness, he flows through a Goat woman's life and comes out the other end without touching down on her compost heap. If he does, he may have to face life at the bottom, and that, for a Leo man, is like being dead.

CAPRICORN MAN – VIRGO WOMAN

If a Goat has reached the top of his own special mountain, he might be glad of the respect and admiration that the Virgo girl can give him. He never actually gets too excited about anything apart from personal hard-lining. If this includes making a permanent fixture of the Virgo girl in his life, then he may find he has chosen the best course of action. The road to his success is littered with women who can be useful, carry him up the golden stairway, or leave him cold and bitter. He is a cynic, but the Virgo girl is equally able to understand he's had a few rough-and-tumble relationships before he met her. But she is convinced that he will find her the perfect, trusting and sensible partner. She won't necessarily want to be his prop, more like his companion. Both strong characters will find much stability in this well-balanced and sensible relationship. She needs to communicate in her own strident way, and he rather likes her fine and highly critical mind, it does enhance his mountain top. She will occasionally unnerve him with her hypercritical nit-picking over breakfast, or the necessity of getting to the train on time when he was actually planning a very important take-over bid for the next-door neighbour's building plot. She might have to be wary of his habit as he grows older actually to play the genial youth. The need for order and for control in his relationship might occasionally be undermined by her pig-headed affront at being treated that way. She is a feminine but strong woman, and he is a very powerful man who needs her.

CAPRICORN WOMAN – VIRGO MAN

This sensible pair is matched well for any partnership, but essentially it will be the partnership of a business-style arrangement rather than a love-affair. Both the Virgo Man and the Goat girl are after stability and firm foundations to build their mutual need for success. The Capricorn girl can often be more ambitious than her Virgo mate, and this could work very well to her advantage. She has no contest over who leads, and there will be sensible meetings between them, ready to face the boardroom and take the consequences of their actions. However, both of them are stubborn to varying degrees. She because Goats really are rigid and reserved in their opinions and won't budge if they are goaded. A Virgo will mentally attempt to budge as he enjoys mind-games, but he doesn't like to disagree, nor to argue. He likes to put things in their place and let them stay there, unless he feels they may be changed. The Goat girl will find him a bit chilly in the bedroom, but her own desire for privacy and her more important need for a dependable and reliable service (she may treat him rather like a bus timetable) are the needs in her life which outweigh basic sexuality and love. The Goat may tire of the rather purist tactics the Virgo man attributes to her success.

Neither is interested in emotion and they will find their rapport built on belief in commitment and sharing the good and pleasant things in life. As they grow older together, their bond will be usually unbreakable.

CAPRICORN MAN – LIBRA WOMAN

The great and overwhelming self-opinionated Goat is quite frankly the sort of man a Libran girl won't fall in love with easily. In fact, to begin with, she may quite genuinely detest him to begin with. Goat men have this absurd notion that if they dress up in their glad-rags, appear charming, fun and willing to let laughter enter their lives, and can keep a glamorous image on permanent hold, it will bring all the gentle-natured, quick-witted, funny women rushing to their sides. Actually Goats aren't good at deception, and they aren't capable of passing themselves off as a Fire sign or a charmer like one of the Air signs. The Libran girl, whose wits are as finely tuned as her brain cells, may be amused by the Goat's antics, but can see right through his deception. Down the pub he may appear as if he could have fun at parties, and enjoy the romance of making love in the woods, or in the attic, but somehow, for this pretend eccentricity, she can see quite clearly that he is restrained, grumpy, and a prig beneath that clever guise. Now, being unfair about a Goat is actually the only time a Libran girl will make a biased judgment. In fact, it's because he is so taciturn, so imposing, so powerful, that she actually would rather not get involved. He might just turn into Prince Charming and prove her wrong.

The Goat will, however, be enchanted by her smile and her charm. He desperately would like to escape into her romantic dreamland, but he has a slightly martyrish attitude about the lifestyle he has chosen, and being power-driven, and old from the day he was born, he can only carry through what he has set out to do. This kind of ambitious Goat may well strike a more interesting vocal chord for the Libran girl, but she needs fun in her life more than solidity. Sure, she would love to have a partnership, needs to have a permanent relationship and still maintain her social ramblings. This man will be very unlikely to allow her either. He wants his relationship to be like his business: ordered, prudent and winning. He lives with too much self-discipline for this girl to understand and, although he might try to let go of the rope that has tethered him, romance and floating dreams are not the answer.

CAPRICORN WOMAN – LIBRA MAN

There are some very notorious and difficult differences between these two signs that might make relationships between them more intriguing than any other pair. For a start, Libran men are gregarious mixers who actually like people and need harmony and peace and fun in their lives. The Goat lady is ambitious for herself, would rather not expose her private life to passing strangers and, as much as she is peace-loving, it will be because she is controlling it. She has the power to cause war if she wants.

Frightening as she can seem to the fairly laid-back and affable Libran, he might actually find that her cautious and taciturn personality has a few faulty chinks on which he might be able to improve. He likes to share his optimism, and also likes to prove he's irresistible to women. In the nicest possible way, of course, which is why he often falls in love with love first and then gets caught out in sticky affairs with women who really aren't his type. He never looks before he leaps, but the Capricorn girl always does. She is a Goat, remember, and through many travels up that rocky ledge to the top of the mountain she's learnt wisely what it's like to slip and fall down the precipice of love. But the Libran never learns, and never really wants to. Whatever life brings to him, even a quiet, dominating and power-mad woman, he believes he will be able shrug her off when, and if, he has to.

This unnerving faith in his own ability to fall in and out of love is one of his charms. And for the Goat the Libran's amicable detente is the kind of ground she can build her ambitions upon, without involving the usual annoyances that go with love. They could combine that positive energy, that force that both have and use so differently. The Goat will see this, but the Libran will probably abandon it. He would prefer to live in romance and the party spirit a bit longer. Sadly he can become involved and some-times used by the Goat, who will then decide she was justified in her belief that too much of a good thing is not all it's cracked up to be.

CAPRICORN MAN – SCORPIO WOMAN

The witty and amusing Goat may prop up the bar down the local pub, be the business whizz-kid in the office, driven by a wise power, but Goat men certainly have a problem when it comes to not being possessive. If anyone can get him out of his rather stuffy ways a Scorpio woman can. Not only has she the strength and determination to soften his rigid views, turn havoc inside his usually reserved emotions, but she can turn him on like a Goat at stud once they pass the initial power-struggle of who is going to run this relationship.

The Goat treats his affairs with women on the same level as his business affairs. They need to be organised, ordered and mostly subject to his demands. He secretly longs to be a more wild and egalitarian type and, although he reserves his humour and imagination for the ears of men rather than women, he can find that a Scorpio woman will see right through his shy, gruff mask into his quite genuine love of the pleasures of life. He will be intrigued, and that's not often, because Goats are usually unaffected by subterfuge, they have enough of their own to digest. Being a brave Goat, if he's one who has climbed to the top rather than resigned himself to a circle of self-restraint, he will fearlessly suggest that they might have something in common apart from the desire to win. The Goat is possessive, so is the Scorpio, but the Goat also seeks permanence and security and is in need of less personal freedom. It's not that the Snake woman wants to dash madly around the world picking up men like pebbles on a beach, but she is proud of her very private and personal self, that needs to be away from even a reserved Goat at times. It is her regenerative process which, unless allowed to work, can only retaliate into their relationship instead. They will be comfortable with each other in bed, as much as they are out of it. Her passion will instil a bit more imagination into his rather practical and sometimes alarming, rough sexual activities. This relationship grows with time and, once past the initial physical and sexual attraction, can turn into a solid partnership.

CAPRICORN WOMAN – SCORPIO MAN

Both these signs live a sinister life behind a backdrop of a rather more lively act. The Scorpio is particularly good at pulling down the curtain and pretending he is an extrovert and a lively chatterbox with an open heart. The Capricorn woman is actually very shy, and can also play the interested, willing listener, when actually she finds most events dull, and at their best, unnecessary. The Scorpio male immediately may drop his act to test out what it is this girl really wants. He is fascinated by everything under any surface: every stone will be turned and tossed until the problem is solved. The Capricorn girl, on the other hand, is neither curious nor interested in finding out the meaning of life, she just wants to get on with it. When he realises that she is also intensely power-mad like himself and that this woman can live up to his very high expectations, not try to investigate his private self, and still be a wilful and able partner, he might decide he's met the perfect woman. The Goat lady may be attracted to him physically at first. He is very self-willed, passionate and rather intense. And he has ambition. Although the Goat lady would prefer to be the controlling force in their relationship, she can realistically accept that she is the practical driving force, and he is the emotive and sexual one. If the Scorpio also excels in business and family matters, then she will be impressed. They are both furtive people, and sense the loneliness within each other. Her restrained love-making can become more expressive in his bed, and they will certainly feel like they belong in the same environment.

At first the Scorpio may find the Goat's rather stubborn and rigid lifestyle depressing. But the Snake is as fixed in his self-seclusion, as she is in her self-restriction. There may be a struggle for power of the mind, but the Goat will always leave the Scorpio's deeper psyche to himself, and he will always let her appear to win. He's good at that, because then he knows he really is in control!

CAPRICORN MAN – SAGITTARIUS WOMAN

The economics of any situation, whether it is to do with business or love, are what interests the Capricorn man. The first thing he may notice about the Archer girl is that she is uneconomical in the way she spends her money so quickly, and in the way she spreads herself around the world, in some vain attempt to bring ideals to every man. The Goat immediately would like to step in and organise her, order her life and in return (for there's always a return on a Goat's investment) take advantage of her very appealing and forthright charm. Capricorns are rigid and controlled, and Archers are not. The more discipline the Sagittarian girl feels around her the more she will attempt to escape, and so it goes on. The chances that she will pull herself together and accept the ambitious Goat's interest in her are very slim, unless she has spent too long on the road, and has finally given up her wild and changeable spirit.

The Sagittarian girl can see a lot of faults in the Goat and will probably quite bluntly let him know about them. Whether she can actually love this man is another matter. She is inconsistent, whereas the Goat will always want to know where she stands and where she is. If it's out of range, he won't be unduly jealous; he fears emotion and very rarely lets it creep up on him, but he will feel out of control and, when a Goat is not in charge, he can resort to stern measures to keep the status quo.

Being forced to do anything is against the Archer's natural habit of surprise. She won't mind giving him surprises, but not on demand. They are a very different pair, and that might be enough to send them into a brief ecstasy about each other for a while. Archers like the newness of love, and the romance of the first bites, and the Goat is always ready to try and make order out of anyone's chaos, especially if she's fast-moving, challenging and distinctly invigorating.

CAPRICORN WOMAN – SAGITTARIUS MAN

The truth of the matter is always what the Archer searches for, the ideals of life are always waiting to be sprung and, like the big bag of surprises he is, he wants to be the one to release the eject button on life. Because he meets so many characters the chances are that bumping into a Goat woman will be one of his more exciting adventures, but it may prove to be more than he bargained for. Goat ladies don't like casual acquaintances any more than casual relationships. And if the Capricorn girl thinks he's only interested in her to work off some Fiery energy, then she will give him the greatest run for his money he could ever imagine. Falling in love with her might seem the only route to forming a relationship with her and he is a connoisseur of falling in love, as he is at falling out of it. The resilient Goat will immediately pull over the cloak of calm poise and self-restraint to prevent any obvious challenge. He is all right, but he's a flirt, he's vain and he's a bit too cocksure. He has a boyish charm, and she can be quite easily flattered by his faith in her, but will she actually let him any closer than arm's length?

For the Sagittarian, it's not so much a question of getting any closer, its actually dragging her along for the ride. Archers don't need closeness in their frantic lives. He won't mind as long as she doesn't try and control him, order him about and generally throw mud on his Fire. He needs to feel free, and if she's clever enough and wise enough, which Goat girls usually are, especially as they grow older, she will be able to let him have as much distance and as much space between them as he wants. And she'll find, not with surprise, but with a smug satisfaction, that the Archer *does* want to come back. He needs a lot of affection, and trust, and a Capricorn girl can give it to him. She's learnt to be patient, to succeed. It's part of her reason for love. But she needs faithfulness and stability, and if she can hang on in and let him feel the power of freedom she could be assured of that faith.

Aquarius
COMPATIBILITIES

AQUARIUS MAN – AQUARIUS WOMAN

The individualistic spirit of two Aquarians together is often, to an outsider, an extremist relationship where both seem to lead separate lives and really have little to do with one another. Actually this is far from the truth. When they first meet, the Aquarians' natural inclination is to be platonic and close friends. There may be a hint of sexual desire, a knowing that they are so similar and that sex will probably be good between them. But that is not why they become involved, and it is the last reason why they actually stay in a permanent partnership.

They are both fascinated by life and the theories that they can make about it. The Aquarian girl may be less inventive, but she is just as cranky in her habits and often much pushier and more stubborn than the Aquarian male. They both think love is about friendship, and any romantic involvement always comes later rather than sooner. Essentially they are mistrustful and often cynical about romantic and sexual love. Both are so single-minded that they will often have their own exclusive circle of friends. Abstract Air signs are able to understand each other's need to live an extra-terrestrial form of life. They may be mentally in tune, and reasonable about each other's freedom, but what they often find troublesome is the unfortunate fact that both are extremely stubborn about their own weird habits. This can produce tension when she wants to eat breakfast at the kitchen able, and he insists on having his in the garden. The Aquarian girl will never be able to persuade him otherwise, and she is certainly not going to change her ways to suit anyone. They like trying to change others and, if they meet with resistance, they can turn very cold, which is why their relationship can often appear indifferent. But if they have established a firm friendship, and this they trust deeply because they both will have analysed it to the core before they even decided to become hitched, they are generally fixed enough to stick together like a pair of outlaws.

AQUARIUS MAN – PISCES WOMAN

The Fish out of water can sense the ideals of the Aquarian man before she realises that his detached attitude to life will always make him aloof and rather cold. A Pisces woman needs his type of strength and determination, but she can do without the analysis and the constant reminder that he is not interested in individual, only humanitarian love. She will agree. In fact the Fish people are also very much concerned with compassion and the welfare of others, over and above themselves and their true strength lies in their ability to rise like dolphins in moments of crisis. Pisces women, sensitive and sometimes gullible as they seem, are fighters for their ideals as much as their partners, and the Aquarian man could find that a Fish is better equipped at handling his detached and Airy dissidence better than most. She will have to learn to tolerate his temperamental attitude to problems, for he must always solve them, however insignificant they appear to anyone else. He's the first to investigate the reason why there are dog turds in their garden. She won't particularly care why and would be happier just shovelling them in the earth. But the know-it-all Aquarian will be down there with his magnifying glass, and possibly a few plastic bags, to perform an autopsy and check out which dog it was. Colour, breed, sex, you name it, the Aquarian will find out the answer.

The Aquarian's ability to play the forensic scientist is an irritation from which the Fish girl will wish to escape. Sexually he can't really give her the affection and indulgence she needs, and she is too ephemeral and emotional for his own peculiar taste.

It's not that she doesn't agree with his high ideals, nor that she loves change and non-conformity any less than he, but she really can't be bothered with inspection and analysis. Retreating is easier, and the Aquarian must accept that she may well disappear quite frequently for solitude or for being with her own circle of less ineffectual friends.

AQUARIUS WOMAN – PISCES MAN

The benevolent and quite sincerely compassionate Piscean man can find a lot in common with the independent and highly spirited Aquarian girl. For starters, they are both idealistic. He lives in dreams and she is attracted by the intangibilities of life. Theorising her problems, her ideas and her thoughts can become addictive with this very receptive and intuitive man. She will find that life never gets boring with him, because he is constantly shifting ideas, changing his attitudes and generally slipping around the ocean like a poetic flying Fish. They need their individual freedom. She will often have a very separate life from his and he often disappears into dream land to escape from reality. She will mind if he doesn't tell her (she does like to be informed about everything), but she realises that her own freedom is important too and will learn to respect his quieter one.

The mental affinity between them is what counts first. The Aquarian girl will probably have made friends with this man a long time before she actually embarks on a more romantic or sexual relationship with him. But Fish make friends easily, and he'll be easy-going about his emotions, letting them stay hidden in the darker caves of his mind and heart until he feels she is ready to accept them. He is not a particularly decisive person, but he is able to switch off from the truth if need be. He will not happily face conflict or emotional scenes. Aquarians aren't emotional types either, but they do flare up and get on their high horses if things aren't done how they think they should be done. Her stubbornness could be the reason the Fish gets uptight, and the Fish hates having his sea disturbed! He will quite rightly put his own case forward, however visionary and idealistic it is, and often, because the Aquarian feeds on such unconventional behaviour, she will begin to enjoy the Fish's more inconsistent and inconstant nature, by the very fact that he is such a non-conformist himself. Living with her awkward strain to be different won't be easy for a Fish, he needs peace and solitude, but he also needs someone just a bit crazy like himself.

AQUARIUS MAN – ARIES WOMAN

Aries women are number one in their own life, and also number one in every relationship. If she doesn't win the risks and the dice rolls of love that she's set her heart on, then she can storm out of a man's life quicker than she stormed into it. With an Aquarian man she is never quite sure if she is winning. He is capable of an almost devious game in which he will never let on who he is or what he really wants. This can infuriate the Aries girl, but only makes him a more challenging prospect. His friendship is important, his social life revolves with apparent unselfishness, and yet he is always holding something back. She can never be sure if it's love he feels or humanitarian compassion. The Aries girl wants to be the be-all of his life, but the Aquarian is more generous with his love and would rather share himself and his relationship with the world. This can make an Aries woman invariably jealous, and it can cause a strain whereby she never feels superior, and he really doesn't have the time to begin to care.

Sexually she will enjoy running the show to begin with but an Aquarian doesn't like being bossed around, as much as he doesn't want to be the boss. Eventually their bedtime fun will suffer when his aloof and sometimes cold passion deflates her vulnerable but beautiful ego.

AQUARIUS WOMAN – ARIES MAN

A brilliant but probably short-lived affair. The Aquarian girl will probably check out everything about this man before even allowing him near her front door, let alone her bed. He will be after a far more physical relationship than she is. But if the Aries man can accept friendship as the most important part of their relationship, they may stand a good chance. Aries men want adventure and excitement in bed, romance and the promise of passionate fulfilment. The Aquarian girl is more likely to be interested in his brain and he may not be quirky enough to amuse her for long. But Aquarian women must defy convention and maybe the sexual antics of this egotistic man will keep her fascinated longer than she imagined. Like most Air signs, her boredom level is reached more quickly than anyone else's and, if he can keep her mind active as well as her body, they will need little emotion in their relationship. Sexual activity is only part of the whole deal to an Aquarian, but to an Aries it represents his ego. She might want intimate conversation by the Thames at midnight, and an awful lot of respect. He might just want a night making love in a tent on a bare mountain. She is an anarchist, and sometimes Aries can be incredibly old-fashioned. This is where they differ deeply. Intellectually Aries men aren't quite on the same planet; it's almost as if they've been left on Mars when the Aquarian girl took off for Earth, and a better place. She might encourage him to think laterally, but her individual and odd habits will leave him cold.

AQUARIUS MAN – TAURUS WOMAN

The aloof and unresponsive Aquarian man has great trouble dealing with the warm responsive Taurean woman who has just touched his arm and offered to cook him dinner at his place one night. The distance this man puts between himself and a possible romantic involvement is further than Uranus from Earth, and this is where these two are far apart. He is Uranus, and she is the Earth: erotic, tactile, needing all the sensual and romantic notions to sharpen her determined and committed motives. Uranians can only be the awkward, straining, unconventional friend who really would rather study your books and work out your background than fall into bed and into love.

Earthy Taurus will want to put her hand round his as soon as she feels comfortable in his presence. But the trouble with Aquarians is that they really have no need for any physical contact. They live resolutely in their heads and no one is going to change their dippy behaviour, especially not such a warm and trusting woman as a Bull. Some Aquarians have been known to get quickly allergic to a girl's cat, just to avoid getting into a relationship. He needs to live alone with a million friends, and a million ideas to test. He wants considerable freedom in a relationship, and a lonely Aquarian is better than a restricted one. Permanency with a possessive woman will cramp his unpredictable and eccentric behaviour. He can find peace with a like-minded being, but the Taurean is too different, too real, and too much of a woman for him. If he falls in love with her it will be short-lived and relies on the fact only that she can tolerate his madness!

AQUARIUS WOMAN – TAURUS MAN

Aquarians are eccentric and radical, both intellectually and sexually. Taurus is conservative and basic in his own love life. The Airy woman isn't usually turned on by erotic and sensual sex, she also needs mental fantasy or intellectual excitement to appreciate the truth of tactile feeling. Aquarians are abstract lovers, and Taureans are direct, forthright and feel the sensual pleasures in life. The Aquarian woman will admire his straightforward motives but, unless she is also in one of her equally direct moods, she can turn him off more quickly than her personal convictions can. This can spill over into their bedtime routine like HP sauce. The Aquarian girl shares with the Taurean the ability to choose stubbornness for its own sake, and why should she clean up their domestic rows, when he makes no effort either? Pig-headed people get on well on the surface, but once they become pig-headed with each other there's a volatile relationship on the cards.

Taurus will seem incredibly selfish about sex to the rather colder and independent-minded Aquarian who is more interested in the invention of the wheel than the local cookery classes and washing the dishes. She won't be told when to go to bed any more than she will be told when to get up. The Bull won't be able to cope with her non-conformist sallies down the local pub either. She may be tempted to put him down publicly, her abstraction of his character may seem a simple test to her, but, for a Bull, it will not only outrage his dignity but also his manhood. He has to feel the dominant partner, and it could be very hard with this self-assured woman. Not a very good match as they are both too self-opinionated, and the Bull's pride is easily deflated by the Aquarian girl's lack of warmth or any genuine sexual response.

AQUARIUS MAN – GEMINI WOMAN

Both Air signs, but she is mutable, restless and changing; he is fixed and stubborn, wanting the world to change rather than him. Luckily for the Aquarian man, the Gemini woman rather likes flitting from job to job, or desire to desire. But unluckily for the Gemini girl, the Aquarian man, although mentally in tune with her, can seem dull and too regularly stuck in the mud. At first she will be amused by his strange advances: not like most men who instantly attempt to guide her towards the bedroom, but more like Frankenstein, who would love to create a monster out of her mind! The Aquarian actually finds her impossibly devious, and has a hard time picking her brain and, of course, the further he has to delve, the more likely he is to be sure that she will prove an intellectual equal and perhaps even be worth considering for a permanent relationship. Neither of them desires commitment. The Aquarian has a need for a rather oblique loneliness and independence. He has to have friends, or he'll die but, within that circle, however close, he will remain aloof and free-spirited. Tying herself to an Aquarian may be the funniest thing she's ever done. She will adore his sudden and weird behaviour, and he will get turned on by her spontaneous and Airy lightness about life, including him. She will at times take him too lightly, maybe frustrated by his commitment to emancipation but, ironically, this can often keep her sparked and interested. For her restless nature feeds on dissension as long as it is not of her own making.

Sexually they are fairly similar: emotion and sensuality aren't for them particularly necessary in bed. In fact they would both prefer to talk all night about the universe, set their deckchairs up on the lawn at midnight and watch the stars.

AQUARIUS WOMAN – GEMINI MAN

The nosy Gemini man will find a great deal of genuine, though not emotional sympathy from the equally inquisitive Aquarian girl. She will immediately want to dissect the bright, witty man she's found at the party, and he will at once be talking non-stop about everything, teasing her with words, playing a game of his own while at the same time checking out what she is all about. They both have the same easy attitude to life, although at times the Aquarian can be downright stubborn and downright awkward, if she chooses. Being awkward is not a Geminian trait. He will always want to express himself, and getting out of tricky situations is as much fun to him as getting into them. Getting into a nosegay of Aquarian eccentricity is better than good; not only will her unpredictability keep him on his toes, but her mentality can champion his own. But the Uranian girl will at times find the mood changes of this youthful rogue just as capricious as her own change in stance. She needs a friend first and a lover second. For a Gemini this is the perfect balance for his wide variety of free-range ideas. He has emotions that change with the wind and she has emotions that remain constant but cold. Together they can unlock each other from the fear of failure which they both possess about their sexuality.

AQUARIUS MAN – CANCER WOMAN

The more a Crab girl attempts to circumnavigate this cranky man with her ideals about home life, permanence and stability, about emotional input and sexual fulfilment, the more the Aquarian will run for his independence and resort to his full and varied circle of friends. If he met her, was fascinated by her ability to keep every secret back from him, he will be determined (for Aquarians are awfully stubborn) to find out everything he can before he can attempt to analyse forming a relationship with her. His rather aloof glamour will have attracted her initially; she can appear very aloof too. She loves his sense of fun and his rather strange behaviour which is always fighting against tradition. This is where his fixed attitude lies: not to change and rebel inwardly against the normal constraints of society, but to see society and those around him change with the world. He has the catharsis of others at heart, not his own. The Cancerian girl is very adaptable, she has to be because of that shifting Moon, but she is not fond of change. If the Aquarian man digs deep enough and finds her emotional responses too intense, he may expect her to give up her secrets and be as crazy about living as he. She is serious about everything; he is serious but only about his effect on abstraction. The Moon girl needs to take a position of control in their relationship, and he will certainly find this unacceptable. He not only needs freedom and a lot of choice in his friendships, but also he certainly won't be tied down to commitment.

Sex is something he's always enjoyed, as any other pleasure. He can over-analyse, and is not exactly filled with deep feelings, but he can provide the passion, for she instils in him a need to find out exactly what is going on in her heart, and in her head. Her secretiveness is her magnetism for this man, and he won't rest until he finds out what all this love and tenderness is about.

AQUARIUS WOMAN – CANCER MAN

The lunatic in the corner will not obviously show his intentions towards any girl. He is a flippant impressionist at times and, at others, the cynical blues player. These extremes of behaviour remind the Aquarian woman that she might like to quiz this man about his inner nature when she begins to suss him out, and she will become more fascinated by his antics when he poses no threat to her quirkiness. Aquarians believe everyone should be their friends, and the constant struggle to keep all their present and past relationships going is part of their stubborn need to be different. The Aquarian woman is nosy, not with the inquisitive curiosity of a Gemini, because she wants to bare the facts, the sordid

COMPATIBILITIES – AQUARIUS

details of life and then, if a man lives up to her analysis, he might find a place in her social calendar. Unpredictable as ever, she is most likely to instigate a meeting with a Crab. The independent spirit and genuine friendliness of this girl will make the Crab feel comfortable and at home (which is where he likes to be immediately). He may step out of that shell just for a while and agree to ridiculous and alien behaviour. To the Crab any behaviour which is unconventional has got to be attractive. He is often the most conventional and passive of signs when it comes to love, and this girl isn't. Sooner or later the Crab will begin to resent her blunt speech, and her inquiring mind. He has secrets that he desperately wants to admit to, even to himself. To be strung up like an intellectual and emotional corpse will make him retreat fast. Cancerians really like their love and their partner's love to be exclusive and Aquarians don't. The other problem is that Aquarian women aren't too bothered about sex. They like it, of course, but it has nothing to do with love. Love is between friends, good friends; being in love is about romance, and sex, – well, sex is somewhere in the middle. It's fun, and fun with a Crab is a matter of luck and the Moon. Of course, she might laugh at his conventional ideas, put him into a black mood of rejection and the termination of their relationship will seem inevitable. It usually is, unless they can appreciate each other's very different qualities.

AQUARIUS MAN – LEO WOMAN

The Aquarian man will immediately want to unravel the secrets of the Leo woman's character. She is so full of up-front insolence and so full of passion he can hardly believe why he is so attracted to her. The Lion lady will not be particularly surprised by his aloof interest in her. Most men are interested in Leo ladies, and she really can pick and choose most of the time. But this rather Bohemian man, resembling a mad scientist or an anarchist, is not so much fascinated by her image and her shining, regal appearance but by something actually inside her. He will analyse her quickly, more quickly than anyone he has ever met, and he will find it hard to resist the magnetic pull of her sexual attraction. Opposite signs are always attracted by the physical chemistry of the other sign immediately, and once an Aquarian man realises that this Leo lady is so different from him, he will want to know more, to test her out, see if she comes up to scratch.

Sexually, the Leo girl will find this man doubly attractive because he is so aloof. Cold men are a challenge, and she likes to prove her strength. But emotionally the Uranian man is an out-of-space man, and the chances that he will be able to fulfil her need for warmth, compliments and much admiration are slim. He may initially find this an amusing pastime, he does love his pastimes, but he will eventually tire of the game, as he tires of a worn out jumper, and revert to his social life. The Leo lady, whose pride is the mistletoe of her sexuality, can turn frigid very quickly, and look for a greater deal of comfort and warmth.

AQUARIUS WOMAN – LEO MAN

The girl who breaks all the rules will seem a prey of a delectable new species to be tasted by a Lion. Her unpredictable nature, her rather strange, analytical approach to life, are things that get the Lion's mane slightly ruffled when he first meets her. He is used to women who listen to him with very open ears and nods a lot, which makes him feel smug. Leos need to feel smug and this enhances his image of himself. This Aquarian girl won't ever make him feel smug, she's more likely to knock him over with her extraordinary, quite challenging rebellion. His Fiery emotions are vulnerable with this carefree and very independent spirit. She is not tamable, and he won't even dare try. She will find him quite vain, and wonder what he has got to feel so haughty about. His generosity will intrigue her and his enthusiasm for everything will actually provide the spark for her own inquisitive nature to burn. There is more to their emotional relationship than appears on the surface. The Aquarian stubbornness will resist any obvious signs of emotion, and the Leo will spend most of his time trying to impress her to avoid her ever really knowing how belittled he can feel in her company,

There will be times when her need to rise against the norms of society will infuriate him. Leos like to feel that they are above everybody, and that includes even a dissident Aquarian. Their sexual relationship can be passionate but often tainted by the Aquarian girl's coldness. Sex isn't a big thing for an Aquarian girl, but it is for a Leo. If he can understand that their friendship is more important than love, she can provide him with the sort of experiences in bed that are wildly entertaining, and certainly unconventional.

AQUARIUS MAN – VIRGO WOMAN

The first thing an Aquarius man must do is respect the fact that the Virgo girl he's become fascinated by is as independent as he is, but not interested in his friends. This may come as a shock to him, because he really dotes on his friends, more than he possibly would a dog. Why can't she just be another friend? Why does she insist on being someone special? Aquarians don't like to think anyone is more special in their life than themselves. Their friends, relatives, spouses, business partners share his equality rule. He will give pleasure to the world with the same amount of attention and will hope that those around him benefit from his ability to change them. The Virgo woman might not enjoy this at all. She can adapt to anything, with great ease, but she won't want to be changed for the sake of change. He will stubbornly exert his contrary opinions upon her most of the time, and she will attempt to remind herself that she saw in him a dreamer, a visionary who could make the world a better place. But he does keep trying so hard to be difficult and different. Turning a relationship upside down for the sake of it is the kind of tactic to alienate even a Virgo girl.

She is difficult to please, so there will be times when he will slump off with his friends and ignore any conflict. He can get angry with her nit-picking and the way she has to clean up his chaos. He likes a rather obscure orderliness, one that he has designed. He will choose the most austere furniture, or the most way-out central heating system, refuse to have animals around because he gets allergic to dust and hairs, and stubbornly believes she would be a better woman for his cranky habits. If she can resist criticising his friends and accept that she will never be the only woman in his unorthodox life, then he might just agree to try eating toast in the morning instead of a piece of lettuce.

AQUARIUS WOMAN – VIRGO MAN

The Virgo man is essentially a loner and the Aquarian girl is mostly everybody's friend. She needs people around as if they are part of her very being. However, the Virgo man who has taken a keen interest in her extraordinary and unpredictable behaviour might be able to understand her humanitarian and extrovert nature. Aquarian girls like analysing and subjecting people to bold and frank inquiry. It's interesting for her to see how they tick, and whether they get upset by her form of character analysis. Funnily enough, the Virgo man can get quite happy on criticism and analysis too, but on a fussier level. Mentally they have much in common, but their differences can cause friction and tensions which may never get them further than a first encounter.

Being an Air sign makes the Aquarian girl fairly immune to emotion and also fairly uninterested in sex. She insists on maintaining an awful lot of freedom in her relationships, mostly so that her rebellious and lawless attitude is never subjected to restraint. The Virgo will attempt to let her have free rein, but he won't enjoy the company of friends in the kitchen, on the telephone, or hanging round their flat at all hours of the night. He has his routine and he has his order. She has no routine, the less routine the better, and she loves her chaos.

This can make them become either inextricably fascinated with each other or separate them quickly. Sex is not something either finds at the core of their lives, so if friendship and partnership are handled carefully they may stick it out. Not an exciting romance, but the chance of a lasting partnership.

AQUARIUS MAN – LIBRA WOMAN

The tactless and rather eccentric behaviour of the Aquarian man will usually make the Libran girl smile quite charmingly and ask questions later. She is nosy and would like to know why he is so fanatical about being different, and why he has to have so many friends. She loves people too, but she loves love as well, and the Aquarian seems to be about the coldest man she has met. His aloof and rather glamorous appeal will often at first seem a challenge to this quite strong and mentally fair girl. She will quite calmly seduce him, with her usual easy-going and apparent harmless charm.

The Aquarian will be naturally suspicious, will put on a cold confrontation to protect himself from her undoubtable attraction, and may even show her how territorial he is, either by planning her life before he's even got her to the bedroom, or by getting her to the bedroom before he even knows her name.

This touching girl won't be touched for long by his law-unto-himself behaviour and this is where they can suffer most in what could be a rather challenging and exciting relationship. What's fair to an Aquarian is not necessarily fair to a Libran girl. Actually she likes fairness, but it's the surface fairness, the closeness of it to her own life and love. The Aquarian will make generalisations, wrongly or rightly, and the only fairness to him is that the world should be a better place and everyone in it should be treated fairly. The Libran girl hates conflict, hates ugliness in her own personal world, but the Aquarian would rather take on the whole of life and change it on behalf of change. He will love her loveliness, very much like his own idealistic truth. But she will find times when even their sexual compatibility, a rare thing for an Aquarian, will remind him that harmony is important in his own life, and the only way sometimes is perhaps to accept one person as more special than the rest.

AQUARIUS WOMAN – LIBRA MAN

The trouble with Air signs is that they need fresh mental inspiration for life's rather tousling affair with their jumbled heads. The Libran man could fall desperately in love with this rather mad and rebellious Air sign, and she could quite easily find that his fair and lovely charm will instil in her the right sort of Air that she needs to breathe. And the mental fencing that these two play in their relationship can be more fun than the Olympic Games. Libra is quite bossy when he wants to be and, once the initial infatuation has worn off, he might find he's tempted to goad the wilder side of the Aquarian girl's unpredictability into livening up the office party. She is incredibly stubborn and insists on being awkward just for the sake of it. She is more likely to have decided he was charming enough to be one of her friends to begin with rather than a lover. She is not usually the sort of female who goes around actively searching for a mate. The Aquarian female is in need of friends, friends and mostly friends! One day she will like the Libran's soft smile, and the next day she won't. She's not fickle like Gemini, she just wants to be different. The more unconventional and crazy she is, the more the Libran will be forced to admit he can't keep control. But he has to accept that the Uranus girl has to trust him first before she even thinks about letting him into her private life. If his romantic notions include sex (which is inevitable with a Libran), he might have to be prepared for some pretty cold nights warming up the bed alone, while she's out spreading the news about him and analysing his friends.

The Aquarian woman can be one of the most independent women of the zodiac. If the Libran man is forced to find solace in drink and women while she's trying to understand what happened to their friendship, he may come back to a lonely bed and a lonely heart. However cantankerous she appears, she won't tolerate infidelity, unless it's her own. He needs love and affection more than she does, and he needs to feel the solidarity of team spirit. She needs harmony in her life too, but it can be exhausting for a Libran man to have to be the Aquarian girl's friend rather than her lover: she can be too cold with his very special heart.

AQUARIUS MAN – SCORPIO WOMAN

The strong-willed and evasive nature of the Scorpio girl's emotional life is an instant hit with the Aquarian man. He is unconventional, eccentric, fascinated by the intellect, and prefers the company of disparate characters and oddballs to the normal beings that make up most of the population. (You may ask what star signs they are, and no doubt the whole of the 'normal' population is not necessarily made up only of the other eleven signs of the zodiac, but normal people can be Aquarians and not be aware of their eccentricities.)

Meanwhile, back down the romantic path, the Scorpio girl will have found a man who will seem as full of surprises as she is herself. She can hide behind a range of masks to suit her mood, but the Uranian man will have already analysed and poked deep enough to make his own judgments and theories, quickly concluded that she is vulnerable and tender, whether she cares to admit it or not. She usually won't.

If they get beyond the car door together he might have to remember that this woman needs sexual love with a big S. Being friends, and she is capable at having male platonic friends, is one thing, but if a relationship that involves love is ever to get off the ground, then she needs to feel that passion is in his loins as well as in his head full of ideas. Aquarians, being a bit intellectual, can give the impression that sex is very much in their loins. But they will play that game to suit whoever it is they are experimenting on at the time. Sometimes a Scorpio girl can get the wrong message from his body language, and yet know intuitively that his heart and loins are not involved. She is possessive. He wants to get out and meet as many weirdos, as many women, as many of anything, as he can. She likes her personal freedom too, but his contempt for society, and his need to change the world and leave himself out of it, can be a small hint that actually the Scorpio girl is no more special than the man on the bus, which is where she may leave without a word, and jump off, before he really gets to know her deepest secrets!

AQUARIUS WOMAN – SCORPIO MAN

The compelling antics of a Scorpio man in full attack and battle gear, ready to ride over any competitor and to win the object of his desire, can be daunting to the self-reliant and independent Aquarian girl. She might laugh at him initially, she does behave erratically and unpredictably, and then she may find him fascinating. How can anyone be so mysterious and yet so calculating about life? Scorpio by now will have already set his target high. The bigger the challenge, the longer it takes, the better. Yet he will be slightly confused by the Aquarian girl's very eccentric and determined sense of herself. It reminds him of his own personal integrity, but his is living life dangerously, it is being alive, and feeling every feeling intensely. The Aquarian's is about analysing life, changing it theoretically, and as awkwardly as she can. She may find him quite magnetic, a wonderful subject for dissection, mentally and even spiritually, and he, of course, will be thinking and feeling along very different lines, usually sexual ones.

It isn't that he wants to notch up another female spirit on his ouija board, but he does find the enigma of this very individual and proud woman a compelling challenge.

For all her inquisitions, the Aquarian girl only wants a sensible and intellectual equal, a companion who will be as willing to inspire change, to get on in life and look at it. Unfortunately, the possessive and emotional Scorpio will find it hard to bring out in her the depth of passion and strong sexual instinct that he lives for. She may seem cold when he is a living furnace of passion, she may seem contradictory when he wants to know where and who she is seeing. She needs friends, not lovers so much, and the Scorpio needs lovers rather than friends.

AQUARIUS MAN – SAGITTARIUS WOMAN

The inventions of the Uranian man are often better in his head than let out on unsuspecting females whom he, at times, uses as part of his experiments. He is a genius of eccentricity and unpredictability, but he is not awfully good at being the lover of most girls' dreams. Aquarians are mentally fascinating, and physically often aloof and glamorous, poised with a feral instinct. And yet the fumblings of the Aquarian man can sometimes seem as distant as his heart. To the Sagittarian girl this man seems ideal. She needs romance, yes, but she adores his brain, gets off on his distance, because it keeps away from her own, and is intrigued by his cranky ideas and rather blunt admission to knowing that life is what you make it. He has ideals, and so does she, but he breaks rules and makes rules and puts up with her ridiculous forays into freedom. For this reason she may seriously consider forming a romantic attachment to him, but the problem arises when she finds that the Aquarian prefers to keep friends as friends, rather than engage in any special and distracting love-affair.

If the Aquarian man realises that this is the sort of woman who can put up with his mad-professor behaviour and his stubborn need to change those around him, he may slip into the relationship for its originality. She seems able to accept that he wants no ties, and also that he can't consider her more special than anyone else. She's also headstrong, open and honest, and has the guts to go where she wants to go and not to ask permission. Finally she may find his coldness doesn't always turn the pillow to ice. He may live on a different planet, but he is inventive in bed, and he does do some quite ridiculous things to make her laugh. Could be an ideal relationship if she has the patience to get past the lengthy friendship stage!

AQUARIUS WOMAN – SAGITTARIUS MAN

The honesty between these two is probably what first draws them together into a comfortable but spirited rapport. The Archer needs an 'honest injun' in his life, and he also needs to feel that she, like him, is free, independent and not likely to crack up emotionally at the change of the wind. An Aquarian girl provides a mental accessory to the normal high octaves of the Sagittarian train of thought. He will change subjects within seconds, and she will give him the fuel and fire to deal with it. She loves talking about every subject under the sun, and they both share the same need to have friends and oddballs in their life first, and lovers second. Who needs lovers when you can have friends? The Archer is probably more romantic at the beginning of any relationship with an Aquarian girl, and probably more willing to express his real feelings, but the Aquarian girl is also in need of an idealist, and one who has the sense and courage to spread that idealism. She isn't possessive, but Aquarians, like Sagittarians, are some-times jealous. She can be stubborn about doing things her way. But because he has no need to be dominated, nor to dominate, he can accept her as an equal. When she sets her mind to some crazy scheme and becomes coolly distant, he is able to shrug it off with his usual adaptable carelessness. He avoids conflict with her, and that is the answer to their success. Passion runs deep through the Archer's sexuality, and at times she may seem too light and Airy, too interested in reading the next section of her book, when he would rather be looning around the bedroom. But both want similar amounts of freedom: the Aquarian for her friends, and he for his ideals. Both are optimistic about life and the future, and this can be a highly successful and mutually beneficial relationship.

AQUARIUS MAN – CAPRICORN WOMAN

The relationship between an Aquarius and a Capricorn is better suited when the Goat is a woman. The Aquarian man will be quickly attracted to this rather shy, undemanding girl with the strength of a rock and the ability to support him in his wilder, eccentric moments. If he would rather be building a computer in his garage, or riding a bicycle backwards, the Goat girl will be quite determined that he should succeed, as long as her own ambitions are rewarded. Goats live in reality, not in the abstract world of the Aquarian. But she can tolerate his need for non-conformity, as long as it doesn't threaten her own conventional way of life. The Aquarian rather admires the realism of the Goat, but he will be frustrated by her need for commitment, and promises of faithfulness. He can hardly promise himself what he's doing tomorrow, let alone commit himself to a woman for the rest of his life. He needs friends, lots of freedom and he needs to form new partnerships so that none is ever more special than any other. This humanitarian aspect may make the Goat lady shudder.

He will admire her practical common sense, and her quiet ambitions. She has calm and strength, and she is not excessive in anything. Both will enjoy sex together as they don't like to make a fuss about it, and they don't believe it to be the total meaning of their life. The Aquarian can be more variable about sex than she, but she has the understanding to accept his rather unpredictable behaviour when he goes off to spend the night with the chickens to see if they *really* go to sleep. She needs affirmation of her trust, but the Aquarian isn't awfully good at reliable words of love. But he can and he will attempt any challenge, and that includes the Goat he first saw at the top of that mountain.

AQUARIUS WOMAN – CAPRICORN MAN

These two are like the washers on a tap that's started to leak: one fits perfectly and never goes wrong, usually the cold tap, the other constantly needs mending, drips as soon as you change it, and then suddenly breaks, and it's hot. The first washer is the Capricorn man, and the second is the Aquarian girl who, although a cold and aloof star sign, can also get very heated about the injustices of life. Capricorn man will be reasonable about life, as long as he's in charge, and as long as it stays down-to-earth and tangible. The Aquarian girl will prefer the theory, the abstract qualities that make life work, and why we wonder why. This will seem nonsense to the taciturn Goat who will find her individuality too far removed from reality. He neither cares about why the universe began nor if there is a God, as long as it all works, and he's succeeding in where he wants to go. What is the point of skidding around trying to upset the balance, or telling the world it's going to end? The Uranian girl is not conservative-minded, she rebels for the sake of rebellion, and will incite total anarchy against the Goat and his conventional ways. One possible chance for this strange relationship is that they both have a very strong sense of integrity. If she can reasonably (which is part of her Airy nature) accept that the Goat needs to be shown that someone cares, then he may be able to communicate his feelings better. In the end the compromises will probably be hers alone. The Goat is rigid and unmovable, even though he admires her sense of purpose. This could be a very successful partnership, for a business-like marriage, but romantic love doesn't have much place here. They are not passionate by nature, her attitude to sex is detached and his is a basic instinct which he draws on as a reminder of power.

Pisces
COMPATIBILITIES

PISCES MAN – PISCES WOMAN

The very unreliability and driftwood mentality of the Fish is what attracts another Fish to his mirror image. They are both gentle, solitary yet gregarious creatures who live in a haze of life, the mist on the shore, or the frost on the trees, never actually there. When they first meet, intuitively, and with great insight, they sense the dependence they have on each other. Pisceans can get awfully dependent on a lot of things that aren't good for them, like alcohol and drugs. As strong as they are in moments of crisis, their weakness is their ability to be led astray by things that appeal to them and help them escape the harshness of truth. Ironically, too much of a good thing can bring them back to that reality quicker than it led them away from it. Meeting another, easy-going, dithery Fish, who doesn't struggle against what is, just goes with it and lets it be, is an enormous shot in the arm of relief. Here is someone who won't try and rush through life, won't expect her to get up in the morning at the crack of dawn, and she won't expect him necessarily to give up his creative talent to hold down a steady job.

Yet although they perceive the relationship as an ideal it is possible that both will rely too much on the other for emotional support. The one thing a Piscean doesn't enjoy is emotional conflict. It makes her insecure and it makes him begin to feel niggling doubts about whether clinging to a woman who is as shifty about life as he is claustrophobic in an out-of-order lift.

Romance may have played the sea shanties to begin with, and there is always poetry and romance in any relationship between these two but, once they have actually sunk into the reality of the partnership, there is a strong chance that sex becomes a pure escape for both of them, neither knowing what the other is wanting. Often one will hold on to the dream that brought them together rather than the actuality. Sexually, they can find a physical release from the cruel world and, maybe, if they learn to communicate more, their indulgent relationship won't suffer the draw of freedom that can often lead them away to other shores.

PISCES MAN – ARIES WOMAN

The Fire and spirit of the Aries girl will find it hard to be enflamed by the sensitive and instinctive behaviour of the gentle Piscean man. She is independent, forceful, bossy and essentially in need of strength and a big-brother-type to support her and to carry her pain and her vulnerability. The Piscean man is quite able to be all these things to her, but he can irritate her beyond her wildest dreams when he disappears into a dream world. When he takes for ever to get up and out in the morning, when he would rather be playing the piano, or working out why the universe is, she would rather be running across the beach or throwing snowballs at the postman. Aries will find his gregarious nature attractive and this is often how they will meet. Sexually he can stir the kind of emotion and feeling in her that she needs, but her impatience and impulsive nature will want him to be a little more passionate and wild in bed. He finds her upfront and dare-devil approach to life more of a threat to his tranquility than fun, and a Piscean would always rather retreat than face conflicts head on. Fish can be weak-willed in the face of arguments and an Aries girl is tempting fate if she tries to rile him with words just to stir his drifting emotions. Aries are usually frustrated with the Fish's tendency to escape every time she gets excited about life. He is likely to leave for peace and a cool lake. The Fish man doesn't take kindly to earthquakes.

PISCES WOMAN – ARIES MAN

This relationship appears to travel the same route as the doom-laden affair from which Romeo and Juliet and other literary lovers never recovered. These two are so opposite in temperament, in their motivations and characteristics, that it seems unlikely that they should ever meet, let alone stick together. But strangely this can be a pure and perfect sexual relationship at its best. At its worst the Pisces girl is too emotional and can turn the Aries optimism into a coffin of depression.

The shunting pace, and the rushing lifestyle of the Aries man can be a times too demanding for the gentle Pisces girl. If she can be tolerant of his self-seeking and selfish aims, which a Piscean girl often can, then she will have found the strength and honesty that she yearns for in her dreams. He might not be burning the midnight candle for her every night, his self-centred need to explore the world may lead him further away more often then she might wish. However, he will expect her to be there for him while he's off up the Amazon, or touring Africa in a jeep. It's not necessarily that he doesn't care, it's just that he doesn't think. The doer of the zodiac will be infatuated immediately with the deep stirrings the Piscean woman can make in his heart. In a long term relationship she could become escapist if he spends too much time out and about, and he could get incredibly bored with her passive and changeable emotions. He could also get jealous of her ability to listen to every soul's problem with the deepest compassion and sympathy, but often won't listen to his own. Joan of Arc martyrdom can cause him to get angry and lose his temper with her, especially if the Fish girl has purposely gone cold on him and herself. He is vivacious and fun and likes male and female company. She is compassionate and gregarious and loves men. And an Aries inflamed by fear and jealousy can toss his love on his own funeral fire, and lose a woman who could truly love him.

PISCES MAN – TAURUS WOMAN

The Fish man doesn't go looking for trouble and would rather live in his world of dreams locked away from the rat-race and hurly-burly of real life. When he meets the quiet, dependable Taurean girl he will instinctively and intuitively know that she shares the same love of peace and tranquility, even though she is tough and determined to succeed. The Taurus woman loves romance, and the Piscean man will fulfil her romantic notions of candlelit dinners, music (she adores music and Pisceans are often very gifted musically) and journeys into faraway lands. She can be a bit too possessive, for the average Piscean needs to escape for a while, even from such a tender woman, and the other quicksand they may fall into is the tendency to be led astray by each other's moods, rather than to lighten the other's darkness with some Airy or Fiery light. There's something almost sombre and shadowy about a Taurus woman and her Piscean. As if down there in the ocean, in the deepest part where the sun never shines, the Bull drowned and never quite recovered her usual charisma.

Sexually they are both sensuous and romantic. They can get lost in his world of fantasy and hers of too much flesh as opposed to feeling. But she will never try to dominate his gentleness, and he's unlikely ever to want to turn into a coldwater Fish with this girl around. He's stronger than she knows, and she is deeper than he believes.

PISCES WOMAN – TAURUS MAN

There is an instinctive rapport between these two oddly matching Sun signs. The Piscean girl will immediately feel comfortable and at ease in the basic sensual company of the Bull. She knows that she can wash his socks and he won't get het up about that word 'commitment'. He likes it deeply, and she needs it unfathomably. Mentally they are worlds apart: she lives in an ethereal romantic existence, preferring dreams to reality; he is down-to-earth and can be coarse and ungracious, but somehow his strength is what she needs, and her weakness is what he finds

attractive and fragile, and in need of protection. His possessiveness can irritate her rather fly-by-night temperament, and she is
also a million times more gregarious than he is. But he can
accept her desire to escape more easily than with any other girl.
Although he doesn't quite understand how she soaks up the
world's problems and every feeling in it, intuitively he provides
the right tenderness when the Pisces woman reminds him how
unthinking and stubborn he can be. She does it with a seductive
and child-like vulnerability and, of course, there he is, to protect
and, perhaps clumsily, to prop her up. Both of these signs are
very self-indulgent and she can drink him under the table if
love is in her eyes. So much ephemeral and misty dreaming
about sex and love will probably rouse the Bull from the dinner-
table more quickly than he is used to. Maybe, after all, love is a
more sensual turn-on than food, just this once.

PISCES MAN – GEMINI WOMAN

When the Fish first catches a glimpse of the Gemini girl above the
murky water she may be shimmering on the surface like a maggot
on a line waiting to catch him. She is fascinated by talent, by
beauty and by that elusive quality that, although part of her own
make-up, can seem doubly attractive in someone else. To begin
with, Fish and Gemini girls communicate well and both are adept
at socialising, although the Piscean man actually finds it quite
exhausting. The Gemini girl has more energy to invest than the
Fish because then life will always be changing, always be moving
on. The Fish will be infatuated by her energy, her wit and her
little-girl appeal. He is gentle and undemanding, and Gemini
women don't like bossy, dominant, or chauvinist men. She is
attracted by surface characteristics, by the way he might play the
piano, or the way his hair falls across his ears. And the Pisces man
has always some mystique which will make her instantly infatuated. In bed the Gemini woman isn't as sensual as the Piscean
man would like. She can be romantic when it suits her, passionate
if she thinks it's time to play the role of a Leo, and downright
bored with sex on the next occasion. This can puzzle the gentle,

loving Piscean soul and at times her lack of feeling can hurt him. The Piscean will always want to dream, to escape from any truth or reality, he is the undercurrent of the ocean, and she is the surface of the same sea. They will frustrate each other because of this. She can get quite annoyed by the way he takes all morning before he's finished shaving, when she is already out walking the dog within minutes of showering. They have many differences, but they have similar attitudes to life. The Gemini woman needs a man who can understand her search for herself, and the Fish man is probably the only one apart from another Gemini who can.

PISCES WOMAN – GEMINI MAN

The ups and downs of the Gemini man's changeable and restless nature can cause a few eddies in the quiet and passive pool of the Pisces girl's heart. He never seems to sit still, and is always on the go, when she would rather slide into a dream or a good book than be organised into another outing, or another party. It's not that she doesn't socialise, far from it, she is as gregarious as the Gemini, which is probably how they met. He will play the little boy lost and she will play the wistful, beautiful dreamy woman that a Gemini man really can't resist. To begin with, her rather dreamy existence may fascinate him, because it seems so unlike his own rather factual approach to life. And then there are the dozen ways she can seem so compassionate and caring; emotions and feelings well up inside of her and she is quite charming. But, after a while, the Gemini man may find it all rather frustrating, because she never seems to get anywhere for all her psychic awareness. The Piscean girl could also soon tire of the gossiping and the witty remarks, the dusting of life that he wipes across every comment she makes.

Sexually, Water and Air signs can often find much in common. When the Piscean girl first climbs into bed with the teasing, lighthearted Gemini man she may begin to feel as though she is alive. The human side of her Mermaid existence won't be floundering for long and the Gemini man might conclude that perhaps feelings and intuitive love are not so bad after all. They both believe in personal freedom, and neither will be possessive. But she can be too slow, too laid-back and dreamy, when he would rather be solving another fascinating riddle, or rushing off on another trip, just for the sake of change.

PISCES MAN – CANCER WOMAN

If the Pisces man surfaces for one moment he might glimpse across the ocean a strange Moon. One that rises quite slowly over the horizon. It isn't Full, it's a new Moon, glinting soft light on the darkness of the black sea. When a Pisces man first meets a Crab girl he will find her own shimmering and spooky light an encompassing magnet. He will intuitively know that she will fulfil all his dreams. Reality is something to escape from and with this woman he can both escape and find a true and delightful relationship. She will be a little possessive, but he shines in the attention, and the need to drift like the tides of his Moon. He is restless and changeable, for he is a dual sign, and she is adaptable and driven by the moods of her loony tunes. He admires her ability to save money, and regulate life so that she is secure and comfortable, while he is actually hopeless with finances, and can get frustrated by her need always to keep an eye on every penny. But he trusts her judgment. He would rather let her lead than any other woman.

Their romance will be long-lived. Both escapists, both dreamers, although she can wail buckets of self-pity, the Fish will prefer to retreat into the water and avoid confrontation. He hates scenes, hates emotional conflict, and if she does drop into one of her more forbidding moods he will escape to the bath tub, or go for a long walk, or play music until he's sure she'll come back out of her shell. But he is equally vulnerable to his own mood changes; it's not so much that he broods, or breeds resentment, for a Piscean is incapable of bitterness, but he will turn silent. He prefers his own company and turns often to solitude as his true companion.

PISCES WOMAN - CANCER MAN

The perception of a Fish woman is dazzling, it's almost like the sensitivity of the Cancerian man. Both are immediately attracted to one another and will flow into each other's hearts before they have even had time to think. Mind you, neither of these two does much thinking, they live in their emotions and their intuitions. The Fish girl will feel secure and comfortable in the Crab's company. He may have his swings of mood, from depressive to manic, but if anyone can understand and tolerate them, a Mermaid can. Her insight can be a shock even to herself and, even though the Crab won't want anyone to penetrate his inner self, he won't be able to resist the Fish lady and her innocent sense of knowing him, without even asking!

The Crab will love her sometimes helpless child-like appeal, and her gregarious charm. The quiet way she can let him feel in charge is actually rather soothing to both of them, because she needs his strength, although sometimes she could do without his weaker, more depressive moments. She can soak up his emotions so easily that she can turn into a rather melancholic dreamer with him, but she lives for the moment, and does not indulge herself as much as most people would imagine.

The Crabby claws may cling a little too much at times for this very independent girl, but she loves to be needed, and her compassionate nature will hold him close to her, if he feels alone and unwanted. They both live in their hearts, and they are both quietly private together. Sexually they can find much inspiration in each other, although the Crab may feel the Fish is sometimes too far away and too lost in her world of dreams. But then the Crab never really believes enough in anyone. His suspicious soul is an eternal battle within himself.

PISCES MAN - LEO WOMAN

The vague and rather elusive quality of the Pisces man can set the seeds of being in love in the Leo woman very quickly. The Fish will generate in her heart pangs of affection for the rather lost and forlorn act that she doesn't often come across. The Leo lady is dominant and haughty, and also rather loud about herself, which can initially make the Pisces man hesitate about getting involved with such an arrogant girl. His feelings may churn and send him back down his whirlpool of retreat unless, of course, the Leo softens, becomes the tragic figure and for a moment listens. Intuitively they should get on as friends first, and then maybe she will begin to be less overpowering. Somehow he knows that her inner nature is fraught with fears similar to his own. He will not have a power struggle with her, because he doesn't feel any need for anyone to be in charge. If she can let him escape from her cat-like claws occasionally she will find that he is more likely to hang around longer. He needs solitude, a lazy languid trip through life's impossible waters. She will need company, lots of company and a Force Ten gale to keep her on a trip of dramas. She would prefer life to be like the *Complete Works of Shakespeare*, and he would like it be a slowboat down a muddy river, time to dream, time to write those words instead of play them.

At first he may seem the ideal lover, always feeling and intuitively knowing what she needs. But he is too ephemeral, too intangible for her feral passion, and the more demanding she is, the more likely he will return to his slowboat and find himself alone.

PISCES WOMAN - LEO MAN

When you're a burning inferno of passion, sunlight and romantic combustion like a Lion, to find a woman who is romantic, dreamy and feminine can turn your whiskers up and make you sharpen your claws on the nearest sofa. The Leo's enthusiasm for love and a warm, eternal relationship can be easily highlighted by the soft gentle rhythms of this sea lady. He is also rather fond of the way she's not pushy, not bossy and listens to him as if she really means it. As if she might actually believe in him, and that his words are of value. Dramatic Cats enjoy the initial romance of any relationship. It means they can play the lead role without anyone knowing about their vulnerability. It's only later in a relationship that any wise woman will begin to sense the Cat needs a good deal of stroking. But the Piscean girl will immediately feel this when she first meets the Pussy Cat. She will find him at once delightful, for although she is of water, drifting through life with misty eyes in search of an ideal, here is an equally idealistic man but one who is fired by ambition, and is full of genuine altruism.

The Leo will always fear, however, that the rather placid and laid-back Fish will drown him in his own sense of rejection. She may reject him, however, if he becomes too vain or arrogant, too loud and over-protective. For this is when she will need to return to the depths of the sea to escape the onslaught of the sometimes over-bombastic lectures of the flashy Leo. The passion of the Lion might also wash over her rather faraway and distant love-making. She needs mystical love, spiritual awareness between two souls, and the Leo needs human flesh, to feel the blood pounding in his loins and real affection in his partner's arms. Unfortunately the Fish girl can turn from this over-dramatised man to seek a deeper freedom.

PISCES MAN – VIRGO WOMAN

For a while, when he comes dripping out of the ocean in search of romance on solid ground, the Fish will realise that there are very few true and pure women, very few ideals are really ever better than the ones you can dream. But as he slithers on to the shoreline of the Virgo girl's quite sharp and bright-eyed affection, he will begin to wonder if, maybe, dreams can be made on dry land.

He will be wary of her rather private, solitary way of life. His own is friendly and humane and, although he is renowned for his disappearances into lonely woods and solitary sea-shores, he actually needs people very much. There will be arguments between Virgo and her Fish because the Piscean is basically a ditherer, always vague and not quite ready to make a definite commitment, either verbally or emotionally. Virgo on the other hand wants to know the truth, and will pull him to pieces with her caustic mouth, if he messes around too long. But she faces another nagging problem. She really hates spending money, and he loves spending it. When she realises that his extravagance can lead him to be addictive in many of the more escapist pleasures of life, she will try desperately to stop him. But the Fish can turn cold and unresponsive if anyone throws too many demands on his sensitive scales.

She can be the seductress in his bed, and the restrictive force in his life. He will enjoy her romantic side but will have to tolerate the restraints she imposes on his natural freedom. And Fish are better at tolerating than Virgos. She will need his gentle sexuality, his dreamy, always mystical and faraway love-making. They may be mutually fulfilled if they learn to see in one another what is lacking within themselves.

PISCES WOMAN – VIRGO MAN

The Fish girl is by nature sensitive, sweet and gentle, but she also has a certain Watery deviousness which often pops to the surface like the bubbles from her Fishy gills. The times that these slippery and spicier facets of this girl arise is usually when she's met a Virgo man. Virgo men have this uncanny ability either to bring out the worst in a girl (usually if she's one of the Water signs) or the best (another Earth). Of course, what happens to the Air and Fire signs is up to them! The Piscean girl meeting the rather mean and uncompromising Virgo with a wad of cash and no one to spend it on, can become masochistically infatuated by his very tight personality. The Virgo hangs out his role of perfect lover like a Daz advert exposes the whiteness that it claims is unique to Daz. But the Fish can see right through this charade. Beneath that perfect gentleman act is a man who is an idealist and one who is in love with purity. He will immediately believe she is the purest form of woman. Not only is she a dreamer, wistful and difficult to catch, she is not interested in his robotic seduction. He hasn't, of course, the intuition or sixth sense that she has to realise she is being the rather slippery character that Mermaids often are.

When he finally beavers in to claim her, to seduce her with words which have a finer chance of working than just male lust, he might just find that their sexual encounter will bring the true purity that he needs, and the idealistic love that she always feels is wanting. He may find her gregarious nature clashes with his rather lonely one, but she feels deeply, and will usually come back to listen to him with an open heart.

PISCES MAN – LIBRA WOMAN

Firmness, tact and reality are not easy for the Piscean man to attempt with much success in his life. If a Libran woman should dance past his eyes while he is in one of his escapist moments, he will be as easily deceived by her as by most beautiful things in his life. He has vision, and his intuition is so natural that he rarely realises that he uses it. But if a flirtatious, gregarious girl should flit through the waves and give that enigmatic smile, he can be swept into the tide of love without a moment's reflection, with no rational thought as to whether this could be a wise move.

Surprisingly they have a good chance of a firm, romantic and quite lengthy sexual relationship. But she is logical, cool and poised, not ready for emotional depth, and would prefer to fly through life rather than swim through it. He will drift quite happily beside her while the going is good, but if her compassion and her common sense take over, if the practicalities of their relationship begin to outweigh the dreamy quality that they first discovered, then he will have trouble adapting himself to rational discussions such as who should be earning the money and how it should be spent. If the Libran woman handles this alone, and she is very adept at doing so, then the Fish can carry on drifting with romance and unreality. She is more likely to be out earning the pennies while he still lies in the bath, but she will find his similar laid-back lethargy easy to live with. However hard a Libran works, she makes sure she has time for his languid moments and her own. The Fish will be attracted to her spiritually first, and she physically to him. Yet they will be able to ensure a passionate and affectionate sexual harmony which can hold them together better than any commitment they may both be uncertain of making.

PISCES WOMAN – LIBRA MAN

The Pisces girl is invariably drawn to men who are either independent and spirited, to complement their own self-expressive style, or to those who are gregarious, idealistic and possibly more dithery than she is. The Libran man is all these things, and very often they will be drawn to one another by an intense physical attraction. The Libran's ideal of beauty will often materialise in the seductive and sympathetic Fish, a catalyst of visions. She soothes, he entices, and together they can make an harmonious and sensitive partnership. Their problems arise because her perceptiveness and the way she takes on every trouble of the world, can, to the Libran, be impartial and not really fair at all. He believes that everyone's opinion is valid, that to take sides, or to be judgmental has little to do with pacification. The Pisces woman often comforts those in the middle of disastrous love-affairs and the Libran man often interrupts to speak up for the defence. He will defend the Fish to the hilt if she is fair and not judgmental, but being able to bend in both directions of any argument could upset their own balance.

Their very different approach to living can end the initial and physical attraction very quickly. But they do share the need to escape. The Libran man can lead the Fish astray into party land, night clubbing and general hedonistic delights, which he has the strength to handle, and she often does not. She can become as addicted to love as to any other pursuit and, if the charm of the lovely Libran keeps her emotional and intuitive side happy, then she will accept his rather cold and rational mentality that precludes most of their disagreements. This is a good romantic association, rather than a highly sexed one. But they can provide each other with lighthearted dreaming if he stops balancing logic with every moment of feeling.

PISCES MAN – SCORPIO WOMAN

As much as the Pisces man would like to resist, he cannot hold back from dreaming when he first meets this mysterious and enigmatic woman. They both have in common a wonderful affinity for the deepest oceans of each other's hearts. Although the Scorpio woman is renowned for her jealousy, and this man will often incite hurt in her unthinkingly, the Fish is about the only man who can also remind her that his secrets are as intense as her own. Scorpio needs to know exactly where they are going, and how they are going to get there. Scorpios plan quite craftily if it involves attracting a Fish man, because a Fish is as devious as a Scorpio is menacing. The Fish is happy to drift, rather than to go on a crusade for emotional happiness. If a Scorpio girl appears too desperate in her love for him, he may retreat further to avoid being shaken by too much life. His fantasy land may not be able to escape her stinging tail. But the Fish is usually able to talk himself out of conflict, and in-depth emotional scenes, neither of which he can stomach, because it drags him back to harsh reality. He has much tolerance, and he doesn't need to be a dominant force in anyone's life, let alone his own. If things go the way they go, then let them. It is not a weakness, and it can be his redeeming strength. If the Scorpio woman is determined for their relationship to survive, then it probably will. He cares, and he loves deeply, but sometimes he has to remember to face the Scorpion passion head-on, and not leave her suspicious and resentful because he is more elusive than she could ever be. Sexually they will fulfil each other, gently and quietly. Their passion will be one of quality, not quantity, as long as the Piscean keeps his freedom and Scorpio feels a rich and emotive bond.

PISCES WOMAN – SCORPIO MAN

Water signs together tend to generate their own deep-seated feelings and lock their experiences into floods of emotional ecstasy, or agony. For the intensely passionate Scorpio to find an intuitive, understanding and compassionate girl like a Fish can be to him the whole meaning of his existence. Except that he might have rashly, in his egotistic way, forgotten that she is actually a good deal stronger than he at first noticed. His own acutely penetrating and compulsive nature will seem alarming to the girl Fish. When she realises that he is so charmed and magnetised by her depth, a depth that even a Scorpio cannot possibly ever be able to discover properly, then she knows she is actually the more powerful of the partnership. Her instincts and intuitions are more perceptive than his, and the floundering Scorpion's tail will miss its mark if it so much as attempts to sting the slithery Fish.

They have great wiles and are the great whales in the sea. Mermaids are whale maids too, whose strength is often forgotten when they appear on the ocean surface with only their human form showing. The temptation to catch such a creature is irresistible to a Scorpion. He longs for her serenity, her elusive charisma and her often doubting self. She does make vague, dreamy promises, and can change them at a whim, which will infuriate the Scorpio who needs to know exactly where he is to feel in control. She may find he is over-possessive, and at times will retreat paradoxically to her gregarious lifestyle to avoid his over-demanding need for her. This can cause much jealousy from him. For the Fish wishes to find a man with whom she can share both her heart and maybe her soul. The fact that sexually they have more to give one another than any other sign should be pasted up on her noticeboard in big red letters! But she can stray from him just once too often, if he expects too much of her soul. He will retaliate like no other man but, if his high moral and egotistic standard has been threatened he will be lost, ready to sacrifice her for his integrity. With this woman a Scorpio can finally perhaps surrender himself; his passion, always held on the precipice of total fulfilment, could be released and exalted in the Fish girl. And he has to remember that she holds the key to nurture his vulnerable soul.

PISCES MAN - SAGITTARIUS WOMAN

In time, if the Sagittarian girl is patient enough to wait, she may find that the dithery, dreamy quality of the man to whom she has been romantically attracted has an inner strength comparable to her own. On the surface, Pisces men often appear weak and wishy-washy. They seem sentimental dreamers, without thought for the reality of life, with no practical sense and ambition. But they are dual signs and, like their Gemini and Sagittarian friends, they are capable both of an adaptable nature and of a variety of guises to suit the weather. Geminis wear more hats than either of the others, but a Piscean will play better and the Sagittarian will enjoy the game and gamble more. When a Sagittarian woman gets into her head that the Pisces man is a far more devious and slippery character than he first appeared, she might try to throw a few blunt and dangerous remarks to sort him out, and see who he really is.

However, if she is too blunt he may disappear to the seashore. He will find her free spirit and her generous nature attractive, but she will become frustrated by his dithery changeability. She is Fire and he is Water and, however hard she tries to stay open-minded and easy-going, it can be very hard with this man. He can drown her in his passivity, infuriate her because he takes so long to get up in the morning and never seems to get anything done. He walks round in a dream, while she has already tackled ten jobs and made enough money to go and fritter it away on an impulse. She'll gamble on his love too, and he will respond with a great sexual intuition for what she needs. Piscean men are always sensitive and sexually imaginative and will always want to give rather than take. 'But sometimes too much giving can be just as self-centred!' shrieks the Sagittarian girl in frustration as the Fish listens to the troubles of the world. But she is only teasing.

PISCES WOMAN – SAGITTARIUS MAN

If you have a problem the simplest thing to do about it is to forget it, then it goes away – usually the solution given by the Piscean woman, and also by the Sagittarian man. Their differences, however, are based on the fact that a Fish girl will evade conflict, and evade anything that suggests she may be put on a hook and dissected, and the Archer just doesn't really give a hoot and prefers to walk away because walking away might lead to another avenue of amusement for his ever-changing spirit. He is an honest man, and will ask direct questions and expect direct answers. On the other hand the Piscean girl is known for her elusive replies, and her ability to change the subject to avoid his ever knowing how she truly feels or what she really thinks. This can irritate the Archer. He does have a lot of anger if he's pushed, and getting rattled is something he would prefer not to do, even though he has the wilder passions of a Fire sign. If he gets angry with the Fish girl she may either take two courses of action, the first being quite cleverly to crumple into a heap of tears and hurt, or coldly to swim off to a different pool to be alone with the only one she can trust: herself.

Archers won't enjoy the tears very much. They care very much about people's feelings, and don't intentionally like to hurt anyone. They can't stand emotional scenes and recriminations. If the Fish escapes to shadowland, then he won't try to follow her.

He will always find the Piscean girl physically attractive, sexually she is very different from him, although because he admires strength in women who are his feminine ideals. He will be more impulsive about sex, preferring to make love when he feels like it. The Pisces girl sometimes prefers her solitude to sex, and this can shoot tremendous holes in his very delicate ego. They both need freedom, and they both need understanding, but she finds his bluntness too demanding, and he will probably think her secretiveness too closed.

PISCES MAN – CAPRICORN WOMAN

As the Piscean man cruises his way up the rungs of success in a profession that enhances his talent he often comes across a wealthy successful woman, an ambitious and uncompromising lady with her head firmly committed to power and glory and a lot of fame. Now Capricorn men are quite well known for their ability to sponge off successful women, to marry into money to achieve and gain advancement in their careers. Piscean men don't even think, let alone plot, along these lines, unless, of course, they happen to come across the Goat lady who is quick-stepping up the rocky path to the top, and is quite bedazzled by the talent and success in others. Her love of fame and fortune can be of benefit to the Piscean man. And the devious and often rather weak-willed side of the Fish may rise to make use of her expertise, direction and cash. The mercenary Goat will make use of his talent, his attractiveness to the world and his ideals. Even in other walks of life, these two can actually cash in on each other for their own advantage, but is there ever love involved in this rather cold and relentless partnership? She lacks romance and she lacks the thrill of the open road. He lacks commitment and would rather dream than go and sort out the neighbours' racket. The Goat can quite coldly accept that 'using' someone is just another relationship; not a particularly genuine reason, but it can improve her own trust. She really has to trust her own judgment, and she really has to believe that she can make it with this man to succeed.

The Piscean is often intuitive about character, and normally will make instant judgments. Finding a Goat lady who is resistant to his charm, unless he has something to offer her in return and thus make it a business arrangement, can be hard. She looks for romance at first, because it is so elusive in her own life. But when she looks more carefully and finds a man who will slip through her fingers, and cause her to feel she has lost control with every smile he makes at a passing friend, it can turn her frigid overnight, unless, of course, he is the means to her own very determined ends.

PISCES WOMAN – CAPRICORN MAN

Lo and behold the Mermaid has slipped into the room and quietly taken the Goat by surprise! She is enchanting, deep and lost in some ephemeral time warp. The more elusive she is, the more she will draw his attention. She slithered past him out by the front door as he cautiously checked his filofax for the next party on his list. Business and pleasure don't mix, he says easily, and when he smiles she knows she can slip perhaps a little further into his heart. Although the Fish is gregarious she is actually quite introverted. Covering up her true feelings is not dissimilar to the introverted Goat's tendency to blot his out altogether. With a bit of luck he will immediately sense in her a quite similar illusion, and it really is the only one: silence. His silence is not as golden as hers, though. She would rather trip off to dream land, but via the bank. She wastes money, plays with it and looks upon life as a game, a surface attraction that can be abandoned when she feels vulnerable to its reality. She hates male chauvinists and the Capricorn is the nearest thing to one when he's driven by the undercurrent of power that motivates his life. The Goat has to control and make sure that finances and practicalities are under his wing. Being with a spendthrift like a Mermaid is not going to make his life very easy. Her retreats and sensitivity will depress him and she will find there is little to lighten her mood when she is melancholic. He is funny, but only when it serves his purpose. He is not uncaring, but he is more interested in his own reputation, his own ambitions, and his own satisfaction. If a Fish girl wants to aid and abet him in life, then fine. But he won't tolerate her own struggle for success, and he won't put up with her flirtatious and gregarious lifestyle for long. Yet they both secretly envy one another: she his spartan detachment from love, his silent power, and he her dream land ideals. They are both loners, but often two loners don't make it right!

PISCES MAN – AQUARIUS WOMAN

The benevolent and quite sincerely compassionate Piscean man can find a lot in common with the independent and highly spirited Aquarian girl. For starters they are both idealistic. He lives in dreams and she is attracted by the intangibilities of life. Theorising her problems, her ideas and her thoughts can become addictive with this very receptive and intuitive man. She will find that life never gets boring with him, because he is constantly shifting ideas, changing his attitudes and generally slipping around the ocean like a poetic flying Fish. They need their individual freedom. She will often have a very separate life from his and he often disappears into dream land, to escape from reality. She will mind if he doesn't tell her (she does like to be informed about everything), but she realises that her own freedom is important too, and will learn to respect his quieter one.

The mental affinity between them is what counts first. The Aquarian girl will probably have made friends with this man a long time before she actually embarks on a more romantic or sexual relationship with him. But Fish make friends easily, and he'll be easy-going about his emotions, letting them stay hidden in the darker caves of his mind and heart until he feels she is ready to accept them. He is not a particularly decisive person, but he is able to switch off from the truth if need be. He will not happily face conflict, or emotional scenes. Aquarians aren't emotional types either, but they do flare up and get on their high horses if things aren't done how they think they should be done. Her stubbornness could be the reason the Fish gets uptight, and the Fish hates having his sea disturbed! He will quite rightly put his own case forward, however visionary and idealistic it is, and often, because the Aquarian feeds on such unconventional behaviour, she will begin to enjoy the Fish's more inconsistent and inconstant nature, by the very fact that he is such a non-conformist himself. Living with her awkward efforts to be different won't be easy for a Fish; he needs peace and solitude, but he also needs someone just a bit crazy like himself.

PISCES WOMAN – AQUARIUS MAN

The Fish out of water can sense the ideals of the Aquarian man before she realises that his detached attitude to life will always make him aloof and rather cold. A Pisces woman needs his type of strength and determination, but she can do without the analysis and the constant reminder that he is not interested in individual, only humanitarian love. She will agree. In fact the Fish people are also very much concerned with compassion and the welfare of others, over and above themselves and their true strength lies in their ability to arise like dolphins in moments of crisis. Pisces women, sensitive and sometimes gullible as they seem, are fighters for their ideals as much as their partners, and the Aquarian man could find that a Fish is better equipped at handling his detached and Airy dissidence better than most. She will have to learn to tolerate his temperamental attitude to problems, for he must always solve them, however insignificant they appear to anyone else. He's the first to investigate the reason why there are dog turds in their garden. She won't particularly care why and would be happier just shovelling them in the earth. But the know-it-all Aquarian will be down there with his magnifying glass, and possibly a few plastic bags, to perform an autopsy and check out which dog it was. Colour, breed, sex, you name it, the Aquarian will find out the answer.

The Aquarian's ability to play the forensic scientist is an irritation from which the Fish girl will wish to escape. Sexually he can't really give her the affection and indulgence she needs, and she is too ephemeral and emotional for his own peculiar taste. It's not that she doesn't agree with his high ideals, nor that she loves change and non-conformity any less than he, but she really can't be bothered with inspection and analysis. Retreating is easier, and the Aquarian must accept that she may well disappear quite frequently for solitude, or for being with her own circle of less ineffectual friends.

Aries

BIRTHDAY PREDICTIONS
FOR THE YEAR AHEAD

March 21st   This year could see both love and impulse running hand in hand! Positive commitment needs strong leadership.

March 22nd   Romantically and socially this year could be the turning point for your honest and forthright endeavours.

March 23rd   Self-sufficiency in love should get you out of any great and long standing routines you have been trying for so long to avoid.

March 24th   Take the road towards a new challenge and you may find the love you have been anticipating makes your year go with a bang.

March 25th   Partners may play the best games of their lives this year, but there is no one who can challenge your leadership.

March 26th   Friends may inspire you this year to get on and take advantage of their genuine trust in your incredible and exciting lifestyle.

March 27th   Enthusiasm and zest for life could ensure a fun-packed and thrilling year for romance and all the energetic pursuits that you love.

March 28th   This year may well be a time for investing more energy into close relationships and discovering that impulse can test more than your integrity.

March 29th With so much confidence and belief in yourself, this is the year of opportunity and reward in all social matters.

March 30th A wonderful year for all aspects of love and close personal relationships.

March 31st Passions and feelings could run high on your list of priorities for the next twelve months, so take advantage of high living.

April 1st 1995 should prove to be one of your most active and exciting years, but don't forget to let others near your heart!

April 2nd Your drive and thrill for risk taking could lighten this year with determination and spontaneity and put paid to any doubts others may have of your self-expression.

April 3rd The year should kick off to a wild start. Be prepared to take a side stall later on when a partner begins to take the lead.

April 4th A new challenge may broaden your whole outlook on love this year and remind you who comes first in all your relationships!

April 5th Without reservations you should excel in romantic matters this year, as long as you remember that friends need your enthusiasm to keep them sparkling.

April 6th You have never been known to hesitate before, and this year sees your impulse and impetuous spirit take on bigger and greater affairs of the heart.

April 7th Leisure pursuits are fast-paced and reckless this year, but you should have time to lavish attention on those you love.

April 8th A perfect year for new beginnings, however hard it is to cut old ties, and compromise more.

April 9th Regrets are hastily forgotten and wisely so. This year brings equanimity to your lifestyle.

April 10th With 1995 comes the humour and reserves of energy you can use to best advantage to ensure your power of leadership.

April 11th Your ally this year is your strong sense of purpose, keep it by you and you can't go wrong.

April 12th Relationships could blossom this year and you'll need all your strength to energise love if you really want it.

April 13th A wonderful year to achieve your highest intentions, even if they involve emotional commitment.

April 14th The line between love and friendship should be drawn firmly this year and you may have to make startling choices!

April 15th Docility is for less Fiery signs and you certainly won't be cuddling up in front of any one else's fire this year. Get out and blaze through your life!

April 16th Reminders of the past may hang on this year, but then you are always able to face new adventures with enterprise and courage.

April 17th The truth is never far from your lips and this year all the honesty in the world can only benefit your romantic interests.

April 18th Don't expect miracles this year, but if you play the right games there is always chance on your side; and don't you love risks?!

April 19th The is year may show you how partnerships can wobble even in the strongest winds. But take advantage of the storm and get on with your exciting life.

April 20th The remarkable year could see you both achieving all the goals you have set for yourself and finding new ones to strive for.

Taurus

BIRTHDAY PREDICTIONS
FOR THE YEAR AHEAD

April 21st   This year you may feel grounded and relaxed with the new comfort in your own determination to succeed.

April 22nd   Invest your love in the right quarter this year and you could find a beneficial reward.

April 23rd   All that could be yours this year can be if you remember to persevere and break through the barriers.

April 24th   Your solid affection and strength of purpose should keep this year a happy one for you.

April 25th   Locked doors may open in the next twelve months and you should see the light at least.

April 26th   Down to earth with a bump this year, but you will be pleasantly surprised by what occurs.

April 27th   This year should see the beginning of a new challenge, however static you would like your life to be.

April 28th   All the powers of your stubborn pride could be put to the test this year, but you'll enjoy every minute.

April 29th   Progress in your love life should take great strides this year after so many past disappointments.

April 30th   A great year for the home front; at last you can relax in the lifestyle you really enjoy.

May 1st   Patience and enterprise should ensure that this year, companionship and friends become of greater importance.

May 2nd   Don't let your social life dampen your spirits, for now more than ever should you find contentment in future ideals.

May 3rd   At last a barrier has been brought down and your daily life enhanced by a harmonious relationship that offers you peace and stability.

May 4th   This year puts the icing powder on the cake, and you should feel resolved to accept the demands of others.

May 5th   Only you can make this year really what you want it to be. Placid, full of warmth, and affection.

May 6th   Bear-hugs should be enough this year to see you through the pacier days that you would rather were gone.

May 7th   Your comfortable and possessive habits should enable you to have a year when all is right with the world, and everyone in it.

May 8th   A good year for making the best of your social life, and encouraging more love into others' hearts.

May 9th   A wonderful year for new beginnings, even though you prefer not to let go of the past.

May 10th   Remember to let patience direct you to what lies ahead and use the sound knowledge of your principles to guide you.

May 11th   The next twelve months should not only remind you of your personal commitments, but astound you with loyalty.

May 12th   Friends and social activities make this year one that should be high on your list for remembering.

May 13th   The benefits of secure possessions may encourage you to try out investment in love as well as finances!

May 14th   Close partners could give you a new outlook on life and give as much stability as you are always seeking.

May 15th   The nest is secure and with it comes the best year for making the most of a well-established and secure relationship.

May 16th   Never doubt your stubborn pride but this year let it bend a little for the less rigid and intolerant.

May 17th   Slow progress in a relationship could now come to fruition and the struggles of the past year could resolve as happiness for 1995.

May 18th   Only time can work with you this year and you should at last feel that the struggles are over.

May 19th   Long-term relationships may take up most of your time, but you should enjoy the warmth and affection all year.

May 20th   Any tugs-of-war you have recently been involved in should now break and you could make 1995 your winning year.

May 21st   1995 will ensure that partners and loved ones are the answer to all your problems and will back you throughout all your endeavours.

ron

Gemini

BIRTHDAY PREDICTIONS
FOR THE YEAR AHEAD

May 22nd This year should be filled with new ideas and new reactions to old romance and love-affairs that may be turning cold.

May 23rd Take the year in your heart, instead of your mind, and watch out for partners or friends who are not what they seem!

May 24th The only thing to stop you having a ball this year is trying to slow down to another's pace. Keep your fun fast and you won't go wrong.

May 25th This year should enhance all the romance and sparkle that you have yearned for.

May 26th The surface attractions that you long to share with someone could finally be adapted and brought to fruition.

May 27th 1995 is one of those years when the spirit of life could make the year pass with changes that only you could ever instigate.

May 28th Long-term relationships may encourage you to take on new and exciting challenges, but socially you might find little time for fun.

May 29th This year you may find that love has at last found you ready to take on a more stable and committed approach than ever before.

May 30th	Your restless nature should enjoy the year as the changes that occur only serve to highlight your need for adventure.
May 31st	Changing course midway through any endeavour is your usual way through life, and this year should prove no exception to the rule!
June 1st	The proof of the pudding is sometimes in the eating, and this year maybe even you can try it out and see!
June 2nd	Try to say what you really mean this year, instead of covering up truths with what you like to believe.
June 3rd	A great year for relationships, and also for a heady social life.
June 4th	Leisure and fun take up most of your time this year, but you may meet intellectual challenges with a fresher approach than ever before.
June 5th	All the cards on the table seem to signify a wonderful year for love and romance, if you take care to follow your intuition.
June 6th	Don't let your dual nature stop you from making the right decisions this year. A testing time, but certainly invigorating.
June 7th	Platonic friendships should make this year a social and active one with lots of amusement and diversions.
June 8th	Keeping constantly on the move may mean you miss some of the deeper mysteries of life, but this year you should only miss those you chose to miss.
June 9th	1995 is a year for you to take the initiative and seek out change as well as compassion for those you love.
June 10th	Adaptable as you are you could find this year demands more versatility than ever before!
June 11th	Mental companionship should be highlighted this year and with love on the cards you could have many wonderful moments.
June 12th	Restless activities this year ensure you are never bored, and past-times and pleasures may keep your active mind on a high if you take the time.

June 13th Love could come slowly to you this year but, when it does, the speed with which you confront it may be astounding!

June 14th Don't let indecision take over and you should find that a partner can make this year one of your happiest.

June 15th Versatility is your watchword this year and if you can keep friends happy then you may find they are full of pleasant surprises.

June 16th Nobody has ever realised the skill with which you can play a million guises, but 1995 could at last show you for your true colours.

June 17th The sky's the limit both socially and romantically this year, so take advantage of all the favourable aspects!

June 18th A great year for close relationships, particularly any that are new and not yet committed.

June 19th You aren't one for making a drama out of a crisis, but this year you might find yourself in deeper waters than you ever thought possible!

June 20th You seek change and adapt to it immediately. Therefore on on account this year allow others to put you off what you know is right romantically.

June 21st 1995 should show you the paths that you take and the tangents you make are always the answer to your success, however hard others may try to dissuade you.

Cancer

BIRTHDAY PREDICTIONS
FOR THE YEAR AHEAD

June 22nd A year when all emotional resources could be put to the test but you find security comes with determination.

June 23rd 1995 should herald the beginning of new commitments and promises that can only bear heavily on the past.

June 24th A great year for you to begin to come to terms with your sensitivity regarding one particular relationship.

June 25th Remember that your moods can often confound others, but this year forget to hide in your shell and the sun may truly shine!

June 26th 1995 may make you realise that tenacity and caution have at last achieved what you wanted from a close partnership.

June 27th Romance and the lighter side of living should be the focus of this year. Enjoy it, don't shrink from the limelight.

June 28th Paths that have so far been uncrossed could soon be bridged with your usual powerful and imaginative resources.

June 29th	Love this year is something that can only grow, however slowly and carefully you try to administer your emotions.
June 30th	A year when you can dance for once in the contentment of the emotional conflicts you have finally resolved.
July 1st	Only those who inspire you can be the answer to your romantic dreams this year.
July 2nd	In spite of your wariness to make a final commitment,this year should see you make a brave front and accept your love is cherished.
July 3rd	This year you may at last take very close partners into your confidence and, with the relief it brings, find a new haven for security.
July 4th	A wonderful year for friends and close partners to begin to understand your very introverted needs.
July 4th	You love your friends and a small social circle where you can feel at home, and this year you may feel rewarded by those who are special in your heart.
July 5th	Forgetting a former romance could be hard this year, and you may find you are put to the test.
July 6th	The home is where you are happiest and this year you should feel the stability of a loved one around you.
July 7th	The year looks set to fill you with so many amusements that you could be richly rewarded by skills you never felt you possessed.
July 8th	Long standing worries and fears may subside this year bringing a new and fresher approach to your personal relationships.
July 9th	All the heartaches you have had in the past will remind you how safe it is in your shell, but this year you will polish it and cautiously emerge like a new and sparkling Crab!
July 10th	Your life is often a mixture of great happiness and sadness, but his year you could find that all you have invested in love will be rewarded.
July 11th	However cautiously you take this year, there will be

wonderful chances to clear the air and make amends.

July 12th The year should bring you new friends and a warmth and security in any new endeavour.

July 13th Not only have you the time and energy to look at your close relationships but, when you do you may realise how much you are truly cherished.

July 14th Forgiving others could be the keyword this year, so make all the effort and reap all the gains.

July 15th A remarkable year for romantic and social occasions of all kinds.

July 16th Put your powers of imagination to good use this year and you should uncover the best love you have ever known.

July 17th Reflect on the past too much and you may miss the year and its challenge to improve or amend a relationship.

July 18th Although partners and relatives could be in the forefront this year you should at last realise that you have nothing to lose by feeling content.

July 19th Begin to take loved ones into your confidence and you may be assured a happy and successful year.

July 20th This year you should be on better terms than ever with loved ones and partners.

July 21st Not only a year for love and romance but also for new beginnings and much social activity.

July 22nd As each day passes you may draw more and more on your intuitive instincts to ensure a stable and confident approach to your close partnerships.

July 23rd Only looking back now can remind you how this year you could be successful in inspiring relatives to your trust.

Leo

BIRTHDAY PREDICTIONS
FOR THE YEAR AHEAD

July 24th	All that can be said about this sort of year is get out and enjoy it, and as usual, be enthusiastic about life!
July 25th	The zest for living you have this year should at last give you a chance to feel really loved.
July 26th	1995 is a year when you may attract warmth and love from the person you least expected!
July 27th	This year could be a turning point for all aspects of love and romance, if you let the fire burn.
July 28th	Your flamboyant nature should enable you to discover the true meaning of love this year.
July 29th	The next twelve months may show you that deep feelings and passions are returned, as long as you communicate your own.
July 30th	Even with the warmest heart in the world you may find in 1995 that your feelings are more important than your partner's commitment.
July 31st	A passionate year when a close relationship will test your highest personal integrity.
August 1st	Take advantage of your close friends' genuine loyalty and you may begin to feel the adoration you yearn for.
August 2nd	Love is expressed easily this year, but you must remember that it should also be shared too.

August 3rd   1995 could be the one year when you end the drama scenes and begin to enjoy more comedy roles!

August 4th   A glittering 1995, with passion up front in your heart you may be able to steal every show you stage.

August 5th   Your self-importance may dwindle this year when you come face to face with a dominating challenge and romance!

August 6th   A year of energy and enterprise, when you can let friends and romance take you through a crash course in pride.

August 7th   Partners may seem stubborn and resilient to your usual flash and ostentatious displays this year, so let them know that your love is for real.

August 8th   Close partners may seem like obstacles to your happiness this year, so take time out to put the zest back into your own life.

August 9th   Your strength is your generous heart and your love of passion, and this year you could find that it wins over any odds.

August 10th   Communicating love is as essential as making it and, in 1995, you should find the energy that should enable you to do both.

August 11th   Hearts may be lost, but this year new hearts may also be found, and broaden your whole outlook on love and sexuality.

August 12th   Passions and feelings could run high for 1995, but with them you should be able to put paid to any doubts as to where your true loyalty lies.

August 13th   Friends may play an important part in all your romantic attachments this year, so give them your loyalty and trust.

August 14th   A year when you may encourage impulsive and dramatic meetings, and throw yourself in at your own deep end!

August 15th   Others may think you conceited at times, but this year you could show that your real magnanimity can outshine any one-off lack of compassion.

August 16th 1995 could bring a year of sparkle and return you to being the centre of attention, which is where you always perform best.

August 17th Confidence and self-esteem keep you on top, and they may bring you to realise in 1995 where a new and deep love can be found.

August 18th Let others feel the heat of your passion this year and you should generate more than enough love and romance for twelve months!

August 19th A year of new beginnings, but don't over-dramatise your desires, or you may have to compromise.

August 20th Close friends could encourage in you the necessary power and excitement to succeed in all romantic matters this year.

August 21st You may be rewarded this year with the starring role for as long as you want it, if you lavish attention on the one you love!

August 22nd The heat of passion may see you through any regrets that others may be having, but this can only be to your advantage for an exciting year.

August 23rd This is a wonderful year for making new relationships, and energising all the love in your heart and giving it freely.

Virgo

BIRTHDAY PREDICTIONS
FOR THE YEAR AHEAD

August 24th   Any barriers that you have recently felt were built between you and love should finally break down this year and allow you to discover a new ideal.

August 25th   This year should give you the time to take a hard and long look at the real aspects of any emotional involvement and realise what is required of your conviction.

August 26th   Inhibitions about expressing your love may be finally brought down this year, and you have the chance to communicate more openly and with it receive genuine feelings.

August 27th   However conventional you like your life to be, this year looks set to offer new and more bizarre challenges with even tame partners!

August 28th   1995 should bring your social life more into focus, although you prefer less company it could bring you the ideal you are searching for.

August 29th   The purity of a relationship may finally be brought into focus this year with accurate and enticing results.

August 30th   This year locked doors may be opened, and old and inferior ones well and truly closed!

August 31st	Discriminating between what you love and what you need will become of major significance to you this year with exacting results.
September 1st	A year when you can relax your mental activity and now begin to concentrate on close friends and partners.
September 2nd	Any analysis of the truth is better than none, and this year you should have good grounds at last to see love grow.
September 3rd	Working at love and emotions could this year be changed to a more playful and happier set of rules!
September 4th	Freedom of expression is something you often lack, but this year may find you can offer words that are in line with your heart.
September 5th	Struggles in any past relationships could now be resolved, and you may realise you have more to share than you thought!
September 6th	This may be the year when you allow acquaintances to turn into genuine and trustworthy friends, rather than keeping your distance.
September 7th	Looking for the perfect love can often elude you, but this year, if you chose to express your feelings, you may be presently surprised.
September 8th	A renewed energy to communicate more openly and to criticise less should make one relationship feel charged with happiness this year.
September 9th	Never doubt your need to improve on others faults, but this year let love take over where coldness usually hides.
September 10th	You are often modest in words, and also in love, but this year take advantage of feeling and let yourself flow into emotion.
September 11th	A long-term relationship may well take up all your time this year, but the commitment and purpose will all be worthwhile.

September 12th   A year when you can be sure that partners and loved ones will always back you 100 per cent in any endeavour.

September 13th   A wonderful year for your quiet but active social life to form new friends and closer companions, and maybe even a light romance.

September 14th   Love will enter your heart this year if you desire it, but fault-finding can only lead to a colder spirit.

September 15th   Your support and commitment to friends and partners is unparalleled, but this year take a break and pamper yourself for a change.

September 16th   You may feel that inwardly you are never satisfied in your search for perfect love, but this year you may encounter pure romance without even knowing it!

September 17th   Your ideals are high, and if you allow others to express their feelings, you may be pleasantly surprised how your own heart opens too.

September 18th   Never doubt your ability to analyse and to discriminate, and this year use it to its full and powerful advantage in all matters of love.

September 19th   Happiness is only what you make it, and this year you should be able to put all your mental energy into achieving it.

September 20th   This year sees romance and your high ideals gather a new strength and with it a new long-term commitment.

September 21st   A harmonious year, when not only friends and family will support your commitments, but partners may grow closer than ever before.

September 22nd   Only you can know that perfection is truly in someone's eyes. And this year you may be lucky enough to glimpse the true love, if you look hard enough.

September 23rd Passion is not high on your list for romantic happiness, but you may have to contend with it to enjoy this year's emotional stability.

Libra

BIRTHDAY PREDICTIONS
FOR THE YEAR AHEAD

September 24th   A highly romantic and sparkling year, but beware of being too easily influenced by others.

September 25th   A year when love and a deep emotional relationship may be formed on a permanent basis.

September 26th   Charming you may be, but this year tests more than romance and keeps you, literally, on your toes.

September 27th   Communicating your love is never hard, and this year you may have to express yourself more frequently than ever before.

September 28th   Retrieving your feelings from a past relationships is never easy, but the relief and the future look brighter than you could possibly have imagined.

September 29th   You may be locked into someone else's opinions this year, but at least you will never be alone again!

September 30th   A social and highly flirtatious year and the changes that occur should keep you amused and very alive.

October 1st   You could have a ball this year if you don't let

others think you are more committed than
you really are.

October 2nd   Avoiding conflict is the way to make this
year as pleasant and harmonious as the last,
but you may be confronted with more
romantic challenges than you can handle!

October 3rd   However strong the pull of commitment this
year, you may still feel drawn to seek the fun
and laughter of a varied and exciting social
life.

October 4th   A restorative and relaxing year whereby you
can enjoy the pleasures of home and the
company of harmonious and sociable friends.

October 5th   Being in love is never far from your mind or
your heart, and this year you can expect
more than your fair share of the heart!

October 6th   Diplomacy is your ally, but don't get
involved in arguments among friends, or you
may find yourself torn between two parting
hearts.

October 7th   Hesitation, rather than indecision, is often
how you flounder when love is offered. This
year, hesitating too long could lose you a
very precious gift.

October 8th   Being in need of a permanent relationships is
usually your dream and this year, if you take
a less middle of the road course, you may at
last find it.

October 9th   Being starved of affection and pleasure can
make you resentful and hurt, but you always
jump back and enjoy your social whirl, this
year more than ever before.

October 10th   A great year for all relationships, and also for
a heady social life.

October 11th   This year you may not only be drawn to the
surface attractions of life, but also find
hidden depths in your heart.

October 12th   Communication is essential this year if you

	are to place any happiness into a commitment with a loved one.
October 13th	You are always happy to be led astray if it brings you romantic fun, but this year take care to follow your intuition, rather than your heart.
October 14th	Gentle and usually passive by nature, you may find the year brings more than your usual amount of extremes of energy.
October 15th	Sometimes frivolous, but always charming, you could find this year's social activities leading you into deeper waters.
October 16th	Any relationship that is currently running short of air should take off with new breath this year.
October 17th	Any socialising you do this year may bring with it new friends, and the chances of finding out whom need.
October 18th	A lovely romantic encounter could occur this year if you use more of your charming self-expression, and less of your small talk!
October 19th	You love the company of the opposite sex and this year you may find that you really are the centre of attraction in any social setting.
October 20th	Close partners should now be letting you know that you need to make a choice, rather than sit back and wait for it to happen!
October 21st	You are forever fascinated by the pleasures of life, and 1995 should bring with it the company of friends you so badly rely on.
October 22nd	A fulfilling year romantically, as the chance of a wrong decision may be far from your mind.
October 23rd	Loving the surface attractions of life may mean you miss out on deeper mysteries, but this year might see you begin to look beyond the physical appearance!

Scorpio

BIRTHDAY PREDICTIONS
FOR THE YEAR AHEAD

October 24th   The powerful force behind your attraction may at last be experienced by the very person you had least expected.

October 25th   A year when you may trust your closest friends to reassure you about a relationship you had begun to doubt.

October 26th   Although you are deadly serious about everything you do, take this year on a lighter note and you may find it equally rewarding.

October 27th   Discovering your inner feelings have hardened to a difficult romance may bring you nearer to seeing your way to cut all ties.

October 28th   The intensity of love you may have felt for someone could be replaced by intense hate this year, but either way you will enjoy feeling the passion!

October 29th   Looking inwards is something you do easily, but this year take a fresh look at the outside of other people's love.

October 30th   Love is a serious game for you, and this year is no exception to the number of subtle plots and intrigues you can manipulate powerfully with a close partner.

October 31st   Friends may find your commitment to a cause over-intense this year, but when you come through it they should realise the strength of your involvement.

November 1st There could be a major emotional upheaval in your life this year, but you always come through any upsets with the strength to start afresh and accept the inevitable.

November 2nd Love and sexuality are crucial for your existence and this year, although they may cause a break or instigate a major crisis in your life, you will handle it all superbly.

November 3rd Only you can know the truth of your emotions and how far you can let others go before you call a halt. This year will prove that regenerating your heart is the answer to careless love.

November 4th Being a detective is one thing, but when others try to infiltrate your heart your barriers are firmly shut. You may need to put up a solid wall this year to hold back the flood!

November 5th Always a victim of your own passion, you may this year seek out bizarre and unusual love and sexual activity to enable you to maintain the romance.

November 6th Total love and total loyalty are your desire in any relationship, and this year may prove that you can only trust what you believe, rather than dwelling on it.

November 7th Emotion and dark jealousies may be given full vent this year, but you could find that clearing the air brings with it only sweeter rain.

November 8th Your determination to overcome disaster in a relationship may find it relieves the crisis by bringing a new and sudden reversal of the odds.

November 9th Your sexuality will be at a peak this year, and a partner should provide you with all the loyalty and response you really need.

November 10th Your suspicions may at last be allayed this year when a deep and sexual relationship finally allows you to see the truth.

November 11th This year broadening your outlook should enhance your vision and clarify any difficulties in your close personal relationships.

November 12th Over-indulgence in love and in play might this year be given a break as new horizons and a new relationship looks set to lighten your life!

November 13th 1995 could be a year in which you can open your heart and let others come a little nearer than you really ever dared.

November 14th Winning against the odds may set a new precedent this year when you finally realise your emotional ambitions.

November 15th Sometimes ruthless, yet always passionate you may instil the intensity of ambition and your powerful image into a close and sexually rewarding relationship.

November 16th Intimate friends could play a big part in how you reach a very important turning point in your life and take the challenge with discernment.

November 17th Any emotional changes this year could put your belief in loyalty to the test, and enable you to know who your real friends are.

November 18th Loved ones could get closer to your heart this year than you had ever dreamed was possible; and you might even let them stay!

November 19th The sky's the limit this year, when you finally adjust to a deep and lasting relationship, and give it all you've got.

November 20th Only you know how deep and penetrating your feelings run, but this year might be the time to let others feel the strength behind that self-control.

November 21st Your life is often extremes of happiness and despair, but this year you could find that giving more in love earns a return that you would never have anticipated.

November 22nd Your imagination is intense and penetrating; put it to good use this year and discover how someone close to you may care far more than you believe.

Sagittarius

BIRTHDAY PREDICTIONS
FOR THE YEAR AHEAD

November 23rd Adventure is in your heart as well as your head this year, so make the most of it and get out and have fun!

November 24th Your versatility in all relationships could be put to the test this year, with startling results.

November 25th There may be restrictions on your ideals this year, but your social life should stay buoyant.

November 26th Your integrity and trust may be put to the test in 1995, but with its confirmation you can be assured of a true and deep friendship.

November 27th A year when your friends will be waiting on your every word, but you may open your mouth wider than ever before!

November 28th Communicate openly this year with those you love and you should have a year free from emotional responsibility.

November 29th Your home life could keep your feet firmly on the ground in 1995, but you should still have time for light romance.

November 30th Family and friends play a big part in your life this year, yet you may feel the pull of stronger and freer challenges.

December 1st   Romantic attachments look set to flourish this year, if you can find the time between escapades!

December 2nd   Love takes the high spot of the year, but any social life may keep it relaxed, just as you like it.

December 3rd   With so much confidence in your ability to work and play, this year should see you juggling both in just the right proportions!

December 4th   Friends may make more demands on you this year, but every one may be welcomed and happily explored.

December 5th   Your optimistic and cheery nature could make this year swing with light flirtations and amiable company.

December 6th   Love is certainly in the air this year, but watch out for commitments you can't or won't be able to afford to make.

December 7th   The only thing that can stop you in your quest for idealistic love is not opening your eyes to the truth this year.

December 8th   With casual friends and lovers taking up all your time, you might find that your sex life is finely tuned for most of this year.

December 9th   1995 should prove to be sexually inventive and the chance is there to form a new and closer relationship.

December 10th   Partners may make you feel trapped this year, so with your usual verve get out and play more, but still ensure they have trust in their hearts.

December 11th   Expanding your vision and your circle of friends could go hand-in-hand this year as you broaden your whole outlook on relationships.

December 12th   A year when careless and irresponsible attachments fly out the window, for a more philosophical and worldly awareness of love.

December 13th   Setting your sights on an ideal love could be the biggest challenge you could have to face this year, but you'll enjoy every minute of it!

December 14th   Your frank and sincere approach to new relationships should at least give you the foresight to sense any difficult emotional traps this year.

December 15th   Travelling through life you often meet new friends and encounter many lovers, and this year should see the road widen into a motorway of love!

December 16th   Friends and close partners should make this an eventful and fun-packed year.

December 17th   Socialising and enjoying a casual laid-back way of life is the key to your heart, and others may unlock it this year in a big way!

December 18th   However far away you wander you always travel light, and this year with little baggage in your heart you can now expand both your mind and your heart.

December 19th   Sometimes your extremism produces conflict in close partners, but this year you should be more willing to settle into a fun-packed but calmer lifestyle.

December 20th   Passion and romance look set to heat up your year and ensure you are never bored, or lacking in adventure.

December 21st   Any new enterprise you take regarding friends or lovers can only result in finding the freedom you need this year.

Capricorn

BIRTHDAY PREDICTIONS
FOR THE YEAR AHEAD

December 22nd The success you have so long awaited in a personal relationship should now begin to see the light of a very charming day.

December 23rd Any plan that you have persevered to put into action regarding your relationships should now provide you with all the satisfaction you need.

December 24th Possessions and very close attachments form the basis of your stability and love life this year.

December 25th Your need for a secure relationship should this year keep you actively happy and firmly in charge.

December 26th Ambitions in love are as crucial as ambitions in work, and this year should see the coming to fruition of both.

December 27th Communicating your feelings is always hard, but this year you could find a more relaxed and liberal approach grow in your heart.

December 28th Home and family ensure that you have a secure and committed lifestyle, yet this may be the time to allow a little more passion into your routine.

December 29th However committed you are to your family life, you should this year open your eyes a little wider, and stop taking others close to you for granted.

December 30th Romantic involvement comes as a shock to you at times, but your secret desire for adventure may be rewarded this year.

December 31st Pleasure, fun and romantic involvement look likely to keep you occupied for most of this year.

January 1st All the shyness and suspicion in the world won't stop you this year finally letting someone very special know how much you care.

January 2nd With cautious and deliberate force you may find this year fulfils all your expectations for a deeper relationship.

January 3rd Your attitudes towards others may have to be reassessed this year, as you begin to find your patience wearing thin with a close partner.

January 4th Barriers could be broken down in 1995, and you may find more truth in a harmonious relationship than you ever believed possible.

January 5th Conventional though you are, you may this year begin to communicate your feelings, and find that love is not solid, but often made of air!

January 6th 1995 may see you being able to express your needs and your love, rather than indulging in fantasy and losing chances.

January 7th However much your family put security and strength into your beliefs, this year you could find release from tensions in close friends and companions.

January 8th Your self-discipline is admirable, and yet there are times this year when you may have to let yourself fly, rather than hide behind your powerful image.

January 9th   Romantic and social activities become more serious and less restrained this year, and you should begin to have a self-imposed ball!

January 10th   Your humour should stand you in good stead this year, as your social life climbs to the sort of heights where you can be in charge.

January 11th   Identifying with emotional freedom could be your biggest reward this year, as you start to unravel the secret of someone's heart.

January 12th   Friends may support you this year with all the time and love they can muster, and romance may see you through any cynicism you had about relationships!

January 13th   The routine of your relationship may take on a different course this year, and you may find any difficult periods essentially rewarding ones.

January 14th   Calculating you are, but this year you might not even have time to plan a love campaign, as someone beats you to it!

January 15th   Close partners may find your ambitions over-protective this year, and could force you to reassess your true feelings.

January 16th   Any emotional relationship could this year have an added spark as your ambitions will be made the make or break of it.

January 17th   Your sex life could dramatically change this year, either because you meet a new partner, or because your current love relationship could finally take on a new meaning.

January 18th   Aspirations for success are never far from your mind, and this year, both sexually and romantically you could achieve the highs you are seeking.

January 19th   By anyone's standards you might find this year that reaching the pinnacle and finally committing yourself to a special partner can only rekindle your own personal ambitions.

January 20th   A year when friends are the key to your success and every social event should be scrutinised for the achievements it could bring you.

Aquarius

BIRTHDAY PREDICTIONS
FOR THE YEAR AHEAD

January 21st   Unpredictable though you are, this year should see the change inspired by love from a perspective different from your own.

January 22nd   Your fixed opinions may subtly be influenced by the vision of a new and lasting friendship this year.

January 23rd   Broadening your outlook and meeting new friends is always easy, and this year you should find even more to fascinate you in bizarre encounters.

January 24th   Friends play a huge part in your life this year, and you may find they rely on your loyalty more than ever before.

January 25th   Without your social life, you would suffer severe intellectual frigidity! But this year you may have to give out more warmth than you care to admit.

January 26th   You can feel confident that this year your progressive attitude to life will rub off on those you want to be your closest friends.

January 27th   Independent and single-minded though you are, this year you can't do without the trust and stamina of your closest partners or friends.

January 28th Instead of inventing mind-games about your emotional relationships, invent a little more romance this year, and you could come out winning.

January 29th However ordinary you think your relationship with someone is, you may be pleasantly surprised by a change of attitude this year.

January 30th No one can challenge your reformist and analytical mind, but be prepared for a confrontation in 1995, however faithful you are.

January 31st Your personal freedom may at last be accepted by someone very close to you, and it looks like a loyal and trusting relationship could gradually develop.

February 1st Communicate more about your feelings this year, and you should inspire the close confidence and love of a friend.

February 2nd Friends may find your self-expression less idealistic this year, but you should still find delight in changing visions.

February 3rd Try to be more understanding for 1995, and less insensitive, for someone special may hold the secret weapon to love.

February 4th A long-term relationship may have been suffering, but now it looks set to take on a new course, and with it new meaning.

February 5th Your attitudes to others may modulate your behaviour this year, and any eccentric notions you have about love can now be put into action.

February 6th Take time out this year to put more energy into your family and home life, and the original lifestyle you enjoy should thrive.

February 7th Self-sufficient as you are, you still need the support of close friends and relatives especially now you are about to take on new responsibilities.

February 8th Pleasure and romance might make you more extrovert than ever this year, and ensure a constant flow on new and sparky ideas.

February 9th Love can sometimes jump up at you from unexpected quarters, and this year it does exactly that. And don't you just adore the unexpected!

February 10th Romantic and idealistic progress should be made this year in all your social and pleasurable pursuits. Make the most of it.

February 11th You may have to keep on your toes, rather than observe from a detached position, as love tempts you from afar.

February 12th This year get down to basics and accept that a close partner is able to give you the freedom you need so much.

February 13th Mental harmony and a long-lasting rapport could be achieved this year, if you adopt a warmer outlook on your love life.

February 14th All emotional conflicts should be far from your heart, as someone makes an impact upon you that you cannot resist.

February 15th Love can be as unconventional as you want it to be and you now have the chance to renew an old and deep relationship or change your whole path through life.

February 16th There is more to your life than a happy sexual relationship, but this year you may be in for more physical fun than you anticipated.

February 17th However inventive your sex life this year, you must make time to let others know that you have a heart too.

February 18th Rash promises have a habit of coming back at you with heavier demands, but this year you might escape taking the plunge and thank your closest friends for their wisdom.

February 19th   Insensitivity can only serve to establish where your true feelings lie this year, and where you stand with regard to any new emotional relationships.

Pisces

BIRTHDAY PREDICTIONS
FOR THE YEAR AHEAD

February 20th   Your intuition should give you cause to relax this year and enjoy the flow of good company and a more outgoing social life.

February 21st   Expanding your horizons makes you more receptive than ever this year to the influences of genuine love around you.

February 22nd   Dependence on love could be temporarily put on hold this year as you now have a chance to feel free of any decision you would rather not make.

February 23rd   Romance is easy for you to follow, but be on your guard this year against those who would lead you down dangerous emotional paths.

February 24th   A highly social and gregarious year to turn all your talents of romance and fun to good and beneficial use.

February 25th   You might find the practical aspects of running your life difficult, but your social life should take the sweat out of any reality you would prefer to avoid.

February 26th   You can easily get confused about whether to remain loyal to certain friends, but this year there will at last be no doubt about who you can really trust.

February 27th Compassionate as ever, you can now put to good use all the love you have for your closest companions.

February 28th Dreams are made and fulfilled this year if you learn to connect your feelings to the real world.

March 1st Escaping from commitment and conflict this year can only make you realise that you have more to offer and less to feel responsible for.

March 2nd Being so receptive to others' moods may make this year exhausting emotionally, but you could find its rewards more illuminating than you dared to imagine.

March 3rd Romance and all social pleasures should sparkle for you this year even though sometimes you seem to have only one foot in reality!

March 4th You live in your feelings rather than in your head, and this year a strong emotional commitment might make you search deeper within yourself.

March 5th Your communication is always direct and friendly and this year you may at last be able to tackle a deeper and more emotional expression of love.

March 6th Your ideas about love may at times be muddled, but the change in the air this year can only make you realise what you truly feel and need.

March 7th Attraction to the ideals of romantic love can now be put into reality, as this year sees a wonderful time for new and exciting relationships.

March 8th This year you may be drawn closer to home life and your family, but without a doubt it can only make you more aware of how easily you can get carried away.

March 9th Pressures from the family may conflict with

your need for personal freedom this year, so make time for both and you should feel less under pressure.

March 10th Without any attempt at making the first move you might find yourself in at the deep end of a dramatic and romantic liaison this year.

March 11th Any lack of purpose in your life may now be suddenly diffused into reality and love could step into your life with real meaning.

March 12th The amiable pleasures of your romantic attachments could become more serious if you don't take a step back to see the real truth.

March 13th Creativity is a positive channel for your need to escape, and this year you may be forced to escape more to avoid the harsh routine of life.

March 14th A good year for all routine partnerships and any creative outlets that you may wish to pursue, even though it means a quieter social round.

March 15th Close partners and loved ones could this year finally begin to make you feel that you are loved and needed again.

March 16th Your weak will may find a renewed strength to carry you through a difficult emotional storm and come out for once unscathed.

March 17th Soaking up the world and its problems can inflict great emotional wounds upon you, and this year you will need more time to recover from friends, weighty emotions.

March 18th Your sexuality should be on a high this year and you could find that love plays more than an important part in your life.

March 19th Emotional clouds will lift this year and your intuitions about a close friend could be deadly accurate.

March 20th Letting someone close to your heart could be the best thing you do this year, and stabilise for once your restless and idealistic mind.